P9-CCP-796

Abolishing Performance Appraisals

Abolishing Performance Appraisals

WHY THEY BACKFIRE AND WHAT TO DO INSTEAD

Tom Coens and **Mary Jenkins**

BK

BERRETT–KOEHLER PUBLISHERS, INC.
San Francisco

Berrett-Koehler Publishers, Inc.
450 Sansome Street, Suite 1200
San Francisco, CA 94111-3320
Tel: 415-288-0260   Fax: 415-362-2512
Website: www.bkpub.com

Ordering Information

Individual sales. Berrett-Koehler publications are available through most bookstores. They can also be ordered direct from Berrett-Koehler Publishers by calling, toll-free; 800-929-2929; fax 802-864-7626.

Quantity sales. Special discounts are available on quantity purchases by corporations, associations, and others. For details, contact the "Special Sales Department" at the Berrett-Koehler address above.

Orders for college textbook/course adoption use. Please contact Berrett-Koehler Publishers toll-free; 800-929-2929; fax 802-864-7626.

Orders by U.S. trade bookstores and wholesalers. Please contact Publishers Group West, 1700 Fourth Street, Berkeley, CA 94710; 510-528-1444; 1-800-788-3123; fax 510-528-9555.

Printed in the United States of America

 Printed on acid-free and recycled paper that is composed of 85 percent recycled waste, including 10 percent postconsumer waste.

Library of Congress Cataloging-in-Publication Data
Coens, Tom, 1947–
   Abolishing performance appraisals : why they backfire
and what to do instead / by Tom Coens and Mary Jenkins.
      p.   cm.
   ISBN 1-57675-076-0 (hard : alk. paper)
   1. Employees—Rating of. 2. Performance standards.
3. Supervision of employees.   I. Jenkins, Mary, 1954–   II. Title.
HF5549.5.R3 C575 2000
658.3′125—dc21   00–010709

First Edition

03 02 01   10 9 8 7 6 5 4 3

Designed by Detta Penna

We dedicate this book

To Peter Scholtes, for his wisdom,
courage, and persistence in boldly
blazing the trail of abolishing
performance appraisals
in the workplace

and

To all the supervisors and managers
who care about people and who
have tried their best to make
performance appraisals work.

Contents

8 Dispelling the Legal Myths and Dealing with Poor Performers   223

Part Three   How to Get There: The Transition to Alternatives   255

9 Disconnecting Appraisal and Designing Alternatives   257

10 Creating Consensus and Confidence for Change   283

Conclusion: Free at Last!   303

What To Do Instead of Appraisal–A Summary   306

Foreword

by Peter Block

This is a foreword that I have been waiting to write. Performance appraisal has become more than a management tool. It has grown into a cultural, almost anthropological symbol of the parental, boss–subordinate relationship that is characteristic of patriarchal organizations. Appraisals are undertaken in good faith, but there is no escape from their basic nature. Their nature is that the boss takes responsibility for the development of the subordinate and exercises that responsibility through a discussion of strengths and weaknesses of the subordinate. This is the exercise of sovereignty, regardless of how lovingly it is done. It make no sense to talk of team- and partnership-oriented cultures, which the marketplace is now demanding, and still hold on to this artifact called performance appraisal.

Now, this does not mean that there is zero value in the appriasal, or that at times it has not been helpful. It has. In fact we all hold our own fatal attraction to the routine; I even made my living from appraisals.

My first assignment in my first job in 1963 was to design a performance appraisal form for fifteen hundred engineers at Esso (to become Exxon, now Exxon Mobil) Research and Engineering Company. I spent six months designing that form. I interviewed engineers, supervisors, and managers until I couldn't stand it anymore. To appease them all, the final form had one hundred and sixty-four different ratable elements of performance. It was designed so that no one could escape unscathed.

When the form was finished and implemented, we began a series of two-day performance appraisal training programs, both to teach people about the form and to train supervisors in how to relate to people in the process. Ten years later, we were still conducting this training program. The form changed and shrank over time, became a blank sheet of paper for a while, was sometimes filled out by the employee, eventually evolved into 360-degree feedback. Regardless of the form, though, the training in how to conduct the appraisal continued unmolested.

After a time, I began to wonder why, if performance appraisal was such a vital and useful happening, did it require perpetual training. At some point I realized that the ultimate purpose of performance appraisal might be to generate gainful employment for staff people and consultants. That might have been acceptable if the appraisal process was benign and did no harm, but this is not the case. Performance appraisal does do harm and this book does a nice job of describing how.

So having begun my career as an advocate, designer, and trainer of appraisal systems, it seems only fitting that I should be a participating witness at its funeral. Perhaps being part of this wake for appraisals will be redemptive and provide forgiveness for all the people fed through the forms and training I so eagerly provided.

I must admit I will feel the loss of performance appraisal, for it has been a wonderful foil for explaining how patriarchal and demeaning institutional life can become. My favorite story, which I will now have to abandon, is to raise the question: If partnership and cooperation are goals of the workplace, does performance appraisal serve that end? I have for years publicly wondered whether, if the appraisal process is so useful, we would consider using it in our personal lives. Would we say to our spouse, significant other, or intimate friend, "Dear, it is time for your annual performance appraisal. For the sake of our relationship and the well-being of the family unit, I want you to prepare for a discussion of your strengths and weaknesses and the ways you have fallen short of your goals for the year. Also, honey, I would like for you to define some stretch goals for the coming year." We might try this at home, but most likely only once.

As if it is not enough to suggest to a life partner that I will be appraising them, would I remind my partner or friend that I am well trained to conduct this discussion? I have been schooled to ask open-ended questions, to maintain eye contact, and to lean forward to indicate interest. And if the appraisal is designed for the development of the subordinate, why is it at the end of the discussion, I am required to say to the grateful subordinate, "That was a great discussion. There is one more thing I need from you . . . would you mind signing this form, just in case of possible future legal action—we need it on record that this discussion was held and that our disappointments in you were duly noted."

Reluctant to do it at home, we still do it at work. We do it even though no one looks forward to it, and most senior managers, who have a little more choice over their fate, do not participate in this ritual. Sold as a developmental experience, I think the real function of performance appraisal and its derivatives is more about maintaining control. It is a time, once a year, when we are reminded by our boss and the institution that they own us. In the name of our development, we have another person involuntarily tell us about our growing edges, where we stand with the institution, what stretch goals we will set, and how we are going to be watched in the coming year.

If this discussion were voluntary, requested, and if the person got to choose whom they got feedback from, then the process might be justified. But the way we do it, it is fundamentally a means of social control. Some day in the distant future, archaeologists will dig up our appraisal forms as major artifacts of our work culture. So, if you stop doing appraisals after reading this book, don't destroy the forms, bury them.

One of my favorite parts of this book is that it explodes the myth that we need appraisals for the sake of a legal defense against the claims of low-rated or fired employees. The authors state clearly that the existence of appraisals do as much harm as good in the company's efforts to defend itself. What a relief.

When we end appraisals as we know them, we have to replace them, for they did fill a need. We all have a need to know where we stand with those we work with. We also need honest dialogue and feedback with each other to learn about ourselves. The goal is to support honest conversation about how we are doing, but do it in a way that is caring and not punitive. Appraisals as we have known them most often have money on the table as part of the discussion, and this brings a weapon into play that gets in the way. When we combine compensation with a developmental discussion, we undermine the openness and vulnerability that development requires, and all our ears can hear is the money.

Hopefully we can reach the point where we can talk about what is good for the individual and what is good for the organization without a coercive dimension to the discussion. We can create cultures where peers can be accountable to each other and bosses can be as open in hearing feedback as they are in giving it. This requires us to choose faith over fear. Faith that most people want to do well, do care about the institution, and are committed to their own learning. If some people violate our faith, then deal strongly with them as an exception, but it is no reason to create low trust practices for all that are needed for just a few.

The book you are about to read is well written and thoughtfully done. The authors' wisdom and advice are needed in a time when the world around us is changing faster than our institutions can adapt. We are all changing our minds about what it means to be an employee. More and more people have contingent, part-time, supplemental, you-name-it jobs, so the old bondage that used to glue us to an organization is weakening. It is a good time to consider more radical changes—and this book pulls us compellingly in that direction.

Peter Block
June 2000

Preface

When we got the idea for this book, we expected to surely find dozens of other books with the same theme. After all, it's common knowledge that every organization struggles with the ritual of performance appraisal, perpetually getting disappointing results. One does not need to consult studies to realize the omnipresent, destructive effects of appraisal. Certainly, in this age of enlightened management, we thought, many others must have condensed appraisal's hopeless track record and offered genuinely different pathways.

To our surprise, however, we found no other books devoted to abolishing appraisal and exploring fresh approaches to the functions of appraisal. We found hundreds of books on various ways of trying to improve, reform, reinvent, or revitalize appraisal, but they largely failed to address appraisal's inherent, inescapable flaws or the idea of dropping it altogether. A good number of books heralded the idea of scrapping appraisal and replacing it with something better. Upon closer examination, however, these "solutions" turned out to be nothing more than appraisal with novel packaging. Beneath the new terminology and promise of something truly different, we invariably found yet another "do-everything-for-everyone" prescription, mandating systematic judgment and regimented collection of paper on every employee. We found no books that seriously attempted to unravel widely-held beliefs underlying appraisal and how to create alternatives upon new premises. Consequently, we bravely undertook the daunting task of taking on the business world's most sacred cow.

We have written this book for *all* of the stakeholders impacted by the process of appraisal. While we have tried to craft a book helpful to human resources and organizational development professionals, we have sought to write from a broader perspective for the executives, business owners, managers, and supervisors who have struggled with appraisal in the trenches. Toward that end, we have included information, stories, and case studies that are of practical value to people at every level, including employees at the bottom rung who, all along, knew deep down that something was terribly wrong. To make the book friendly to this broader audience, we have deliberately de-emphasized the technical and academic aspects, leaving that for others who, hopefully, will join us on this exciting and adventurous new path.

We do not proclaim to have found "the answer" for the dilemmas of appraisal and how to truly accomplish its many worthwhile goals. We do know, however, alternatives will not make a difference unless they are built from new premises and beliefs. As Einstein astutely observed, "The significant problems we face cannot be solved at the same level of thinking we were at when we created them." If, by the close of the book, you understand the critical importance of working from new thinking and assumptions, then we have succeeded in our goal for writing this book.

Tom Coens
Mary Jenkins
August 2000

Acknowledgments

We are deeply indebted to Peter Block for his inspiration and helping us see the true nature of our mission. We likewise are grateful to him for blessing our book with a foreword so befitting our subject. Special thanks also goes to his very able assistant, Maggie Rogers. In the same vein, we extend our heartfelt gratitude to Steven Piersanti, President of Berrett-Koehler Publishers, for his confidence in us, caring personal support, patience, and invaluable suggestions through the writing process.

The writing, reviewing, and rewriting process was far more laborious than we had bargained for, but the generous contribution of others enabled us to persevere. In particular, thanks goes to Amy Gambrell for her skillful editorial assistance throughout the process. We are equally grateful to copy editor Pat Brewer and book producer Detta Penna for their high-quality workmanship, to Elizabeth Swenson for helping us get the right cover, and to so many others at Berrett-Koehler who graciously lent their talents and support. For their diligent assistance in tackling the research, we thank Laura Coens, Thomas M. Coens, Mollie Hunter, and Julia Kooistra. For their many helpful ideas and suggestions in writing and revising the book, we thank Diane Biondi Mukkala, Roger Brice, Eric Budd, Cathie Coens, Joe Farinella, Bob Jenkins, Alfie Kohn, Jim Link, Timothy Schwalm, John Victory, and the talented team of external reviewers retained by Berrett-Koehler.

In writing this book over the past three years, we have received invaluable information and assistance from countless individuals and organizations from around the world. We cannot name them all, but we convey our gratitude to every individual identified in the case studies and stories for their invaluable time and assistance. We likewise thank others who indirectly contributed to the content in significant ways, including Dr. Michael Beer, LuAnn Berry, Kim Bordenkircher, David C. Boyer, Teresa Chappell, Monica Dugan, Joan Holda, David Purcell, and Robert Rodin. In various endnotes, we acknowledge others to whom we are grateful.

Special Acknowledgments from Tom Coens

My life has been a continual blessing of wonderful people who have inspired and enlightened me. Whatever contribution this book may bring is in many ways attributable to them. Though their number is legion, a few played critical roles at pivotal stages of my growth, including Sister Mary Frederick, C.S.J., Prof. Robert McCluggage, Don Heine, Dan New, Phil Granquist, Dr. Arthur Dobbelaere, Ed Graney, Prof. Gerald Berendt, Roger Brice, Dr. Michael Moore, Wayne Harrison, Scottie and Terrill Putman, and Pam Bergeron.

My friend, life companion, and devoted wife, Cathie, has been a pillar of support throughout the arduous years of writing this book. I cannot express in words the extent of my profound gratitude for her loving ways in providing moral and logistical support. The unwavering support of my children Laura (and Ben), Allison and Bill, Tommy (and Laura), and Katie have touched my heart. In the same light, I thank my parents, Ann, my brothers and sisters, and my wife's family. Thanks, too, to my secretary Deanna Kingman for keeping me in some semblance of sanity.

Special Acknowledgments from Mary Jenkins

So many have contributed to my professional growth, generously sharing their knowledge and stimulating my thinking. My passion and undeterred resolve to challenge the status quo, no doubt, evolved from working with colleagues who gave me space and refrained from trying to impose upon me their own view of the world. Much of this repartee took place at General Motors Corporation, and in particular, at the Powertrain division with its great group of people and a courageous leadership team.

No one has contributed to my professional development more than W. Edwards Deming. It was Dr. Deming who encouraged me to examine my thinking, and personally started me down an irreversible path of personal transformation. I will remain forever grateful.

Finally, and most importantly, I am profoundly grateful to my parents, who always encouraged me to openly express my ideas, and to my husband, Bob, and daughter, Katie, who have taught me more about love, support, encouragement, and teamwork than I ever could have learned on my own. Together, they are my constant source of inspiration.

Introduction

Letting Go of a Hopeless Ritual

The world will not be saved by old minds with new programs. If the world is saved, it will be saved by new minds—with no programs.

Daniel Quinn, *The Story of B*

If less than 10% of your customers judged a product effective and seven out of 10 said they were more confused than enlightened by it, you would drop it, right? So, why don't more companies drop their annual job-performance reviews?

Timothy D. Schellhardt, *The Wall Street Journal*

Throughout our work lives, most of us have struggled with performance appraisal. No matter how many times we redesign it, retrain the supervisors, or give it new names, it never comes out right. Again and again, we see supervisors procrastinate or just go through the motions, with little taken to heart. And the supervisors who do take it to heart and give it their best mostly meet disappointment. Earnestly intending to provide constructive feedback and write good development plans and goals, they find that people with less-than-superior ratings are preoccupied with the numerical rating rather than the message. Except for those receiving top ratings, the good conversation they had hoped for rarely happens. Employees tune out and politely complete the interview. Others become defensive and resentful, with shattered relationships sure to follow. Then the supervisors ask themselves, "Where did I go wrong?" knowing they were only doing their job. Some blame themselves. And even more attribute the outcome to the employee's bad attitude in refusing to accept constructive criticism.

After every new experiment with appraisal, word of disappointment filters its way back to the Human Resources department. The H.R. staff reflects on what has happened. They had tried to create a process that would please everyone. They researched and then redesigned the steps, scales, and forms to be friendly and meet organizational objectives. Well-planned and high-spirited training was provided. The new tool was proudly conveyed with sincere enthusiasm. But then the fizzle came, with all the symptoms of the past—the disenchanted supervisors, the procrastination, the employee complaints and appeals. Rather than helping people, the H.R. staff finds itself policing, refereeing, and collecting a lot of paper that doesn't mean much to most people.

Most of us have seen this pattern. We readily recognize the widespread ineffectiveness and resistance to appraisal as well as the unintended, undesirable effects. Most of us tend to treat these outcomes as anomalies to be cast aside, blaming the givers as defective managers and the receivers as malcontents. Because of these beliefs, we continue to hope that people can turn it around and get it right.

Even with our best efforts, however, we cannot get it right. The source of the problem is not the people involved—*it is in the appraisal system itself,* its very nature and its unseen, underlying premises.

In this book, we uproot the underlying premises and beliefs of appraisal so you can see the causes of appraisal outcomes and damaging effects. Upon reflection, we expect you, too, will see that appraisal is a hopeless and futile path. In its place, we offer real hope and entirely new pathways.

We work from the intended purpose of appraisal. Your motives for doing appraisal were never wrong—they were noble and worthy. Good communication, improving performance, motivating and helping employees with their careers, fair promotion and pay practices, reliable legal documentation, and properly documenting counseling and corrective actions—*all* are valid and necessary objectives. Building from these noble intentions, we open new doors and offer alternatives that can bring success and restore joy to people's work. We offer specific guidance on how to transition away from appraisal and even have fun doing it. The pain of policing and the paper-collecting drudgery of appraisal were never fun. In discarding appraisal, however, there are unlimited opportunities for interesting challenges and joy in learning.

The Legacy of Appraisal

Assuredly, challenging the very notion and necessity of appraisal is a daunting task. The practice of giving employees annual ratings or performance evaluations is widely accepted as an essential and valuable tool throughout the business world. Indeed, it is difficult to find large organizations that do not subscribe to the practice of appraisal. Over the past several decades, many books have been written about performance evaluations or performance appraisals (as human resources professionals prefer to call them). At our most recent checking, Amazon.com offers nearly 200 titles that focus on the less-than-fascinating topic of appraisal—more than 50 were published since 1994. The Library of Congress lists more than 500 titles on the topic of appraisal dating back to 1898. Half of these were published after 1975.

While many of these books talk about the pervasive problems associated with appraisal, sparingly few of them engage in any serious, in-depth discussion of the bigger question: *Are they needed at all?* Instead, they give advice and suggestions on how to *improve* appraisals rather than considering the possibility of a work world *without* any kind of performance appraisal.

This book is different. It is not written to give you a better approach in *using* performance appraisals. We have nothing new to sell you. We offer no "newly designed, re-engineered, total-quality, 360-degree, competency-based, high-performance management appraisal process" or any other bottled medicine. Our objective is simple. We wish to challenge you to think about the use of appraisals at a deeper level—to ask yourself the questions rarely contemplated by managers and organizations that perpetuate the use of appraisal today:

- Why do you use performance appraisals?
- Do they accomplish your intended goals?
- What are their real effects?
- Do you really need *any* kind of performance appraisal system?
- If not, are there alternative ways to accomplish your intended goals?

We challenge you to explore these questions with an open mind and then ask you to consider new possibilities to build a more joyful and productive workplace, including, *can* you imagine, work environments *without* any performance appraisal system.

What This Book Is Not About

The confusion and complexities of appraisal are so commonplace that we must briefly say what this book is *not* about before telling you what to expect.

This book is *not* about a better or new way to do performance appraisals. This book is about eliminating appraisals, not doing appraisals in a different way. Nor does this book offer a specific, canned alternative to replace appraisal. As we explain, no one system can address the complex goals of appraisal. And to meet the needs of your unique organization, there are no easy solutions. With examples and a clear-cut strategy at the close of the book, however, we do tell you how to escape the perennial disappointments of appraisal and create alternatives that will really make a difference.

This book is *not* about a new way to do pay-for-performance. The issues surrounding appraisal and merit pay practices overlap to a considerable degree, yet they are different. Incentive pay systems are also fraught with problems, some of which arise from the inability to accurately assess individual performance. Eliminating appraisal does not necessarily mean giving up merit pay practices. For many organizations, however, abolishing performance appraisals will pose new challenges and deeper questions about their merit and incentive pay practices (as we discuss in Chapter 6).

This book is *not* about replacing performance appraisals with a formal mandatory, written feedback system. Managers are increasingly aware that many employees do not like rating scales because of their rather arbitrary and reductionistic nature. To cure these defects, many organizations have moved to a system of annual, written feedback, without rating scales or any connection to pay raises. While this method eliminates some of the problems of traditional appraisal, it nonetheless perpetuates much of the thinking behind appraisal, creating unhealthy effects as we explain in Chapter 5.

Then What Is This Book About?

This book *is* about questioning the underlying assumptions behind the use of performance appraisals. For appraisal to be a reliable and useful tool, certain premises must hold true. For example, we must believe that all employees want to be coached with the same approach, or we must believe that people who rate performance can be unbiased and objective. We have asked thousands of people whether these and other appraisal assumptions are reasonable. The response is always the same—*the key underlying assumptions of appraisals are not logical and realistic*.

This book *is* about a return to authenticity in communication, giving feedback, and partnering with employees. Good communication is critical in today's fast-changing workplace. More than ever before, we rely on employees to be committed and responsible for the functions they serve. We need employees to partner with management in meeting customer needs amid global competition and, in the public and nonprofit sectors, to help us survive life-threatening financial conditions. Far more often than not, appraisal actually *impedes* authentic communication and partnering.

This book *is* about redefining the roles of managers and employees. In this new century, the relationship between managers and employees is undergoing dramatic change. The new workforce, if it is to be energized at all, will more and more demand a genuine say in how the work is to be done. The prevailing mode of work has shifted to empowerment, collaboration, and teams. These changes mean that every manager will serve in a new role. It requires a shift from "managing" people to *helping* people manage themselves and the business. With the information age, new technology, and flattened organizations, a manager's work-knowledge skills will become increasingly less important. More and more workplaces of the future will require managers to excel in *people* skills and the *artful* leadership evinced by a shared sense of purpose and vision.

New roles for managers also means new mental models for employees. Paramount to this book is the idea: *Employees want to be and are fully capable of being responsible for themselves*. With a supportive work culture and access to helpful resources and training, employees will take responsibility to get timely and useful feedback, grow their skills, and improve their performance in alignment with organizational needs.

In asking you to abolish appraisal, we are really challenging you to answer a deeper question: *What type of work culture do you really want to create?* Do you want one where managers are responsible for their employees or where *everyone* through collaborative efforts is accountable for the work to be done?

This book *is* about giving leaders the freedom to choose for themselves the most effective ways of working with people. It is hypocritical and unrealistic to hold executives, managers, and supervisors "accountable" for outcomes or talk about an empowered organization when we mandate one specific coaching approach for everyone who supervises. Though well intended, appraisal uniformly imposes a single method for conveying feedback, managing performance, measuring competencies, developing employees, and the like. Instead, each manager, based on his or her unique personal style and particular assignment, must be given the space and freedom to choose the best methods and timing for coaching, feedback, and fostering performance and development.

Lastly, this book *is* about refocusing on outstanding *organizational* performance. The widespread practice of using *individual* performance appraisals to attain *organizational* improvement stems from the myth that better organizational performance will result from getting each person to do a better job. Substantial organizational improvement can only be achieved by improving the *whole* organization as a complex system. While individual improvement efforts are beneficial and often necessary, too much emphasis is placed on improving the organization by working on individuals. In place of appraisal, we urge organizations to use alternative strategies that seek improvement from a broader perspective. At the same time, we discuss how individual improvement initiatives can better align with the organization as a whole.

Getting to the "Instead"

If you are anything like the audiences we encounter, you anxiously want us to just zip ahead to "what to do instead." The "instead" is not a concise list, a set of new forms, or best practices that you can model. The "instead" can only begin with *new thinking*. And we know no effective way to help you get there unless you first understand the dynamics of appraisal and why it fails. To short-cut this step will only doom your best efforts to start anew.

We are often told about companies that purportedly have abolished appraisal. But when we take a closer look, we find they have adopted merely a *variation* of appraisal—people are still having things done *to* them, paper is collected for the personnel file, and every employee and supervisor is required to use some process that was determined to be in their best interest. Invariably, the symptoms and effects of appraisal pop up again.

To get to an "instead" that will really make a difference, you must design alternatives from an entirely new set of premises and beliefs about people, work, motivation, improvement, and the nature of leadership. For most of us, it is extremely difficult to think in terms of new assumptions— our conventional ways of looking at workplace issues are steeped in hidden, unhealthy assumptions that underscore control and a lack of trust in employees. To keep them from popping up again in designing our "insteads," we must look at what happened in appraisal and clearly identify the operative assumptions. Only then can we avoid repeating our mistakes.

We are as anxious to get to what to do instead as you are, but to create meaningful alternatives, we must work through the assumptions. To ease this arduous task, we provide an overview of appraisal's pervasive assumptions (Chapter 1) and throughout the book discuss assumptions relating to the functions of appraisal. To reinforce the learning, we close chapters with a recap of conventional appraisal assumptions and new assumptions from which we can create alternatives.

A Road Map

The book is organized into three parts: *Why Appraisals Backfire: The Fatal Flaws* (Part One), *What to Do Instead: Five Functions of Appraisal* (Part Two), and *How to Get There: The Transition to Alternatives* (Part Three).

Part One provides foundations that are critical for the remainder of the book. Chapter 1 clarifies what we mean by *appraisal* and spells out its key functions. It further explains the mechanics of *underlying assumptions* and discusses assumptions that repeatedly crop up in the various functions of appraisal. Chapter 2 challenges you to think about organizational improvement in a new light. This new perspective will prove invaluable in designing alternatives to appraisal. In Chapter 3, we examine appraisal's track record as a rating tool. As you probably understand, this is an important underpinning to other functions of appraisals, particularly pay and promotions.

In Part Two, we discretely examine the five major functions of appraisal in separate chapters: coaching (Chapter 4); feedback (Chapter 5); fair pay and motivation (Chapter 6); development and promotions (Chapter 7); and problem performers and legal documentation (Chapter 8). With respect to each function, we identify the most commonly held underlying assumptions. From this foundation, we recommend specific strategies with case studies and examples for designing alternatives.

In Part Three, we lay out a series of sequential steps to phase out appraisal and to design and implement alternatives. Finding the right alternatives for your organizations cannot be expedited—it requires careful inquiry and strategic measures to garner support from the entire organization. Bypassing these measures is a sure formula for failure.

At the end of the book, *What the Sages Say* and *Further Reading and Resources* provide supplemental information.

The most difficult challenge in writing this book was to find a logical, coherent order to present the ideas. We have found it most difficult to write about any one aspect of appraisal functions and problems without concurrently addressing others. After considerable rework, we found this presentation to be the most economical and effective. You may have bought this book with particular interest in a single function, such as feedback, pay, or employee development. However, you will get the most out of this book if you resist the temptation of jumping ahead, or, if you can't resist, then at least read through Chapter 3 before skipping ahead.

Though abolishing appraisal is the prevailing theme of this book, we understand that, in the end, you or your organization may not choose abolishment. If you choose to stay with appraisal, however, we hope, at the very least, that this book enables you to better understand what you are doing and why you are doing it.

Part One

Why Appraisals Backfire: The Fatal Flaws

*How human organizations
can be conceived, organized,
and led in ways that best release
human ingenuity and
maximize human choice
is one of the great conundrums
of the (new) century . . .
Fusing chaos and order
in uncentralized systems
is bound to be the key
to that puzzle.*

—Harlan Cleveland

1

Good Intentions That Never Deliver

It is not enough to change strategies, structures, and systems, unless the thinking that produced those strategies, structures, and systems also changes.

Peter Senge, *The Dance of Change*

It seems quite probable, as we continue to question our current practices, that most systems of performance appraisals . . . will be unmasked as detrimental to human spirit.

Dick Richards, *Artful Work*

Abolish performance appraisal. Yes, it feels uncomfortable to say that. Appraisal represents the conventional wisdom. We've grown accustomed to it, in spite of its inevitable flaws. Letting go of it feels like we're going on a course to abandon people and their needs—the need for feedback, good coaching and development, the need for a measuring stick so people and the organization can know where people stand.

Our discomfort is quite natural. It stems from the truly good intentions behind appraisal. Abolishing appraisal does not mean abandoning its good intentions. It is diametrically the opposite—it is about getting serious about those intentions and finding pathways that *can* deliver without bringing on the perennial problems of appraisal. In this chapter, we separate the wheat from the chaff, keeping the worthy intentions of appraisal while we thresh out its structures and underlying beliefs. It is those potent beliefs and the resulting structures that ensure failure and the unintended toxic side effects.

To bring focus and clarity to this discussion, we begin by defining what we mean by *performance appraisal*. After all, there are innumerable euphemisms for appraisal and many variations in form. At their extreme, the variations may make it difficult to discern whether we are talking about appraisal or something else. Next we examine the noble intentions of appraisal. Before we can intelligently discuss their flaws and what to do instead, we must be clear about what appraisals are trying to achieve. Then, we take a distant look at the *outcomes* and *effects* of appraisals. Finally, as a foundation for the remainder of the book, we examine the beliefs or *underlying assumptions* that cause the repeated failure of appraisal.

■ What Do We Mean by Performance Appraisal?

Confusion prevails over what appraisal is and is not. Many organizations have proclaimed that they have dropped the practice, but what they do instead is merely appraisal with a new name. The goal of this book is to truly *abolish* appraisal. If ultimately this is your goal as well, it is critical to understand what appraisal is and is not. To clarify the difference between a variation of appraisal and *genuine* alternatives to appraisal, we start with a good working definition.

Although management textbooks provide scores of definitions for *performance appraisal*, a mere dictionary gets us off to a good start. *Performance* is defined as "the way in which someone or something functions."[1] *Appraise* comes from the Latin word *pretiare*, meaning *to value*. Hence, appraisal is a process in which we *evaluate, judge,* or *estimate*.[2] Combining these definitions, we may say that performance appraisal is the *process of evaluating or judging the way in which someone is functioning*.

Gertrude Stein ·

"A Rose Is a Rose Is a Rose"

Performance appraisal is the most accepted term describing the subject of this book. It is generally interchangeable with *performance evaluation, performance review, annual review, personal rating, performance rating,* and the like. It also may include appraisal schemes that are called *performance management, 360-degree feedback,* or *competency modeling.* The descriptors *performance review* or *performance evaluation* are perhaps most popular in the vernacular, but human resources professionals prefer to call it *performance appraisal.* Using the word *appraisal* makes this process easily distinguishable from another unrelated process called *job evaluation,* a system used to rate and compare *jobs* (not people) for pay purposes. Throughout this book, we will simply use the term *appraisal* as a cauldron for all the names and variations of performance appraisal.

When we speak of appraisal, our focus is on processes that judge *individual* performance, not the performance of an organization or a business unit. Although widely varying in form, appraisal, as conventionally practiced, will nearly always contain the five distinguishing features we summarize below. If a process is missing some of these features, we would not view it as a systematic appraisal practice but rather as some other type of communication, personal development, or organizational development tool. Regardless of what it is called (see *"A Rose Is a Rose"*), we believe the practice of performance appraisal exists when most or all of the following features are present in a single process or tool:

1. **Employees' individual work performance, behaviors, or traits are rated, judged, and/or described by someone other than the employee.** In many organizations today, appraisal feedback is given by persons other than the immediate supervisor (e.g., co-workers, subordinates, internal or external customers, suppliers, or professional raters). Just because the supervisor is not the sole rater or one of the raters, the process may nonetheless constitute a form of appraisal. A tool in which *the employee* is the sole judge would be a developmental tool rather than a performance appraisal.

2. **Such ratings, judgments, and descriptions relate to a specific time period (e.g., a year, a calendar quarter) rather than a particular work product or project.** A salesperson may get a written evaluation after each sales call from the trainer—feedback of this type on a work product, project, or task is an appraisal of sorts, but it is not the systematic appraisal process that is the target of this book.

3. **The process is systematically applied to all employees or a class of employees.** Sometimes people are selectively evaluated because they are performing poorly or they are asking for special help. Selective evaluations would be an appropriate form of *individual intervention* and

do not constitute systematic appraisal as general practice, and such is not in conflict with the goals of this book.

4. **The process is either mandatory or induced by an extrinsic incentive (e.g., eligibility for a pay raise) as opposed to a process that is purely voluntary or elective.** An employee who freely chooses to seek feedback, without coercion or extrinsic incentive, is engaged in an employee development process.

5. **The results of ratings, judgments, or documentation are kept or preserved by someone in the organization other than the rated employee.** If, for legal or other reasons, the results of the evaluative process are preserved as a record by the organization (in the H.R. department, supervisor's records, or by someone other than the rated employee), this would be consistent with appraisal. However, if the *sole* purpose of the ratings, judgments, or work documentation is to provide information for the *employee's* own use, and there is no requirement to file the documented evidence of the evaluation or feedback with the organization, it is a communication or development tool.

Putting these five characteristics together into a single statement, for purposes of this book we can say:

> The practice of *performance appraisal* is a mandated process in which, for a specified period of time, all or a group of employees' work performance, behaviors, or traits are individually rated, judged, or described by a person other than the rated employee and the results are kept by the organization.

We can illustrate this definition through a couple of examples. Some organizations have pared conventional appraisal down to a process in which all employees simply receive written feedback from supervisors or others. In this approach, the employer systematically requires employees to undergo a feedback session that culminates in a written feedback form. There are no numeric ratings or scales. The outcome of the feedback is disconnected from pay raises, promotion, or layoffs. The human resources department or supervisor keeps a record of the written feedback form. Although such a feedback mechanism would be friendlier than conventional appraisal approaches, it nonetheless is a variation of *performance appraisal*. Even though there are no scales or ratings, there is an *evaluation* or *judgment*, explicitly or implicitly, about the success of that employee. Such documented records, at least implicitly, would reflect upon the quality of work performed. Because the process still mandatorily imposes an evaluation by others, we label this process an *appraisal*.

By contrast, in some organizations, the responsibility for feedback has been shifted to the employee. The employee freely decides if and when to initiate and gather feedback from various sources. When collected, the results are sent only to the rated employee (or, sometimes, 360-degree models utilize a processing center that deletes the identity of contributors but makes no record of the feedback). The employee keeps all of the feedback records but may choose to share and discuss the results with others (supervisor, mentor, career counselor, etc.). Though this process partly resembles appraisal, the elective features and exclusive control by the employee would cause us to characterize it as an employee development tool.

The distinction between the above two examples may seem trivial at this juncture, but it is critical in evaluating alternatives to appraisal. Feedback may be the key action in both processes, but the absence of certain structures in the second suggests an entirely different set of beliefs and this, as we shall explain, will drive entirely different outcomes.

■ The Intentions and Purposes of Appraisal

The above definitions tell us little about the *purposes* of appraisal. When we ask organizations why they use appraisals, we get a variety of answers and a very long list to boot. In one form or another, the items in Figure 1.1 typically are mentioned.

Give feedback	Set and measure goals
Promotion screening/decisions	Motivate/provide recognition
Get performance improvement	Downsize/layoff decisions
Coaching and mentoring	Award pay increases
Counsel problem performers	Measure individual performance
Development/training needs	Legal documentation
Career Advancement	

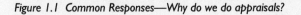

Figure 1.1 Common Responses—Why do we do appraisals?

Various surveys are consistent with our audience's responses. For example, an earlier survey 2,400 members from human resources, finance, marketing, and information systems departments, taken by the American Management Association, found that 86% of the respondents said appraisal was tied to *compensation* decisions. Another 65% of the same respondents reported that the tool was to be used for *counseling*, while 64% identified *training and development*. Other purposes also drew high responses including: *promotion* (45%), *staff planning* (43%), and *retention and discharge* (30%).[3]

A key goal of this book is to explain why appraisals backfire. We can't explain why until we specify the purpose of performance appraisal. In other words, *What are we trying to accomplish?*[4] In most organizations the answer is several items in Figure 1.1. For the sake of economy and logical organization, we have taken the commonly identified purposes of appraisal and allocated them into six broadly defined functional categories, each of which we address in separate chapters. The six functional categories are:

1. **Improvement.** The process should help both the employee and the organization to get better results, improving quality, efficiency, effectiveness, alignment, and the like (Chapter 2).

2. **Coaching and Guidance.** In the traditional management view, appraisal provides a managerial tool and framework for coaching, counseling, and motivating employees (Chapter 4).

3. **Feedback and Communication.** Appraisal is intended to enhance communication between the employee, supervisor, and others in the organization, including feedback on employee performance (Chapter 5).

4. **Compensation.** By tying appraisal to compensation (salary increases, bonuses), purportedly people will work harder. In theory, the pay also will be more fair, rewarding the most deserving employees (Chapter 6).

5. **Staffing Decisions and Professional Development.** Appraisal attempts to provide information to enable the organization to fairly and effectively select employees for promotion, layoffs, or reductions-in-force (RIFs). It's also used to identify staffing and training needs and assist employees in their career development (Chapter 7).

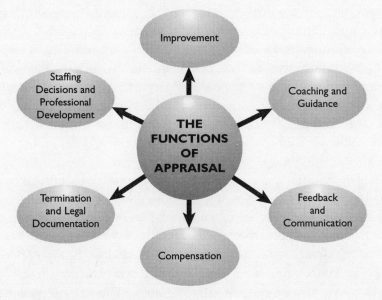

Figure 1.2   The Functions of Appraisal

6. **Termination and Legal Documentation.** Effectively written appraisals should provide objective and impartial documentation that is necessary or useful in disciplinary and discharge decisions—ultimately they may be challenged by the unemployment office, civil rights agencies, and union representatives (Chapter 8).

We have not listed the rating process as a function of appraisal because it is not a function in and of itself, but rather a tool that is used with appraisal functions such as pay, career advancement, promotion, and determination of training needs. The process of rating, however, is so critical to the functions of appraisal that we have devoted an entire chapter to appraisal as a rating tool (Chapter 3).

■ Do Appraisals Work?

Knowing the reasons why we do appraisal, the question is—do they work? As you work your way through this book, we hope that you will see the answer for yourself. In the interest of honesty at the outset, let us say it is our fervent belief that appraisal does not work. It impedes the reception of feedback, and there is no solid evidence that it motivates people or leads to meaningful improvement. Due to its inherent design flaws, appraisal produces distorted and unreliable data about the contribution of employees. Consequently, the resulting documentation is not useful for staffing decisions and often does not hold up in court. Too often, appraisal destroys human spirit and, in the span of a 30-minute meeting, can transform a vibrant, highly committed employee into a demoralized, indifferent wallflower who reads the want ads on the weekend.

Our harsh censure of appraisal rests on a solid foundation. Academia, industry, and professional associations have intensely scrutinized appraisal for more than 50 years now, producing hundreds of studies, surveys, and articles. Despite a strong bias by many researchers who favor appraisal or imply that appraisal is indispensable, these studies and surveys offer scant evidence of appraisal's success. A survey by the Society for Human Resources Management found that more than 90% of appraisal systems were not successful.[5] Another survey by Development Dimensions Incorporated, a leading H.R. consulting firm, found that most employers expressed "overwhelming" dissatisfaction with their performance management systems.[6] In an *Industry Week* survey, only 18% of respondents said their performance reviews were effective, with 48% of respondents calling them "second-guessing sessions."[7] A 1997 survey by Aon Consulting and the Society of Human Resources Management found that a mere 5% of H.R. professionals polled reported that they were "very satisfied" with their performance management systems.[8] Throughout the rest of this book we discuss the reasons for these dismal results.

■ Why Do We Hang onto a Process That Doesn't Work?

Taken as a whole, the research decidedly demonstrates that appraisals are ineffective and cause a spate of undesirable, unintended effects. As we excavated a mountain of research on appraisal, we became increasingly amazed that business scholars and leaders have not collectively called a halt to the practice. With the vast majority of organizations repeatedly experiencing disappointing results and problems with appraisal, we wonder why there isn't more discussion about dropping it, rather than trying to fix it.

As a person who has purchased or checked out this book, you very likely sense that your appraisals are not working. You also likely have observed some of the damage done by appraisal and may have some notions about why it doesn't work. You may have a clear sense that most people in your organization dislike, disregard, and even despise the process. Interestingly, even if your sense is correct, you shouldn't expect the people in your organization to stand up and cheer if you announce the end of appraisal. In fact, if you take a poll without any educational initiative, asking people in your organization if they would like to abolish appraisal, we predict that most employees will say "keep it." Even in organizations with high rates of dissatisfaction and disillusionment about appraisal, you will get this reaction.

Why do people want to keep a process that has never worked? There are many answers to this complex enigma. In part, people want appraisal because its purposes are worthy—the notion of tossing appraisal seemingly means abandoning those purposes. People think that no appraisal means no feedback, no special help on career and performance issues. They believe no appraisal means arbitrary decisions about pay adjustments and career advancement. They also cling to the illusion that they need appraisal to tell them where they stand. As we explain in the pay chapter, most people believe that they are top-notch performers (for example, 80% of people perceive themselves to be in the top quarter of all performers), and they believe that an evaluative system will recognize this and reward them with pay increases, career advancement, promotions, and other perks. To them, dropping appraisal will mean their good efforts will go unnoticed and unrewarded—they will get the same treatment as their sub-par peers. Because they have not examined the underlying assumptions of appraisal, they see its perennial problems only as something that needs to be fixed—a new design or better training could fix the problem.

Given this prevailing view, each organization has two choices in dealing with the futile process of appraisal. Choice one is to appease everyone by continuing the practice, promoting the illusion that appraisal works and pretending not to notice the harmful side effects. Choice two is to begin an organization-wide initiative of *education* in which you help people understand *why* appraisal fails and then, *together*, work on strategies to replace appraisal, looking for genuinely new ways to actually deliver on the high hopes that were placed in appraisal. The rest of this book is aimed at the latter course.

▪ Why Appraisal Fails—Its Underlying Assumptions

When organizations begin to recognize the ineffectiveness and damaging effects of their appraisal system, they embark on fixing it. Usually the "fixing" is focused in one of two areas: (1) improving the *design* of the process (e.g., new criteria, new scales, more interaction, more raters, more frequent appraisals) or (2) improving the *implementation* (e.g., better training, stricter rules to ensure timely execution, checking raters for consistency and bias tendencies). These improvement initiatives do little to help, however, because the problem with appraisal is neither in the design or implementation—it is beneath the surface in the form of *underlying assumptions*, i.e., the basic premises and beliefs upon which the appraisals are built.

Underlying assumptions are unsurfaced beliefs or premises that we take as given or true even though we do not express them. They are present whenever we implement a policy or work rule, establish a practice, or give a directive. Assumptions are not necessarily true, but without evidence or question, we treat them as true. For example, if we tie an incentive bonus to achieving a certain performance outcome, we assume that the bonus will motivate the person to work harder. Or we may assume that, without an incentive, the person will withhold his best efforts. If we mandate supervisors to give feedback once a year, we assume that the employee will be receptive to feedback in a formal setting. We also assume that the feedback will lead to change and improved performance. Assumptions are accepted and presupposed without proof or empirical demonstration. Sometimes our assumptions are clear and easy to identify. More often our assumptions are unsurfaced and obscure; hence, *underlying*. Although we can't see them, we rely on them in designing an appraisal practice.

Underlying assumptions are unavoidable. They underlie all human resources practices, the good, the bad, and the ugly. They may be helpful or undermining. They may be healthy and consistent with idealized corporate values or clash sharply, promoting unhealthy and negative associations about people and work. Some assumptions are true. Some are not. Others are partly true or are sometimes true. The key point is that they will *always* affect your processes—they may even drive the process. To design effective H.R. systems and practices, assumptions must be made explicit so that they may be tested and evaluated for reliability and desirability. The goal is to choose assumptions that are realistic and reliable, to use assumptions that align with the desired organizational culture.

Underlying assumptions reflect an organization's unspoken beliefs and values. Typically these beliefs form a constellation of related assumptions that center on people and work—the nature of people as trustworthy or not, what motivates people and influences their behaviors, how people should be managed, the way the work gets done, and beliefs about how communication, improvement, and change occur. Though not expressed in policies and practices, these assumptions dynamically impact their efficacy. They speak volumes to the people of the organization as to how they are perceived.

The assumptions underlying appraisal are many, complex, and interrelated. To uncover them, organizations must ask: *What underlying beliefs or premises do we hold to be true in the design and implementation of our appraisal?* When organizations take the time to unearth these beliefs, people begin to see why appraisal processes consistently get disappointing results and unintended, harmful side effects. Some of these assumptions are unique to particular functions of appraisal, such as pay, feedback, or legal documentation, but a number of the assumptions cut across most or all of the functions. Several overriding assumptions appear in nearly every design of appraisal, and many of these are faulty or unhelpful. Among many possibilities, the assumptions in Figure 1.3 on pages 22 and 23 seem to be prevalent in conventional appraisal designs, across most or all of the functions.

What we find interesting about these assumptions is their recurrent nature in designing both improvements to appraisal and in purported alternatives to appraisal. In striving to shed the problems of conventional appraisal, H.R. staff and their managerial colleagues earnestly and enthusiastically try to create something better, something that is positive and supportive of people. Yet, with rare exceptions, we find that the end product reflects most or all of the assumptions in Figure 1.3.

To effectively design alternatives to performance appraisal or design any kind of human resources system, we must unearth and examine the assumptions of the system we are replacing. More than a mental exercise, making assumptions explicit is an indispensable step of the design process. Systems thinker Jamshid Gharajedaghi illuminates the importance of this design step:

Assumption	Nature of Defect	Alternative Assumption
One appraisal process can effectively serve several functions at the same time.	Appraisal is overloaded with too many functions—in many cases one function undercuts the other (e.g., money gets in the way of receiving feedback).	The multiple purposes of appraisal can be better achieved through separate designs and processes.
A one-size-fits-all coaching, feedback, and development structure works well for all supervisors and employees in all situations.	Every individual does not effectively relate well to the same style of coaching and feedback. Supervisors also have individual preferences that better align with their strengths and the particular situation.	Employees' and supervisors' preferences and needs for coaching, feedback, and development vary with the individual and the situation, and change over time.
You can get commitment from a forced process.	Without commitment, performance improvement, growth, and development will likely not occur—commitment is thwarted, not encouraged, when it is forced through a compulsory process.	Commitment can best be nurtured through a supportive work environment, encouragement, a compelling vision, education and training, and, most of all, choices.
The organization and supervisors are responsible for employees' feedback, development, and performance.	Empowerment is promoted as an organizational value, yet appraisal imposes processes that make the supervisor, not the employee, the driver of improvement and compiler of feedback.	As healthy adults, people need to be responsible for their own feedback, performance, and development, with and without support from the organization.
Appraisal processes can objectively and reliably evaluate and assess individual performance.	Appraisal is fraught with bias and rater errors and is based on incomplete and unreliable information, even when people are doing their best to get it right.	Evaluative processes are largely subjective; just-in-time ratings provided for a single purpose will be more valid and reliable than multi-use ratings.
Appraisals are required by law or are necessary to assure legal documentation.	With few exceptions, the law does not require appraisals—appraisal evidence tends to help employees in legal actions at least as much as it helps employers—just-in-time, written counseling will provide more reliable documentation.	Employers can defend against employee lawsuits by documenting serious deficiencies and providing deficient employees with prompt notice, good information about the nature of the deficiency, and assistance as appropriate.

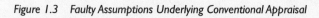

Figure 1.3   Faulty Assumptions Underlying Conventional Appraisal

Assumption	Nature of Defect	Alternative Assumption
Ratings are motivating and let people know where they stand.	Ratings typically don't provide information that is helpful or reflective of employee's true status; ratings also undermine commitment and demoralize because nearly everyone expects to be rated highly and have their efforts appreciated.	In a supportive work climate, people will use good information to improve their performance, if given the training and opportunities. People want to access (and should have access to) the information that influences decisions about their pay, promotion, status, and future.
Feedback, development, and performance improvement are annual (or quarterly events).	Feedback should be viewed as being available *all the time,* not as a calendar-driven event. Improvement opportunities may knock at any time. The need for development differs from one job to another, the particular situation, and each individual's openness at any point in time.	It is the individual's job to seek out the feedback needed to grow and improve performance at the most opportune time. The best time for improvement and development discussions is variable and depends on the situation, individual needs, personal choices, and good timing.
People withhold effort if they feel they are not being extrinsically rewarded.	This assumption suggests that people are uncommitted to their jobs and unmotivated to work. While inadequate money and recognition may *demotivate,* people are intrinsically motivated to do a good job. Rather than rewarding people, organizations need strategies to unleash the intrinsic motivation that is already present.	Healthy people are intrinsically motivated to perform well when the work is meaningful. Pay is not a motivator but can be a powerful demotivator when it is inequitable. Intrinsic motivation may be diminished by encouraging focus on extrinsic motivators.
Inspecting individuals leads to improvement, and improving individual performance improves organizational performance.	Getting improvement comes not from inspection but from looking at opportunities to understand the overall system that drives outcomes. Improving individuals is often important but is a low-yield strategy for improving the organization.	Improving systems and processes improves the performance of the organization. Improvement results from identifying and studying the cause of a problem or specific opportunity for improvement, developing a plan, learning, and acting on the learning that occurs.

The implicitness of the organizing assumptions, residing at the core of the organization's collective memory, is overpowering. Accepted on faith, these assumptions are transformed into unquestioned practices that may obstruct the future. Unless the content and implications of these implicit, cultural codes are made explicit and dismantled, the nature of the beast will outlive the temporary effects of interventions, no matter how well planned.[9]

To effectively start the redesign process, the organization must carefully and thoroughly excavate the underlying assumptions of the practice it intends to replace. If the intent is to design a new system, you may wonder why we advocate examining assumptions of the former system first. This is necessary for two important reasons:

1. Unhealthy underlying assumptions about people and work are deeply ingrained in our thinking. If we don't see them clearly and pull out their roots, they will surface again like weeds in the new system design. By digging up and removing the roots of these weeds (making the assumptions of the former system explicit) in the design of alternative systems, we create integrity between what we say and what we believe.

2. Surfacing and examining the assumptions of the former appraisal process generates the creative sparks needed to effectively design alternative systems. Digging up these unsurfaced beliefs provides a source of new ideas for the healthier assumptions needed to drive a new culture.

In Chapter 9, we discuss strategies for unearthing assumptions, and *Further Reading and Resources* has citations under *Designing New H.R. Systems*. Throughout the remainder of the book, we help you see the recurring assumptions and assumptions related to particular functions (coaching, feedback, pay, etc.). To help you sharpen your skills in seeing the assumptions and developing viable alternative assumptions, the first eight chapters close with a matrix of appraisal and alternative assumptions.

■ Generally Applicable Assumptions of Appraisal

Before going on to assumptions relating to the various functions of appraisal, let us examine some of the broadly applicable, pervasive assumptions and contrast them with what we believe about the real world.

One appraisal process can effectively serve several functions at the same time.

Organizations commonly expect their appraisal process to concurrently accomplish a number of functions—motivate employees; encourage communication and feedback; provide a vehicle for coaching and goal setting; establish reliable data for pay, promotion, and layoff decisions; and assure the organization of legal documentation needed to deal with poor performers. Our inclination to accept this assumption emanates from the idea of economy—if we have to sit down with a person once or twice a year, we might as well take care of coaching, alignment, feedback, career counseling, and personal development all at the same time. Moreover, if we're taking time to rank or rate a person's standing for pay purposes, we might as well use the same data to determine promotions, decide who stays during a reduction-in-force (RIF), and identify sub-par performers who should be shown the door. On the surface, integrating all of these functions into a single process for the sake of efficiency seems to make good sense.

In reality, however, the practice of bundling multiple functions is a key contributor to the dismal track record of appraisals. Because so many functions are associated with appraisal, its purpose is confusing and ambiguous to raters and ratees. When multiple functions are loaded on appraisal, the process becomes cumbersome and time-consuming, perhaps explaining in part supervisors' procrastination and reluctance to execute the process. The aim and purpose also become foggy and distorted, resulting in varying interpretations and emphases. Consequently, mixed messages are sent, learning is impeded, and some purposes of appraisal are undermined or just plop on the floor.

Beyond the confusion, overloading appraisals with multiple tasks creates impediments and conflicts in which the pursuit of one purpose undermines another. If people are focused on pay, it will be difficult for them to really hear, accept, and integrate feedback. If low appraisal ratings are connected to discipline for poor performers, fear will be associated with the process, engendering defensiveness that may undermine learning and the acceptance of coaching in a constructive way. A 1991 survey by Wyatt Company found only 41% of nearly 6,000 employees interviewed had learned something useful during performance appraisals, while the remainder found the experience negative or were noncommittal.[10] Substantial research also has shown that linking appraisals to personnel decisions, such as compensation and promotions, leads to higher incidence of distortion and rater errors.[11] Ratings collected for pay and promotion are significantly higher than ratings of the same individuals collected for the purpose of feedback, research, and other purposes.[12] While an organization's human resources policies and practices need to be cut from a common cloth, loading a multitude of key functions into a single process sacrifices effectiveness for the illusion of efficiency. (See "Have You Had This Experience?")

A True Story

Have You Had This Experience?[13]

Julia Brooks is a Benefits Analyst with Big-3 Auto, reporting to Kathleen Coyle, Director of Benefits. Julia and Kathleen have worked together for three years. In their day-to-day work, they get along very well—they are cordial, open, and supportive with one another. Big-3 Auto requires annual appraisals for feedback, coaching, counseling, and development. They are also tied to pay increases and, in some instances, promotion decisions. The results are kept in the official personnel file.

Weeks before Julia's review, Julia tells Kathleen that she is really looking forward to the appraisal meeting. "I'd really like you to give me some honest feedback so I can learn and strengthen my performance," Julia says. Kathleen is delighted that Julia is so enthusiastic and open to improving. Kathleen puts in hours preparing for the meeting, looking at evidence of Julia's work, thinking about her strengths and weaknesses, and considering opportunities for Julia to improve.

The day arrives and Kathleen meets with Julia in a cozy conference room, sitting next to her at a round table. They crack the ice with a little joking about the event, and it is clear they are both in good spirits and up for the meeting. Kathleen begins talking to Julia about her strengths and her many contributions in keeping the benefit functions humming. Kathleen then artfully delves into the first of three areas where she feels Julia could make some improvement. Julia's response is denial and defense. On the next issue, Julia again puts up a wall, challenging Kathleen's observations and viewpoint. Kathleen, feeling frustrated, takes a deep breath, and then starts to give feedback on the last area for improvement. Before she even finishes, Julia cuts her off with "But this . . ." and "But that . . ." In total exasperation, Kathleen stops and says, "What do you want from me? You asked for some honest feedback. I spent two half days looking over your work, thinking of where you could grow. Today, I'm just trying to honestly tell you what I think and what could go better. You've done nothing but shut me down, telling me I've got it wrong and why the improvement isn't necessary." Julia looked stunned and didn't respond.

After an eternity of silence, Kathleen finished her last point and Julia said nothing. Kathleen nervously covered development goals while Julia passively nodded. Julia signed the review, and it was sent on to her personnel file. Julia's pay raise was as good as anyone's in the department. In the days following the review, it was clear that the relationship had taken a big step downhill. Kathleen gazed out the window, asking herself, "Why did my best efforts to help Julia and give her the feedback she expressly asked for end in such disaster?"

Some would say Julia needs an attitude change. Others would say Kathleen must become more artful. What is seldom asked is—How did the context of the formal process of appraisal affect their conversation? Did the tenor of formal judgment and link to other purposes (pay and promotion) impact the quality of communication and listening?

Assumption

People want to know and need to know where they stand, and appraisals tell people where they stand.

At a recent quality conference, a CEO was questioned as to why his organization continued to use appraisals after shifting to a quality management culture of system and process improvement. After a slight pause, he replied, "We think we owe it to people to let them know where they stand." On its face, his reason seems sensible and sound. It's a rationale we encounter in many organizations. While we would readily concede that most employees would like to know the answer to this question, the question itself raises profound implications and connects to a number of related, dependent assumptions that must be unearthed.

First, it is important to understand what "where do I stand" means. Does it mean—*How am I doing? How do I compare to others? Am I promotable? Where will I be if the downsizing comes?* We have found that it means different things to different people. Most people believe, quite correctly, that their status will impact them in a number of areas, including their pay, job perks, whether they get favorable assignments, career advancement, job security, and even psychological concerns, such as whether they and their opinions and contributions are valued by the organization.

More important than the meaning of the question is—Why do so many people have an urgent need to ask the *where-do-I-stand* question? We believe that, at some level, people know that there are unseen remnants of control in their organization that affect pay, promotions, career

> ### Author and organizational trainer Rick Maurer
> ### on the paternalism of appraisal
>
> Most performance review systems reinforce a paternalistic world, one
> built on distrust and the assumption that the boss knows more about
> our skills, abilities, and commitment than we do. This dependency
> works against empowerment. And focusing on individual problems,
> rather than looking at systems issues, works against the grain of qual-
> ity improvement.[17]

advancement, favorable assignments, and the like. At some level people
recognize that these remnants are largely disconnected from appraisal.
They will quickly tell you that appraisal is unfair, political, and biased.
Paradoxically, these same people steadfastly hold onto the belief that they
need appraisal to tell them where they stand. This is a strange addiction,
considering that the habit of appraisal rarely delivers satisfaction, i.e., appraisals seldom tell people where they *really* stand. All this seems like an
addiction to a hopeless illusion.

What people really want is access to the knowledge and information
that influences the organization's pay, promotion, and status systems and
how these affect or apply to them. In most organizations, these cryptic systems are embedded beneath the surface of the formal systems of appraisal
and other practices that purportedly decide pay, promotion, and status.
People are insatiably curious about *Where do I stand?* because, in most organizations, this query is decided with a maze of unspoken rules, in-
scrutable political influences, and other dynamics of organizational life.
Appraisal is not the system that drives pay, careers, and status; it is an in-
cidental effect of those dynamic systems. Appraisal is primarily the paper-
shuffling that sanctifies decisions already made.

Beyond curiosity, we have found that the question—*Where do I
stand?*—in many organizations signals much more than ambiguity and
angst about status. All too often, it is indicative of paternalism and a disempowered workforce. Over time people see that their pay, promotion,
and favorable status in reality are linked to the opinion of one person
(sometimes two or three people) and where they stand with that person at
a given moment. That opinion, if favorable, may bear fruit. And because
opinion can change like the weather, people must keep checking—*Where
do I stand?* Consequently, the goal becomes staying in good graces with

your boss. Peter Block describes this practice as "patriarchy," noting that most organizations, from the top to bottom, operate on a fundamental belief that control, authority, and decisions are the "domain and prerogative of the leader."[14] People who enable and pay homage to the patriarchal leader are rewarded. They usually get good assignments, ample pay raises, promotions, and a secure status. In an afterthought, these gifts are justified by purportedly "objective" appraisal ratings. When we examine the characteristics of patriarchy (see John Bradshaw's definitions in "Further Thoughts on Patriarchy"), we often deny that it is present, decrying that our workplace values teamwork and empowerment. But if people take time to think about what *really* happens, beneath the surface rhetoric of harmony, they will find patriarchy and paternalism persisting as core values of the organization.

We must sever our unintended yet implicit control mindsets that are steeped in patriarchy and paternalism if we wish to enliven people with a new spirit of authenticity, openness, and partnership. We must choose a radically different workplace culture. A genuinely new culture would be characterized by a sharp shift in underlying beliefs. In such a world, says Peter Block, "Partners each have emotional responsibility for their own present and their own future. Bosses are no longer responsible for the morale, learning, or career of their subordinates."[16] The goal would be to create a culture where the people systems and processes, though subjective in part, are clearly understood by everyone in the organization. The *where-do-I-stand* question would be unnecessary (except relative to the context of a defined process) because people would have the tools, information, knowledge, and understanding to answer this question for themselves.

Further Thoughts On Patriarchy

Psychologist and author John Bradshaw has found that patriarchy is pervasively practiced by both men and women in our workplaces. He says four conditions characterize the practice of patriarchy:

1. Blind obedience—*never question the rules*

2. The repression of all emotions except fear

3. The destruction of individual willpower

4. The repression of thinking whenever it departs from the authority figure's way of thinking.[15]

The organization and the supervisor are responsible for individual employees' morale, performance, and development.

This seldom spoken assumption perhaps pinpoints why organizations rigorously adhere to the practice of appraisal. Like the *where-do-I-stand* assumption, it perpetuates the notion that someone else is taking care of you, setting the stage for paternalism and dependency. "A performance appraisal is about believing that others hold the secret to your own self-worth," says author Dick Richards.[18] He further notes that people cannot take ownership of their work until they let go of "the illusion that a company will take care of us."[19]

We interviewed a Midwestern sales and service company that had dropped performance appraisals and, in its place, challenged its supervisors and managers to exhibit more progressive styles of one-on-one leadership and coaching. While these steps were helpful, we believe their primary focus was misplaced. Even though a shift in leadership style is critical to successful transformation, lasting change will come only when *the employee* takes on a new view of herself, accepting that she is an adult who is responsible for her own growth, development, and self-worth. This is not a reversion to the "me" fad of the 1980s. The ultimate goal is to help people attain an authentic and energized commitment to the organization and its goal of efficiently providing quality service and products. Such a commitment can come only from a whole person, and a whole person can evolve only from a resolute strength of self.

A final broad-sweeping assumption we might discuss here, "You can get commitment from a forced process" is taken up in the discussion of *control* in Chapter 4. The pervasive assumptions pertaining to appraisal as an improvement tool and a rating device are covered in the next two chapters.

Conclusion

The way we think greatly impacts and shapes the outcome of our endeavors. Much of our thinking is unconscious and invisible, yet it profoundly affects every aspect of organizational life—our work methods, practices, policies, strategic planning, and any changes we try to implement. Until we gain a clear understanding of our thinking, we cannot effect the transformational change we desire. Author Danah Zohar astutely has observed that if we want to really transform our structure and leadership, "We have to change the thinking behind our thinking."[20] To accomplish this and truly move on from appraisal, we must surface our assumptions and build alternatives from newer, more hopeful assumptions.

Review of Chapter Assumptions

Conventional Assumption

One appraisal process can effectively serve several functions at the same time.

Alternative Assumption

- The multiple purposes of appraisal can be better achieved by separate processes.

Conventional Assumption

People want to know and need to know where they stand, and appraisals tell people where they stand.

Alternative Assumption

- People want to clearly understand and access the knowledge and information that influences decisions about their pay, promotion, status, and future.

Conventional Assumption

The organization and the supervisor are responsible for individual employees' morale, performance, and development.

Alternative Assumption

- As healthy adults, people need to be responsible for their own morale, performance, and development, with and without support from the organization.

2

The REAL Goal: Improving the Performance of the Organization

We live our lives in webs of interdependence and yet we keep telling our-selves the story that we are independent.

Peter Scholtes

With any turn of a century, it is common for new possibilities to emerge, new approaches to become common practice, new philoso-phies of living to become popular, and new qualities of leadership to give birth to a new world.

Robert Fritz, *The Path of Least Resistance*

As the nineteenth century came to a close, the horse and buggy was the prevailing mode of transportation. The automobile was viewed as an expensive amuse-ment. People laughed at the possibility of the sturdy, re-liable horse and buggy being replaced by a mere machine. With the dawn of the new century, however, the automobile quickly emerged as the preferred choice in transportation. The horse and buggy became an amusement.

And now, having closed the twentieth century, this book proclaims that the performance appraisal is just another "horse and buggy" to be left in the past (though the track record of the horse and buggy was far superior!). Yet, appraisal is still a widely used tool in workplaces that are radically different than those of 100 years ago, 50 years, or even 20 years ago. The appraisal survives more out of unfounded belief and habit than any demonstration of success. As the prevailing paradigm of organizational life continues to shift, the inherent flaws of the performance appraisal are becoming increasingly evident.

In this chapter, we look back over decades to see the thinking that led to the emergence of appraisal as an improvement strategy. Understanding the origins of appraisal will enable you to see its structures and approach to improvement and help you understand why appraisal became so "popular" and persists as part of the conventional wisdom. With this backdrop, we look at the benefit of appraisal in light of emerging workplace values and the new thinking that is shaping today's business world. We focus in particular on appraisal as an organizational improvement tool and offer an alternative perspective that can lead to *real* improvement for the organization.

■ A Tool for Mechanistic Organizations

At the turn of the last century, Frederick Winslow Taylor's theory of scientific management and Henry Ford's assembly line rapidly transformed industry. Unprecedented gains in productivity resulted. Both Taylor's and Ford's approaches were applied with the assumption that an organization operated like one huge machine. People were merely parts of the machine, parts that needed to be *controlled* to enable the machine to operate in alignment. By reducing jobs to simple, repetitive tasks, it became easier to control what people did.

Though these ideas originated in manufacturing, they were transferred to other rapidly growing industries including the service, retail, education, and public sectors. The jobs in these sectors did not easily allow task reduction and control to the degree that manufacturing jobs did. The individual focus of performance appraisal, however, offered a seemingly tangible way to assert control and make people accountable in service, office, and managerial positions.

By the early 1950s, the performance appraisal became commonplace in "machine model" organizations. It offered a comforting perception of accountability and control. Appraisal created the illusion that each *part* (employee) of the *machine* (organization) was *operating* (working) efficiently and effectively. If each part worked well, so would the machine.

A Tad of History on Performance Appraisals

How did the performance appraisal come into being? Its precise origin is unknown, but the practice of giving performance appraisals can definitely be traced back to the third century, when the Wei Dynasty in China rated the performance of workers. It's no surprise that the writings from that period question the fairness of the rater, alleging that, "the Imperial Rater of Nine Grades seldom rates men according to their merits but always according to his likes and dislikes."[1]

Appraisals were used in industry in the early 1800s by societal reformer Robert Owen at his cotton mills in New Lanark, Scotland. Over each employee's workstation was a colored block, displaying particular colors for different degrees of merit. So much for confidentiality!

Appraisals in the U.S. military date back to 1813 when General Cass reported individual ratings of officers to the War Department, depicting them as a "good-natured man," a "knave despised by all," and the like.[2] The origins of appraisals in the Federal Civil Service system reportedly go back to 1842, with the merit rating system firmly in place by 1887. Retailer Lord and Taylor introduced appraisals in 1914.[3]

Data on the growth of appraisals in private industry in the United States is spotty prior to the 1950s. By 1954, however, the National Industrial Conference Board reported that about one half of 400 employers reporting were using merit rating plans.[4] A study in 1962 reported 61% of organizations using the appraisal tool.[5] Several surveys taken over the past two decades indicate that between 74% and 89% of business organizations in the United States use a formal performance evaluation tool.[6]

The top-down organizational chart became the blueprint for the mechanistic organizational model, lining people up like billiard balls to ostensibly create a predictable chain of reactions.

As corporations in the booming post–World War II era grew to an astronomical size, the performance appraisal rapidly became the tool of choice to ensure alignment and control through the layers of bureaucracy. Appraisals were mostly tailored to people's traits and behaviors (such as punctuality, diligence, grooming, cooperation) rather than to individual performance outcomes. "Attitude," often expressly identified, was the focal point of the appraisal process. Employees with good attitudes made it easy to get compliance. Appraisal was a way to hold people accountable for directives. By connecting appraisal outcomes to pay raises, compliance by every worker could be ensured. Or so the theory went.

■ Management-By-Objective (MBO)

By the late 1950s, a new management philosophy, called Management-By-Objective (MBO), emerged as a variation of the machine model. MBO was based on the idea of assigning employees numerical targets that matched overriding objectives determined by the organization. Along with MBO, a new appraisal model emerged. Individual performance was measured by the employee's success in meeting various targets, most of which were quantitatively measured. The "annual review" rated employees on their success or failure in meeting a number of precisely defined targets.

The idea of MBO and objective-driven appraisals initially was quite seductive, even to brilliant people such as Douglas McGregor.[7] Instead of rating people on vague notions of traits or behaviors, MBO-oriented appraisals promised clearly communicated, numerical goals that would lend themselves to comparison against measured results and outcomes. On the surface, the idea of using numerical measurements made MBO appear to be objective, fair, and even reliably scientific. The performance appraisal became more or less a score sheet to ensure individual accountability in meeting targeted objectives. During the 1960s and 1970s, MBO's popularity, along with a later variation called Management-By-Results (MBR), rose rapidly. This surge brought with it the widespread adoption of performance appraisals, particularly in larger organizations. (See "A Tad of History" regarding the growth of appraisals.)

By the 1980s, the popularity of MBO had peaked, and its efficacy was in question. Many organizations recognized that the MBO-driven appraisal had failed to deliver its promised success, despite years of trying to improve the process. The MBO appraisal generally failed as a motivator because people were resistant to and dissatisfied with the process. Both supervisors and employees commonly manipulated the data and the supposed "objective" evidence to ensure desired ratings and compensation outcomes.

The 1980s also brought the nascent quality management (TQM) movement, and it heaped further condemnation on the usage of MBO appraisals. *Real* improvement, the quality management advocates contended, could not be achieved by setting numerical targets—it would only come from studying and changing *the system* and getting all of its elements to work together (i.e., the people, work methods, structures and processes, the tools, resources, and the working environment).

Although many organizations had initially adopted or expanded the use of appraisals in conjunction with using MBO, organizations dropping MBO in the 1990s did not abandon performance appraisals. Believing that appraisal was useful or necessary, organizations continued the annual ritual. Behavior-based appraisals re-emerged, only more often in the form of elaborate scales. Novel variations of appraisal also appeared. For example, "competency-based" appraisals were supposed to measure the skills and competencies that employees demonstrated in performing their jobs. "Performance Management" systems were sold as a replacement for appraisals, but they mirrored the mechanical MBO appraisals of old, only with added rigmarole. The 360-degree appraisal (being rated by everyone—subordinates, co-workers, customers, etc.) was promoted as a solution to the bias problems of appraisal based on the idea that many ratings would water down a single person's bias. Though implemented by well-intending H.R. staff, these designs largely did not alter the underlying assumptions (discussed in Chapter 1), and the results, problems, and unintended effects of these "more progressive" appraisal methods mirrored the past.

■ High Hopes End in Frustration

Aside from the efforts to change appraisal, other trends in the past two decades have begun to reshape the prevailing thinking about improving organizations. Industry journals and best-selling business books have awakened managers to totally new views of the nature of work, people and work, and related values. Though difficult to define, this new perspective has triggered the dawn of a deep-rooted transformation and the emergence of strikingly different approaches to people management. The edges of top-down styles have begun to soften, and the machine model of organizational design seems to be collapsing into amorphous forms. Teams, less structured, and even unstructured approaches have become commonplace. *People skills* have become the hallmark of a good leader.

Organizations have replaced the harsh, dictatorial managers of the past with a new brand of leaders who openly and earnestly espouse more caring and benevolent employee relations. Managers are experimenting with more positive and radically new ways of working with people. Buzzwords and phrases such as "empowerment," "teams," and "putting people first" characterize the early stages of this transformation.

Sadly, these positive and hopeful measures have yielded spotty and temporary successes. After nearly two decades of increased awareness and intense organizational development and experimentation, there is surprisingly scarce evidence of substantial change in the way people are managed. Concerns about employee commitment, motivation, trustworthiness, and cynicism certainly have not diminished. The best intentions and diligent efforts of executives and managers largely have not garnered great success in bringing about meaningful change in the way organizations deal with people. Beneath the buzzwords and softened rhetoric, the people systems and power dynamics have mostly undergone cosmetic changes, even with sincere intentions for something better.

And workers then and now see all of this clearly. They hear the newly espoused values and read them in vision statements proudly posted on the wall. But, at some level, they know there has been no real change. From appraisal and H.R. policies, they still feel an emphasis on *individual* accountability (rather than teams). They also see inconsistencies between professed values of "caring about people" and the way big decisions affecting their work lives come down from the top. The turbulent economics of recent decades and resulting downsizings have further left them feeling *fear* rather than freedom and empowerment. Both the victims of downsizing (who go on elsewhere) and the witness-survivors have become wary and distrustful. Against this backdrop of fear and disappointment, the "team," "empowerment," and "people-first" initiatives have fed the rampant cynicism in today's organizations, where Dilbert-cartoon perceptions prevail.

Executives and managers see this response but cannot understand why employees react negatively to their well-intended overtures to be more caring and supportive. After their sincere efforts produce disappointing results, they too become cynical, only toward their employees rather than the organization. Out of frustration, people managers then retreat from the "softer" approaches, returning to the "old way," more sure than ever that most people just don't give a damn. "I tried it. It doesn't work," they say with a tone of resignation.

The Feeling We Get From Appraisal

Peter Scholtes, author of *The Leader's Handbook* and a man we would call "The Father of Do-We-Really-Need-Appraisals" inquiry, offers the following reflection on feelings people get from appraisal:

The pain of performance appraisal is like a low-grade fever. It doesn't prevent you from working, but you have this vague sense that something is not right, and you don't get over that until you in fact have successfully dismantled the performance appraisal.

But a good number of managers have not given up. Despite repeated failures of progressive initiatives in recent decades, they still possess a deep-felt belief that *something new* can work, that there is a more authentic and effective way to work with people. These ever-hopeful, soul-searching managers also intuitively sense the unseen obstacles—something is wrong, but they're not sure what it is.

And their hunch is right. An undercurrent hangs like a cloud, pervades the workplace atmosphere, and impedes their best efforts. That undercurrent comes from the overall *system* that deals with the *people* part of the organization—the personnel policies, human resources practices, and, most importantly, the organization's unseen culture (values and beliefs) about people. This system of polices, practices, and the work cultures of the past are an albatross that burdens any manager who is striving to shift toward a more positive, people paradigm.

The unseen, underlying assumptions of this system send messages of distrust—messages that people are not interested in working or improving the organization, messages that people are children who need to be directed and controlled in an atmosphere much like a traditional elementary school. The undercurrents of this people system are very insidious and powerful: They suppress the human spirit. They perpetuate an outcome of dependent, de-motivated people. Their power easily negates the intentions of the most well-meaning and caring manager.

These damaging underlying assumptions manifest in various forms. In policies, we see at-will agreements and elaborate rules of conduct (*so we can fire you easily when you screw up*), elaborate *policy* manuals (*we're in control and you're not a responsible adult*), time clocks and leave approval slips (*we don't trust you*), attendance awards and incentive pay (*you really don't like to work*), suggestion programs (*"If you have an idea, put it in a box"*), and, of course the subject of this book, the sacred cow, the Godzilla of them all—yes, the *performance appraisal*.

The performance appraisal, more than any other aspect of our people system, surreptitiously sends a number of resounding, negative messages about the nature and potential of people. As discussed in Chapter 1, these underlying assumptions signal distrust and a belief that people need to be prodded and psyched to put forth their best efforts. The assumption that we can even rank or precisely measure a person's contribution is degrading in a sense. In blindly accepting this assumption, we trivialize an individual's work, often involving heart and soul, from something unique and wonderful into a cold and sterile numerical rating that purportedly signifies that person's total contribution.

Setting the process's underlying assumptions aside momentarily, consider another reason why appraisals have perpetuated when so many managers sense the worst about them. We live in a whole new world we don't even know yet. Uncertainty abounds. The pace of change accelerates at an exponential rate. The world is erratic, volatile, and unpredictable. Our customer bases continually change. New technology and global competition throw curves we can't see coming. Many of our organizations are so large that they seem disjointed and out of control. We don't fully understand the aging baby boomers, Generation X, and the emerging Generation Y or their perceptions toward work. As organizations continue to flatten, supervisors are burdened with an ever-increasing number of direct reports. Our organizations are profoundly affected by this newly emerging world. More and more, in our work worlds we feel lost and as though we have little control over what's happening.

What do we do when we feel we are out of control? Often we hold onto familiar things, what worked in the past, or so it seemed. The performance appraisal allures us with its illusion of control, the illusion that we are tangibly *taking action* to ensure order, accountability, desired outcomes, and improvement in an unpredictable world. Appraisal gives us documentation of people being encouraged to improve. This feels good because, by holding conversations about improvement and filling out forms, we believe we are making people accountable and getting improvement. This alluring but false impression has enabled appraisal to survive amid managers' sincere attempts to apply a new philosophy.

Holding onto the beliefs of the "old way," many organizations have redesigned their appraisal systems and boast that their newly designed systems are humanistic development tools. Despite sincerity in these claims, appraisal perpetuates myths about people, change, and organizational responsiveness that are no longer valid. Appraisal and the machine model of thinking that goes with it impede our ability to create new styles of leadership and find new ways to energize people in the workplace. We must let go of this striving and seek a new model of leadership accompanied by a whole new people system based on a different set of assumptions about the nature of work and people.

■ Emergence of the New Models of Thinking

Despite our fumbling in the dark, the light on the horizon offers new hope. An ever-increasing number of managers perceive the severe drawbacks of the machine model. They sense something is wrong with people systems premised on *control* and *mistrust*. A growing, and soon to be critical mass of managers and human resources professionals are yearning for something new, something genuinely different. Conferences on employee participation, servant leadership, and the like are growing around the world, drawing thousands and thousands of people who truly want new ways to work with people, as well as new approaches to work altogether.

What seems to be burgeoning in place of the mechanistic model is not yet clear, but it appears to be a more dynamic, *organic* model, a model that attributes organizational outcomes to the interaction of organizational systems and structures (sometimes called *systems theory*) rather than individual performance. This model capitalizes on *freedom* rather than maintaining *control*. We see more and more managers who are willing to experiment with leadership styles attuned to this new paradigm. It is based on *trust* and a greater belief in people. It assumes that, with *less* control and greater *autonomy*, commitment and innate motivation will flourish. It rests on the premise that with *less* structure, people can effectively work in concert, within naturally emerging systems that foster optimal work patterns. The new model, whether it is called *organic* or something else, is still evolving. Its precise nature is vague and undefined. Its probable origins are many.

Some people link this new paradigm to the earlier motivational models and humanistic ideas of Abraham Maslow, Douglas McGregor, Frederick Herzberg, Harry Levinson, and more recently, Steven Covey. Others would point to more recent influences such as W. Edwards Deming, Joseph Juran, Russell Ackoff, Peter Block, Peter Senge, and others who give focus to quality management, systems theory, and the true power dynamics in organization life. Many would attribute the evolving model to learning drawn from advanced scientific models, the *new* physics, quantum theory, and chaos and complexity theories, as artfully articulated by Margaret Wheatley, Danah Zohar, H. Thomas Johnson, Dee Hock, and dozens of others.[8]

While these influences ostensibly have separate origins, we see the convergence of a single model that brings a different view of people and organizational dynamics. We see the new model as a confluence of these ideas:

- An organization, because it is a system, cannot be significantly improved by focusing on individuals.

- The choices of commitment and responsibility must be left to individuals if they are to be meaningful and effective.

- Less structure and control over the individual employee often will result in greater motivation and productivity.

- Employees cannot be *motivated* to perform their best, but conditions of openness and trust can unleash intrinsic motivation, spirit, and heart-felt commitment to organization goals.

- Focus on improving the overall "system" of the organization yields better results than trying to get employees to improve their individual performance.

- Organizations can survive and grow only if they are freely evolving systems, where variation, differentiation, and diversity are valued as pathways to innovation and improvement.

This partial list of key underpinnings suggests the emergence of a dramatically different view of organizational dynamics. Meg Wheatley has urged a whole new view of the workplace, stating "Human organizations are not the lifeless machines we wanted them to be."[9] As this century unfolds, our thinking will continue to shift. It will become increasingly clear that organizations are living, constantly evolving, self-organizing systems rather than machines with component parts of people.

As the new view becomes more prevalent, a critical question will be: *Does the performance appraisal fit this new model?* Over the past 50 years, we have learned that appraisal does little to bolster organizational performance. And in helping individuals, its overall track record has been dismal at best. Despite widespread use of appraisals, organizations have increasingly recognized difficulties in motivating workers and aligning their energies.

■ The Clash of Appraisal and the New Thinking

Appraisals have not worked because their underlying assumptions send the wrong messages and cause unintended damaging effects. When we contrast these assumptions with the emergent thinking in the business world, it is clear that appraisal is increasingly out of kilter, undermining and running counter to the values of the postmodern workplace. In Figure 2.1, we see some of the commonly accepted values of organizations moving along these more progressive paths. In the second column, we see the values and messages of appraisal, clashing squarely against these emerging values. It seems heretical to talk about empowering people and at the same time have a process that is imposed on every employee and supervisor "for their own good." If it means anything at all, empowerment must shift responsibility for commitment, performance, feedback, improvement, and development to the employee. As we detail in Chapter 4, supervisors must also have freedom to choose the right style of leadership that best suits them. Appraisal's heavy focus on individual accountability seems to negate the notions of collaborative teams. To some it may suggest:

> Yes, work in teams, but, remember, take credit for yourself, get recognized, watch your back, because *you* are accountable for *you*, and that's what goes in your file, not the team stuff.

A great deal of the most popular business literature in recent years, coming from people such as Steven Covey, Peter Block, and W. Edwards Deming, has focused on the importance of unleashing intrinsic motivation rather than the "do this and you get that" world of incentives. Appraisal designs, however, continue to employ tired extrinsic schemes that tie performance ratings to pay increases, bonuses, and awards. The "one-size-fits-all" approach of appraisal ignores the powerful benefits of managing *for* diversity and capitalizing on the differences in people (more on this in Chapter 4).[10]

With enough said earlier on emerging structures, let us look at the bottom three *emerging thinking* values in Figure 2.1. These come from quality management strategies, which continue as a tidal wave across the business world in varied forms such as TQM, Malcolm Baldridge assessment, Six Sigma, and ISO 9000. A positive effect of this movement is that it shifts the focus away from inspecting people to examining and understanding processes. The common sense notion of just-in-time (JIT) eliminates excessive inventories, rework, and process steps, among other benefits. Yet appraisal causes supervisors to stockpile and rework feedback, guidance, and development—the events are automatically triggered by calendar rather than offering help at just the right time (more on this in Chapters 4, 5, and 7). The mind shift to one of system and process improvement is held back because of certain underlying assumptions that also relate to appraisal, as the next section discusses.

Emerging Thinking	Appraisals
Empower People	Forced Process
Collaborative Teams	Individual Accountability
Unleash Intrinsic Motivation	Motivate with Incentives
Respect Diversity	One Size Fits All
Emerging Structures	Controlling Structures
Just In Time	Annual Event Approach
Improve Processes	Rely on Inspection/MBO
Improve Whole Systems	Improve the Parts

Figure 2.1 Clashing Values

■ Assumptions Around Improvement

Improving performance. The concept seems simple enough, but take the question to a deeper level, and it gets more complicated. The question then becomes: *Whose performance are we trying to improve?* The performance of the organization? Or the performance of individuals? When we ask organizations to clarify their ultimate intentions in improving individuals, we often hear that getting individuals to improve will improve the overall performance of the organization. Let us look at the fundamental assumption of improvement by appraisal:

> *Assumption*
>
> **Improving individuals' performance improves organizational performance.**

Appraisal orchestrates a regimented system of paperwork that trickles down and ultimately aims at *individual* improvement and alignment. The idea is—if we get every person in the organization to do a better job, the organization will be more successful in meeting its objectives. The assumption could be said another way: *Improving the parts improves the whole*. The logic seems solid and sound because this strategy has dominated our thinking and corporate cultures for more than a century. The game plan today is usually called *performance management*. Its execution nearly always depends on some form of *performance appraisal*. These so-called performance management systems call upon individuals, in consultation with their supervisors, to set performance and development goals. Quarterly or periodic follow-ups, a common design feature, attempt to hold people accountable for the attainment of their individual goals.

The idea of *setting goals* is alluring and feels so comfortable—it has become a workplace mantra that is honored at the level of corporate virtue. Its very sound chimes a worthy ring, like *taking responsibility* or *making a commitment*. At bottom line, however, this approach will be helpful toward achieving *organizational* improvement only if the whole can be improved by improving the parts. But is this a valid assumption?

Over the past few decades, highly revered business visionaries, including Russell Ackoff, W. Edwards Deming, Joseph Juran, Peter Senge, and many others, have emphasized that improving *systems*, rather than individual efforts, is the most effective way to leverage improvement for the organization. By the term *system*, we mean: *an indivisible whole consisting of people, behaviors, things, and ideas that act and interact to achieve a common purpose*. The organization itself is *a system*, composed of a number of subsystems. An organizational system is composed of the people who do the work, but far more than that. It also includes the organization's methods, structures, support, materials, equipment, customers, work culture, internal and external environments (such as markets, the community, and government), *and* the interaction of these components. (See Figure 2.2 and "McDonald's Corporation.") Each part of the system has its own purpose but at the same time is dependent on the other parts. While every part is connected to the aim of the whole, no part by itself can achieve that aim. In a system, all of the parts are *inter*dependent.[11] That is, a change in any part of a system will affect one or more other parts of that system. Hence, a system is not the sum of its parts; rather it is the sum of its parts *plus* the interaction of all of its parts.

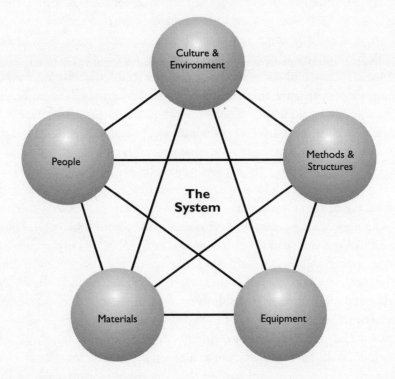

Figure 2.2 The System

McDonald's Corporation: Example of a System

The McDonald's Corporation aims to conveniently provide low-cost, good-quality fast food to people throughout the world. Along with its franchises, it is one *system*, bound with a common aim. The people within the McDonald's *system* include its investors, customers, and employees, as well as the people employed by its franchises and suppliers. McDonald's unique physical work *environment* is plainly visible at its stores. The *work culture* at its establishments seems to be one that values a diversity of people, competency derived from standardized, on-the-job training, and flexible work arrangements, among other characteristics. The *structure* appears to be relatively flat (low ratio of managers to employees) and operates with well-defined jobs. McDonald's is known for prescribing at its stores and franchises highly standardized *methods* in preparing, wrapping, and packaging food, cashiering, and serving customers. Corporate and franchise stores tend to use specific types of *equipment* and *materials* (prescribed for consistency). Together, the people, environment, culture, structure, methods, materials, and equipment of McDonald's interact and act together as one *system* to accomplish a common aim.

Because of the interdependency of the parts, improvement strategies aimed at the parts, such as appraisal, do little or nothing to improve the system. Russell Ackoff often explains this by analogy to an automobile: Assume you wanted to build the greatest automobile in the world. As a means, you find out which manufacturer makes the best motor, transmission, powertrain, chassis, axle, electrical system, dashboard, interior, etc. You order all of these parts and have them delivered to your garage. But could you build a great car? Could you even assemble a car that would run? Certainly not. Improving parts in isolation of the whole is a futile strategy for improvement. Improving parts can help the whole only if such efforts are made in the context of the interactions and interdependencies of the other parts toward a common aim.

Systems theorists believe that individual performance is mostly determined by the system in which the work is done rather than by the individual's initiative, abilities, and efforts. Yes, individual commitment and qualities decidedly impact performance outcomes, but aren't these attributes also greatly impacted by the system? An individual's level of commitment, motivation, and growth in ability is influenced and in large part determined by the system in which she works. The training received, how one is perceived and treated, cooperation of others, support and resources provided, work environment, organizational culture, and other subsystems have a powerful effect on an individual's level of performance (see "How Systems Can Drive Individual Performance"). W. Edwards Deming said that 94% of performance outcomes are attributable to the system.[12]

Over time, appraising people on system-caused performance can lead to bitterness, cynicism, and even deceptive tactics. A fast-food restaurant in Virginia rated its managers on the average time it took for cars to go through the drive-through window, using an electronic camera to record times. The manager learned that if employees waved a large garbage bag by the electronic eye, it would be recorded as a car. The result: The store set records for average drive-through time and the corporate office visited the store to give the manager and his employees a recognition award![13] Rating people does not give them fraudulent dispositions, but when someone is forced to deliver and they see the system largely driving unacceptable results that they cannot control, they may turn to desperate measures (we hear these kinds of stories everywhere we find incentives).

Consider as a customer how systems improvements, rather than employee attitudes and efforts, really make a difference. A hotel clerk who repeatedly experiences long checkout lines in the morning may be counseled and coached to work faster. This may actually worsen his performance because, in his effort to be more efficient, he may make more errors or sound curt and uncaring with the guests. Instead, a systems redesign called *express checkout* enables guests to leave charges on their credit card and leave their key in their room. This frees up the clerk to patiently give high-quality service to guests with special checkout issues or questions about their bills.

Our point here is not to negate all notions of individual responsibility for work performance. Rather, we wish to spotlight the often ignored impact of *the system* on individual performance. Despite widespread acceptance of system theory, managers cling to the belief that the organization can make significant strides in improvement only by getting individuals to improve their performance. Look at the improvement efforts at 95% of organizations, and you will find a decidedly disproportionate focus on individually oriented initiatives such as performance management, MBO, individual competency, and personal development plans.

Performance appraisal is not a tool that improves systems. Appraisal

How Systems Can Drive Individual Performance

To gain a sense of the system effects on individual performance, consider a young, enthusiastic manager named Fred who manages a fast-food franchise restaurant. Fred starts out with great enthusiasm. Assume his performance is rated on volume, costs, margins, overhead, inventory, adherence to standardized practices, cleanliness of the store, etc. He is also compared with managers of other locations, all in better neighborhoods. Fred's store is located two blocks from an inner-city high school with predominantly disadvantaged youngsters. Sales to students comprise a large part of store sales. Fred also relies on the neighborhood as a primary source of labor. Consequently, many of Fred's hires need confidence-building and extra training because they are young and from disadvantaged homes. The extra training time drives up his labor costs. The high-school customers come in throughout the day, peppering the eating areas with litter as they eat and loiter. It is difficult to manage this without driving away his main volume source. Despite his best efforts, Fred gets marked down on cleanliness in every appraisal. At night, the roughness of the neighborhood necessitates a security guard to walk and monitor the premises. While this helps business, it drives up overhead costs.

Earlier Fred was trained for six months by another store manager who did most of the inventory rotation in his head, never giving Fred guidance on effective, standardized approaches for properly rotating inventory and discarding aged products. Without knowing the best method, Fred now conscientiously tries to do a good job on inventory but is criticized in his appraisal for deficiencies as though they were caused by his dereliction. Fred's present boss believes in "free-rein" management and rarely suggests specific methods for improvement. The corporate franchiser initiates promotions intended to increase dollar volume. At Fred's store, however, the student customers are seldom interested in promotional items and higher-priced sandwiches, sticking mostly to traditional menu items. Fred is expected to participate in these promotions, even though past patterns at his store indicate they have scant impact on sales. With typical franchise arrangements, Fred has very little control over the products offered, marketing, suppliers, or even the methods of preparing the food and cashiering, yet he is held responsible for gross sales, costs, margins, etc. Because of his boss's "leniency" and the neighborhood factor, Fred gets appraisal ratings mostly in the middle of the scale, but he still gets the lowest ratings among store managers in the franchise company. This also means Fred gets the lowest pay increase. The franchise company means well in using appraisals and the incentive of pay-for-performance, only wanting its managers to do their best. While people can always improve and learn from feedback, the appraisal of Fred's performance does not alter *the system* and scarcely affects the bottom-line measures. In Fred's case, the main effect of appraisal has been the transforming of an energetic, enthusiastic manager into a discouraged and dispirited employee.

is a process of inspecting and improving the parts, i.e., people as individual employees. Appraisal and improvement initiatives aimed at individuals contribute little to the *organization's* overall performance, and often they undermine improvement because of their unintended effects, such as demoralizing people and rupturing relationships with supervisors. Because of these effects and the low-yield benefit of improving the parts, it makes little sense to design organizational improvement strategies around appraisal while the leveraging power of improving the systems and processes is ignored. A recently published study, looking at 600 companies recognized for practicing quality management (a practice that largely focuses on improving systems and process), indicates the power of a systems approach. Over a five-year period, these companies significantly outperformed comparable companies in growth in income and sales by a 2 to 1 ratio. On an average, the 600 companies experienced a 114% rise in stock price over five years compared with an average increase of 80% for Standard & Poor's 500 Index companies during the same period.[14]

Business people acclaim the power of systems at business conferences across the nation, and systems theory books such as Peter Senge's *The Fifth Discipline* have topped business best-seller lists, yet the lion's share of improvement efforts continue to be aimed at getting individuals to do a better job. The myopic focus on *individual* improvement equates to a religious dogma that is manifested through the rituals and rites of ranking and rating. Case in point: A large hospital in Michigan prominently displays a vision statement in large letters in a decorative frame in its main lobby, which, amid other noble language, states:

> *We are each held accountable by personal evaluation of our individual performance based on clear, concise, and mutually agreed upon expectations.*

Like the Great Reformation, breaking from the religion of performance appraisal will require nothing short of radical reformation in our prevailing business thinking.

We do not advocate abandoning all strategies aimed at individual improvement, personal development, and goal attainment. When combined with serious efforts toward improving the system and work environment, such initiatives can significantly bolster organizational transformation, especially if they are predicated on healthier underlying assumptions.

Conclusion

Appraisal became a conventional practice in the 1950s based in part on the belief that improving individuals improves organizational performance. In spite of innumerable iterations, appraisal has consistently failed to accomplish this goal and continually triggered an assortment of damaging side effects, some of which undermine the very goal of improvement. While there's always been reason to question the efficacy of appraisal, it is increasingly incongruent with today's business world and emerging patterns of work. Systems approaches, self-organizing teams, and humanistic ways of working with people have emerged as the preferred practices among organizations around the globe.

The shift toward systems theory and new values toward work and people are clearly the keys to sustainable improvement. Quality management principles have taught us that substantial improvement in an organization can only be accomplished by understanding, improving, and redesigning the processes and systems that generate outcomes and results.

The notion of rating people, the subject of the next chapter, demonstrates yet another conflict between the values we profess today and what actually happens when we try to rank and rate individual performance.

Review of Chapter Assumptions

Conventional Assumption

Improving individuals' performance improves organizational performance.

Alternative Assumptions

- Improving systems and processes improves the performance of the organization.
- Individual improvement initiatives are most effective when they are combined with serious efforts toward improving the work climate, systems, and processes.

3

Appraisal as a Rating Tool: Fair or Foul?

Detailed studies of performance appraisals show that at their best they are often wildly inconsistent and damaging to the loyalty and commitment that help people do their best.

Jay Mathews, *Washington Post*

Rater distortions of employee appraisals and employee attempts to embellish apparent performance are facts of organizational life that can never be completely eliminated.

Steve W. J. Koslowski, Georgia T. Chao, and Robert F. Morrison, *Performance Appraisal*

At the heart of many appraisal functions is an assessment, an evaluation of performance. Typically this takes the form of numeric or descriptive ratings or a ranking. The goal is fair and "objective" measurement—measurement of the quality of one's work and how it stands up against some standard or in comparison to others. The ratings must be reliable and fair because they are used for important purposes. They decide pay adjustments and bonuses. They determine whether someone can move up on the career ladder. Within competitive, internal promotion processes, screening committees rely on ratings to choose the interview pool and even to select a group of finalists. Ratings also serve as a coaching, feedback, and development tool. They tell individuals in a tangible, concrete way the precise value of their contribution and performance, or at least that's the intent. An unacceptable rating in many organizations triggers remedial measures and even formal disciplinary steps that may lead to discharge. In sum, a lot is riding on ratings.

While the reasons for ratings are important, at some level, we know that the ratings really do not come out right. Without looking at data or research, we see inconsistency. We've even experienced it personally. We sense a certain caprice and arbitrary application of the measuring sticks. We know that the raters do not have all the facts. While we readily see that appraisal is not particularly reliable, we nonetheless pretend that it is a valid measurement. At our gut level, we *know* the filtered lenses and biases of the raters pose insurmountable problems, yet we drift into the dream of believing we can fix them—we just need to get the right criteria, design more precise indicators and scales, and train people on how to be truly "objective."

That gut-level sensor often tells us the truth, but we ignore its insights. Evaluating performance is necessary, we tell ourselves, and the fact that ratings always turn out tainted and inconsistent is no excuse to abandon them and the functions they serve. We must do the best we can, and so we go on. We stay with appraisal.

To a certain degree, our thinking is not illogical or off course. With regard to many personnel functions, assessment of individual performance serves several critical needs. Without some assessment, an organization cannot weed out unacceptable probationary employees. Without some evaluative information, it may be difficult for some employees to identify strengths to build from or weaknesses to work on. Absent a measuring stick, we cannot properly pay (and some would say "reward") those who have grown and advanced their ability to contribute to organizational success. Without assessment, we cannot choose the best candidates for promotion, nor can we identify those who are bad fits and should be encouraged to pursue new career paths. Accordingly, the part of us that senses we cannot let go of evaluation is responding to a legitimate and valid need.

Acknowledging this need, however, does not mean that *systematic performance appraisal* is an inescapable fact of organization life. Yes, some form of evaluation for particular purposes must continue, but appraisal, as a practice of mandated, wholesale, periodic individual assessment, is not reliable or helpful in achieving those purposes. In this chapter, we explain why.

■ Appraisal as a Measuring Tool

We assume that fair and objective measurement can occur within appraisal, but does it? Appraisal's capability for accurate measurement has been a favorite subject of social scientists for decades. Hundreds of studies have attempted to evaluate its impact, efficacy, tendencies, validity, reliability, and unintended effects. Along the path, we have tried every way imaginable to provide a reliable method for one *human being* to make a fair and objective evaluation of another *human being's* performance. With the hope of getting objectivity and consistency, we have painstakingly designed and redesigned innumerable structures, criteria, and standards to measure exhibited traits, behaviors, competencies, and performance targets. We've applied elaborate ratings, scales, boxes, checklists, weighting mechanisms, and mathematical formulas in the context of one new form after another. In striving for accuracy, we have required raters to document their ratings with supporting evidence and detailed narrative statements. We've attempted to bolster objectivity by requiring that people be measured against numerical targets. We've experimented with countless ways to train, monitor, compare, hold accountable, and retrain the raters to get them to do it right. In recent years, we've tried to arrest rater bias by mandating multiple raters and sources of feedback, including the ratee, peers, subordinates, and customers.

Despite many diligent efforts, we've seen scant improvement. True, some methods are slightly more effective. Using specific criteria has worked better than very general criteria. Adding additional raters has increased reliability (i.e., the consistency of ratings) but not necessarily validity (accuracy). Even with purportedly improved methods, we still see a lack of enthusiasm and commitment from supervisors and employees alike, and the unintended side effects never abate. The net effect of fifty years of intense efforts at improving the process has failed to yield any form of appraisal that can consistently and accurately measure an individual's performance over an extended period of time. This may be somewhat overstated in the case of very simple, highly structured, repetitive jobs, but it certainly holds true for more complex jobs, including managerial and professional jobs that are most routinely subjected to appraisal.

■ The Track Record of Appraisal as a Rating Device

The poor track record and widespread dissatisfaction with appraisal as a rating device are well documented in the academic literature. Appraisal's problems of inaccuracy and inconsistency are so commonplace that social scientists have created an entire lexicon to describe the various categories of rater errors, biases, and tendencies that undermine its accuracy. An abbreviated list of the rating problems commonly attributed to appraisal include categorization tendencies, favoritism, bias, and rating errors.

Categorization and Stereotype Tendencies

Categorization tendency is an underlying basis for other kinds of rater errors and biases. *Categorization* is the natural human tendency to perceive and identify people (and things) by categories—it is a way we instinctively and cognitively process information in our minds. In categorizing people, we psychologically divide them into separate groups.[1] From our personal experiences and media portrayals, we adopt beliefs about certain kinds of people based on characteristics and tendencies we have observed. Our mind then sorts and lumps these characteristics and tendencies into a reference category (a do-gooder, Type-A personality, a "good-ol' boy," a computer nerd, one of "those people" from the company we merged with, etc.). When we encounter others of the same category, we ascribe to them, without actually observing such, the characteristics and tendencies in our memory-bank category. When we allow our mind to instinctively assign patterns to groups of people, we are *stereotyping*.

People-I-Like-Favoritism

Though this category is broadly based, it's one that everyone recognizes and quickly acknowledges. In the literature, this kind of bias is sometimes referred to as *affect* (people's reaction in terms of like and dislike, arising from preference, attractiveness, friendship, and even extent of familiarity). Affective reactions, liking people and not liking people, are inevitable, unavoidable consequences of human nature (and perhaps in nature in general—when you take your dog for a walk and encounter other strange dogs, notice how your dog can be indifferent or quickly like or detest the other dog!). Some people call this chemistry. Some researchers seriously question whether humans can set *like* bias aside, even with good intentions.[2]

Consistent with this affect research, the interpersonal relationship *before* appraisal strongly predicts an employee's satisfaction with the appraisal process, and this seemingly holds true under purportedly more objective methods such as competency measurement.[3]

Gender, Race, and Age Bias

As one might expect, appraisal research provides solid evidence of bias based on gender, race, age, and other EEO categories. The research indicates that we have stereotypical beliefs about categories of people (that women are this, Hispanics are that, and so on), and those beliefs distort what we see, for the good or bad. The manifestation of these stereotypes is quite complex. For example, with regard to gender bias, the commonly held belief that women always favor women and men favor men is not true—it varies with the particulars. If we see women as nurturing and men not, regardless of our personal gender, we will rate women higher in jobs where nurturing is important.[4] Surprisingly, one study found that liberal women tended to show more prejudice in favor of males over traditional women.[5] There is also some evidence that gender bias tapers off when women constitute a majority of job holders in a work group.[6] It is not surprising to learn that men rate pregnant women even more negatively than women who are not.[7]

Race bias also operates in perplexing ways. A 1985 review of 88 studies found that "both black and white raters gave significantly higher ratings to members of their own race."[8] Research and analysis since that time, however, show that racial bias is far more complex (e.g., there is evidence that *both blacks and whites* rate white supervisors higher and that negative ratings for blacks diminish when blacks constitute 90% of the work group).[9]

Like race and gender, age bias in appraisal also varies with the situation. Typically, however, ratings for older workers are negatively influenced by the age stereotype that they are less capable and have less "potential."[10]

Of course, with or without appraisal, bias and stereotyping are difficult to eradicate. Efforts in combating bias in appraisal have not yielded great success. In organizations that have strong norms against racial and gender bias, there is evidence of less antagonism toward nonwhites and women, but reportedly an *increase* of favoritism among whites.[11] Altering the method of appraisal or its format does little to prevent bias from influencing outcomes—even outcome-based, MBO-type ratings require interpretation and judgment calls. Training may help somewhat but may trigger exaggerated ratings in the reverse (overrating members of a protected class).[12] With the growing popularity of 360-degree appraisals, effective training against rater errors and bias is several times more costly because of the large number of raters who need to be trained.

Various Types of Rating Errors

In addition to biases, social scientists have identified various kinds of commonly recurring rater errors, including:

- **Leniency Error.** This represents raters' tendencies to give very generous ratings. The tendency may arise from a supervisor's desire to preserve a good working relationship or politicking to advance "my people."

- **Severity Error.** This is the reverse of leniency error. Severity may reflect a cultural view toward appraisal or may be the product of a supervisor who has received a poor rating. Evidence indicates that people's tendency to rate severely or leniently is significantly influenced by the way they are rated ("If I am mediocre, then that must be true of most people!")

- **Central Tendency and Range Restriction Errors.** As these words imply, *central tendency error* reflects a predisposition to cluster most people near the middle. *Range restriction error* is similar but refers to rater's tendency to place people within a specified range (e.g. on a scale of 1–5 and 5 being high, absent very unusual circumstances, everyone will be rated between 3 and 4).[14]

- **Halo and Horn Errors.** These errors refer to our tendency to carry over our perception of a strength (the *halo*) or a weakness (the *horn*) in one dimension of rating into other dimensions. For example, a rater sees a person with high productivity, and this favorable impression unconsciously is carried over in rating the candidate in other dimensions, such as analytical and communication skills. Consequently, the person receives somewhat inflated ratings in these other

---

Performance Ratings in the Changing Workplace

Rutgers University Professors Chao C. Chen and Nancy DiTomaso reviewed more than 125 studies on the impact of demographic diversity and various forms of cultural, racial, and gender bias in appraisal. Looking at appraisal, organizational transition, and related issues, they made these rather interesting findings:

• The processes of categorization, differentiation, and evaluation of people according to race, gender, and age categories can have important effects on appraisal outcomes.

• Some rating formats are less likely to be biased than others, but the evidence tends to show that bias can occur regardless of the particular evaluation format.

• Outcome-based and objective measures are not panaceas for eliminating bias. The growing interdependence of work processes will increasingly make it difficult to determine who has contributed what. Outcomes in a knowledge-based economy may be far less tangible than they were in an industrial economy and, therefore, also much more difficult to measure and evaluate.

• As job occupants become more diverse and as job content becomes more difficult to characterize, the ability to measure performance against an understanding of what the job requires will likely become more subjective.

• The changes underway in the nature of jobs and the structure of network relationships across organizations are creating an environment where appraisals designed for individual assessment are likely to be increasingly out of kilter with the populations most affected by them.[13]

---

areas. An example of *horn effect:* an administrative assistant does a poor job of filing and organizing paperwork, and this results in diminished ratings in an area of strength, such as client communication and resourcefulness.

• **Recency Error.** Everyone who has been a giver or receiver of appraisal knows this one, also known as the *what-have-you-done-for-me-lately* syndrome. While ratings in theory reflect the prior 12-month period of time, the frailties of selective and poor memory tend to cause high focus on events immediately preceding the appraisal. An engineer could do six great projects in a row during the year, but if her last project before review turns out badly, she can expect that project to deflate her ratings for the year. The reverse occurs as well.

- **Fundamental Attribution Error.** *Fundamental attribution error* is our tendency to attribute favorable outcomes for *ourselves* as caused by our internal qualities (I'm smart, hardworking, etc.) while seeing our unfavorable outcomes as caused by external forces beyond our control (the equipment, the customer, etc.). However, when we view the outcomes of *other* people, fundamental attribution causes us to do the opposite—we tend to see others' success as a product of luck and their failure as a reflection of their incompetence, laziness, or something within their control.

- **Self-Serving Bias.** *Self-serving bias* occurs when raters inflate ratings to make themselves look good. Supervisors responsible for training and developing a person will have a favorable bias because the rating reflects on their skill as a supervisor or trainer.[15]

This discussion of rating problems is only a sampling of the many biases and rating error tendencies associated with human evaluation of others.

Another True Story

Can We Assume That Raters Are Consistent?

Cindy works in a department of a big bank in a large Midwestern city. Cindy had grown up with a great deal of pride in herself, always striving to get good grades in school and excelling in her work. In her late thirties, Muriel became her boss. The bank required annual appraisals, using a 5-point scale (2 = needs improvement, 3 = meets expectations, 4 = exceeds expectations). Cindy is an extremely conscientious, bright, and hard-working employee. She expected her appraisal to reflect the same. Muriel, however, quickly deflated this expectation with an overall rating of 3. This meant a mediocre pay raise and some disadvantage if promotion committees screened her application to advance. Crestfallen, Cindy asks, "What do I need to do to get a 4?" Muriel tells her, "A rating of 3 represents good work—nobody should get a 4 unless they're doing something truly extraordinary. And that's not likely to happen. If you're only doing your job well, you're merely doing what's expected and that is a 3 rating." Cindy finds out that everyone in her department got 3s. Cindy nonetheless was discouraged because she really wanted to excel, but Muriel seemed to suggest that a brick wall was in the way.

Cindy later learns that supervisors in other departments, who went to the same appraisal training as did Muriel, had given 4s to many people. When confronted about this by her staff, Muriel steadfastly stuck to her position that 3 is the appropriate grade for people who perform their jobs well. "*Exceeds* means *exceeds*," she explained. Ironically, months later, Cindy finds out that Muriel got a bonus for "exceed-ing" expectations in keeping the labor costs of her department exceptionally low! A short time later, Cindy transferred to another department.

In assessing the inconsistencies, it's not clear whether other supervisors were engaging in *leniency error* or whether Muriel is guilty of *severity error* or both oc-curred. Perhaps, it doesn't matter, except that these inconsistencies always appear whenever people receive appraisal ratings—thus undermining morale and turning positive, supportive people into cynics.

Over the years, various strategies have attempted to eliminate or minimize these errors and tendencies. For example, organizations monitor ratings and give feedback to raters to reduce the above types of errors. Other organizations force ratings into specified parameters (e.g., no more than 5% of a department's employees will get the highest rat-ing). Constricting or reducing the skewing of rating patterns, however, does not necessarily improve the accuracy of the ratings.[16]

Another strategy used to overcome errors (such as *halo* and *recency*) is encouraging supervisors to keep a diary of critical incidents to create a more "objective" basis in evaluating. This sounds good in theory but does not escape another human tendency—our inclination to focus on the negative. Research indicates that people subconsciously tend to perceive and remember the negative—what is wrong or bad, rather than what is good or favorable.[17] While there's speculation that this tendency helped people survive the Stone Age, it surely hampers humans' ability to ob-jectively see and recall the good and bad in others' performance.

■ Our Assumptions About Rating People

Having reviewed what we do know about the dynamics of our biases and potential for rating errors, let's now examine our underlying assumptions in using appraisal as a tool to decide pay raises, career advancements, and otherwise. Two beliefs we commonly accept in designing appraisal are:

Assumptions

An evaluative process can objectively and reliably assess individual performance.

Supervisors and raters are fair, objective, and unbiased.

Yes, we accept these assumptions with a grain of salt, fully recognizing that there will be some degree of inconsistency and imperfection. Despite this allowance, we still hold onto the belief that somehow we're getting reasonably reliable information. The clear weight of evidence, based on fifty years of intensive experience with appraisal, however, does not support this conclusion. Beyond the research, examine your own experiences with the process and your intuitive feelings—do you truly believe that we can measure performance adequately enough to distinguish each employee's level of performance and contribution? And if we set aside the people who are at the very high or very low end of the scale, do you believe that we can discern with any precision where the remaining people stand? Can you say to someone with confidence, "Based on the merit of your work, Jill, you get 3.2% and Joe, you get 4.1%?" If you say yes or still have faith in the process, read the next section on the political abuse of appraisal.

■ Political Problems

Assumption

Supervisors and rated employees will not try to manipulate performance ratings to get desired outcomes.

While rating errors and bias may be subconscious and unintended, research demonstrates that both the rater and ratee deliberately distort, abuse, or misuse the process with political motives. By "political" we're talking about people who play games with appraisal to arrive at a predetermined or desired result connected to the rating.

Managerial Politics

For good or bad reasons, supervisors and managers make advance decisions of what they want to happen and then use ratings as a vehicle to get those results. The goal may be to get someone a hefty pay raise or to ensure that someone is barred from promotion. Connecting rating outcomes to personnel decisions, such as pay and promotion, is a sure way to end up with distortion and inaccurate ratings. Although leniency is the most

---

Will Multiple Raters Overcome Rater Error and Bias?

Multiple raters may increase reliability (getting greater consistency of ratings), but they do not necessarily provide more accurate results. Multiple raters are still human and bring the biases, rater errors, and political motives of other raters. Often 360-degree systems have people (such as customers or peers with different assignments) rate employees with only superficial knowledge of the ratees' performance and work.

Dr. Anthony T. Dalessio, Staff Director at Bell Atlantic, reviewed various studies on multi-rater feedback. He concluded that ratings collected for personnel decisions (pay, advancement, etc.) are significantly higher than ratings collected merely for feedback or development purposes.[18] "(W)hen multisource feedback is used for personnel decisions rather than purely developmental purposes, practitioners should be prepared for ratings that are potentially contaminated by rating errors, which may make distinguishing between genuinely good versus mediocre performers difficult," Dr. Dalessio observed.[19]

---

prevalent form of political abuse and most frequently is done for positive motives (e.g., inflating ratings to help people to qualify for a raise or a promotion), it nonetheless distorts the outcomes and undermines the validity of the ratings.[20]

Politicking with appraisals is so prevalent that people who otherwise would tend to rate straight-up feel compelled to distort ratings. They fear that "their people" will be punished if they don't inflate the ratings as they perceive other raters doing. Appraisal distortion perhaps reaches the extreme in the U.S. military, where appraisal outcomes are inextricably linked to promotion and "any negative information is considered career threatening."[21] One study examined the ratings of 602 military officers who were in their "window of promotion" time frame. The outcome of the study defies logic and mathematical possibility—in excess of 98% of rated officers were ranked as being in the top 1% of all comparable performers![22] These ratings were given by well-intending commanders who merely wanted to support "their" officers.

This approach is rationalized in the military and throughout the corporate world by the idea that "everyone else is doing it, so why should my people be punished?"[23] Well intended or not, this manipulation undermines fairness and the objectives of the organization. In the context of appraisal, it is nearly impossible to eliminate this kind of abuse. It is not significantly lessened by using "performance management" approaches (outcome measurements) or competency-based approaches, both of which leave open many doors for subjective judgment and manipulation.[24]

Distorting ratings to ensure proper distribution of available "merit" raise funds in the budget process is equally common—and yet another example of the tail wagging the dog. Typically, a dollar amount is established before appraisal time to conform to budget parameters. Months later, before appraisal formally begins, managers already know their merit pay target. No one is surprised then when the ratings just happen to turn out so that the total merit pay increases granted equal the exact amount that was budgeted for merit pay months earlier.[25]

Some people believe these and other "adaptations" with positive intentions are necessary for the effective functioning of the organization and may, in effect, serve to help advance the best people.[26] We agree that politics can have a positive, functional purpose for individuals and the organization but wonder why any organization would want to perpetuate rating systems that are not honest and straightforward, and where the real meaning of a particular rating cannot be known except in the context of an obscure, informal, often clandestine system. No doubt, it's precisely these kinds of disingenuous practices that give good fodder for an environment where everyone walks around wondering and asking—*Where do I stand?*

Political Abuse by Employees

Employees, too, attempt to maneuver and distort the system. Researchers call this *impression management*, which comes in many variations more commonly known as brownnosing or *hey-look-what-I-did*. Employees know when appraisal time is coming around—they start saying good morning and take time to chitchat with the boss. The overall effect of apple-polishing? *It works*, says the research. Several studies published in the 1990s support this conclusion, finding that enhancing performance near appraisal time, doing favors for the boss, being polite, and engaging in ingratiation tactics favorably affect supervisors' perceptions, liking, and ratings of subordinates.[27] While obvious or aggressive impression management may backfire, some research indicates that managers give the highest raises to politically connected people who would threaten to complain if they didn't get a substantial pay raise.[28]

In sum, it's safe to say that appraisal connected to pay raises or other personnel decisions will invariably invite politics from raters and ratees alike. Appraisal, however, cannot bear the blame for politics. Politics in any situation is an inevitable aspect of organization life. And, as one moves up the ladder, the intensity of politics increases.[29] Although appraisal does not *cause* politics, it compounds the problems of politics. Conversations and processes take place that have no meaning but to play the game. Absent appraisal, there would still be politics about pay and career advancement, but *the context* might be more open and visible. Perhaps an open context would encourage the parties to talk about what truly should be determinative in a particular situation and what is going on, rather than arguing about or pretending that it has something to do with the particular ratings on a form. In Chapters 6 and 7, we discuss specific strategies to minimize the untoward effect of political abuse in making decisions pertaining to pay raises, career advancement, and promotion.

■ Crediting Performance to Individuals or the System

Assumption

Raters can adequately distinguish an individual's performance from the situational constraints (the system).

If we are going to base compensation on "fair" ratings, the rating method must be able to distinguish what should be credited to or blamed on the employee versus "the system," i.e., the situation and environmental factors that largely affect individual performance. If the goal of fair compensation is to pay more to those who contribute more, then the ratings or appraisal must be able to ascertain each individual's contribution and performance apart from the system. To some degree, in crediting individuals for their performance, we are deciding how much *the individual's* efforts, skills, and abilities have contributed to that performance, albeit good or bad. This may be an insurmountable challenge, says W. Edwards Deming. A trained physicist, he makes his point using an algebraic equation. He said, if X represents the contribution of *the individual,* and Y the effect of *the system* (the inputs, structures, methods, materials, tools, training, supervision and support of other workers, etc.), then an equation for performance would read as follows:

$$X + (YX) = \text{individual performance outcome}$$

Hence, performance is the individual's contribution *plus* the impact of the system and the impact of the individual in that system. Dr. Deming wisely counseled that this equation cannot be solved. "Unfortunately, there are two unknowns and only one equation," he explained. "Johnny in the sixth grade knows that no one can solve this equation for X."[30] Performance ratings try to solve X while essentially ignoring YX.

Some appraisal advocates have encouraged checklists that presumably allow one to separate an employee's performance from the "situational factors." One recommended approach is to make a list of all of the situation factors (lists of 20 or more items are not uncommon) and then matrix them against each of the job duties or objectives, having both the employee and supervisor complete and reconcile a huge matrix.[31] This potentially adds *hundreds* of judgments (if each rating factor is looked at relative to all of the situational elements) to the appraisal process. It also assumes that the parties can see the effects and interactions of a system, a highly doubtful assumption in light of what we know about system dynamics.

If we cannot segregate the impact of the system or the situation in assessing an individual's performance, we need a new "theory." One view adopted by many of the organizations that have successfully abolished appraisal (Glenroy, Inc. and GM–Powertrain, for example) is that performance is largely driven by the system. In a given year, some people perform better and some worse. A single individual's performance may be better one year, worse the next, somewhere in the middle in the year following. These differences, however, may not be the result of some people trying harder or anything else significant. It may just be the random happenstance of events and factors that impact individual performance. People advanced in process improvement skills call these fluctuations *variation*. Variation is the random fluctuation that occurs with everything in the universe.

Let us illustrate our point. When you pop popcorn, the kernels pop at different times. This does not mean you have lazy kernels or a derelict microwave. Some don't pop at all. The size, the shape, the density, the genetic structure of the kernels may contribute to this variation, as may the storage temperature, the room temperature where the microwave is located, how the microwaves are beamed, the wattage, and whether the microwave has a rotating platter. Whether the bag is placed precisely in the center or slightly off center will have an effect, as will the placement of the kernels within the bag. We could go on, but what we are illustrating is that the causes of variation has infinitesimal dimensions, most of which can never be solved. If we can illustrate these many complexities in the performance of a single popcorn kernel, how can we ever unravel the reasons for variations in the performance of a human being?

Look at variation in the work context. Terry, the auto salesman, sold eight cars last week. This week he's sold none. Has he been reading the newspaper while unserved customers walked out of the dealership? No. Zero cars sold is just one of the possibilities of variation for a person performing well. Like the popcorn kernel, we can identify fifty items that contributed to that outcome, none of which are attributable to Terry. Budgets, production runs, and standardized projects all have variation, too, but in the work world we typically attribute their adverse variation to the dereliction of the individual who is "responsible," especially when it is negative.

Figure 3.1 depicts the likely effect of a system driving the performance outcomes of individuals. Typically people's level of performance is scattered at varying points of the spectrum with the largest segment in the middle. Because the system and random variation to a great degree account for the particular placement of most of the individuals depicted, there is no benefit in trying to see or understand why one person is seemingly performing slightly above or below the performance of another. Because individual performance is so highly interdependent and occurs within the complex variables of the work environment, the performance differences of people inside the extremes of the spectrum are in large part attributable to factors unrelated to their individual efforts and skills. The differences arise mostly from the happenstance effects of the system, resulting in varying levels of performance that will randomly change from one year to the next, even with consistent individual efforts. Acceptance of this theory is not saying that there are no good or bad performers. It may, however, require us to be more conservative in making assumptions about who is truly an above-average performer or a below-average performer in need of help. As Figure 3.1

Distinguishing Individual Performance

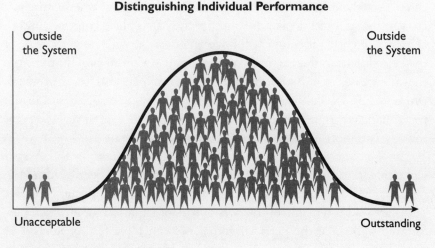

Figure 3.1   Distinguishing Individual Performance

suggests, only a very small percentage of people, perhaps 2–3%, can reliably be identified as *exceptional*, and some would argue that this number is high.

Figure 3.1 is not presented as a new way to evaluate people. It is simply an attempt to illustrate how we might *think differently* about performance and individuals. Rather than thinking we can rank or effectively rate people, we change our assumption. We accept that, while results are measurable, discrete differences in what can be directly attributable to individuals is not measurable. We may only be able to recognize, with a healthy skepticism, people who "stand out" in various settings, thereby warranting special attention. We may also, over *a period of years*, keep data, and if the data are reliable and valid indicators of performance, they may tell us who is exceptional.

To some degree this issue is further sorted out in Chapter 6 on pay. For now, though, recognize that our ability to fairly measure the performance level of an individual is severely hampered by the unknowable effects of systems and random variation. Add to this the unsolvable problems of bias, rating errors, and political abuse, and we clearly understand that our gut feeling about the accuracy of annual ratings is rational and justified.

■ Conclusion

Assume for a moment that annual ratings are not inherently and inexorably defective. Assume we found a way to give people accurate, objective, and fair annual assessments. Would appraisal ratings then be a good idea? Our answer: no, unless they were necessary or legally mandated (discussed in Chapters 4 and 8). The reason: *unintended consequences*—the insidious, destructive, and counterproductive effects of giving people ratings about their work performance. Whether accurate or not, people are psychologically affected by ratings. And except for people rated at the highest end of the scale, the impact is usually negative and consequently counterproductive to the cause of improving performance. Within the function chapters that follow, we sort this out. In Chapters 4, 5, and 6 (coaching, feedback, and pay), we identify and illustrate how annual ratings undermine commitment, impede good communication, and promote the perception of unfair pay practices.

Review of Chapter Assumptions

Conventional Assumptions

An evaluative process can objectively and reliably assess individual performance.

Supervisors and raters are fair, objective, and unbiased.

Alternative Assumptions

- Evaluative processes are largely subjective.

- Most raters and supervisors consciously want to rate people fairly.

- People unknowingly bring perspectives that distort perception and unknown biases when rating other people.

- Training and objective formatting can significantly reduce perceptual and evaluative biases and rating errors, but cannot effectively eliminate these problems.

- Rating formats designed for a single purpose work better than multi-use ratings.

Conventional Assumption

Supervisors and rated employees will not try to manipulate performance ratings to get desired outcomes.

Alternative Assumptions

- As raters and ratees, people will attempt to manipulate and distort ratings to get predetermined or desired results, often with positive motives in mind.

- Multiple raters may be more reliable than a single rater, especially with a collaborative process and clear criteria, to be applied for a specified purpose.

Conventional Assumption

Raters can adequately distinguish an individual's performance from the situational constraints (the system).

Alternative Assumptions

- The system is the greatest influencer of individual performance, making it difficult to ascertain any person's specific level of contribution.

- The few people who are exceptionally good or bad performers may be distinguishable from others, especially over a few years.

Part Two

What to Do Instead: Five Functions of Appraisal

Modern management has
stolen and smothered intrinsic
motivation and dignity.
It has removed joy in work
and learning. We must give
back to people intrinsic motivation:
for innovation, for improvement,
for joy in work, for joy in learning.
The need is to make a person
only responsible to him/herself.
—Henry Neave

4

Coaching Employees in the New Workplace

I have nothing but confidence in you—and not much of that!

Groucho Marx

Leadership must move from the performance appraisal system to appraisal of the performance of the system.

Ronald D. Moen, *Quality Progress*

Coaching. Once a buzzword metaphor, it now capsulizes everything a good supervisor is supposed to do. It's an easy concept to endorse because it has no particular meaning—it means one thing to one person and something else to another. Rarely do we take time to think about or clearly state what we mean by *coaching*. Nor do we ask the important questions: Through *coaching*, what are we trying to accomplish? What are its processes? And who is responsible to ensure that people get the coaching they really need?

Despite a variety of perspectives about coaching, there's one overriding trend pertaining to the concept of coaching—it's called *performance appraisal*. Nearly every design of appraisal touts that it is an effective *coaching* tool. Appraisal is proclaimed as the instrument that facilitates coaching. It's prescribed by well-

73

meaning H.R. departments to ensure that supervisors are doing their job in coaching, guiding, and developing employees. But does it help? Or does it get in the way?

In this chapter, we answer this question by tackling the underlying assumptions of coaching employees in the context of appraisal. We demonstrate how these potent assumptions can foil the most well-intended efforts of supervisors and bring unwanted side effects. Using alternative assumptions, we offer suggestions to deliver coaching needs *without* systematic appraisal, including two in-depth examples of organizations that have found ways to promote effective coaching without appraisal.

■ What Do We Mean by Coaching?

The notion of *coaching* employees means different things to different people. Despite such variability, people usually mention two or three of the following items when asked about coaching:

- Providing and clarifying direction
- Encouraging the development of performance goals
- Giving feedback and listening
- Serving as a source of expert guidance and advice
- Making suggestions for improvement
- Helping people with their work
- Providing encouragement and building self-confidence
- Motivating and keeping up morale
- Removing barriers and providing resources
- Providing technical training (develop skills, knowledge, abilities)
- Assisting and guiding career development (advancement and education)
- Supporting people in personal development (e.g., relationships, political issues).

Some people emphasize the *direction* aspects of coaching more, while others mostly talk about the *development* role. But most of us would recognize everything on the list as a valid need. Cutting a few corners, the list can be boiled down to five primary tasks: (1) guidance and direction,

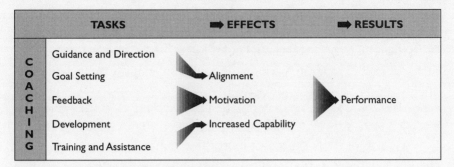

Figure 4.1 Coaching tasks and intended effects

(2) goal setting, (3) feedback, (4) development, and (5) training and assistance (see Figure 4.1).

Figure 4.1 further distills the intended effects of coaching tasks into three categories:

- *Alignment*—ensuring that the right tasks are being done, the targets and priorities are clear, and the work correlates and meshes effectively with other work.

- *Motivation*—building confidence, providing encouragement, challenging people to put forth their best efforts, and attaining unfeigned commitment to do the work.

- *Increased capability*—encouraging and helping employees to develop the knowledge, skills, abilities, competencies, and healthy mental outlook needed now and in the future.

In simplest terms, the ultimate goal or objective of coaching is *performance* or perhaps *improved* performance, i.e., enabling people to increase the net contribution or value of their work.

The remainder of this chapter deals with the roles of coaches and the tools of direction, guidance, and goal setting. The tools of *feedback* and *employee development* are covered in Chapters 5 and 7, respectively.

■ The Changing Role of Supervisors

We expect a great deal from supervisors. In most workplaces, we expect them to deliver the full range of employee coaching needs. We hold them responsible to administer an overloaded appraisal process that rolls together ratings, feedback, improvement goals, development, training plans, pay-raise decisions, and even the triggering of disciplinary measures. With these kinds of processes and tasks, we are really asking every supervisor to act as the "be all" for each of their subordinates, who seem to grow in number every year. It's as though we expect every supervisor to wear a cape, tights, and a blue body shirt with a big red S on it! While appraisal is intended to ease this burden, it mostly has had the effect of *kryptonite*.

And the overload becomes increasingly unrealistic amid the many changes emerging in the business world, including changes in organizational structure, the nature of jobs, work environments, technology, and the accelerating pace of change itself. As a consequence of these changes, coaching needs must be delivered in new ways and the role of the supervisor must be reconfigured. Despite the clear need for new thinking and dramatically different approaches, many workplaces seem wedded to appraisal processes that burden supervisors with unrealistic expectations and wasted time in paper shuffling. We persist in these practices with good intentions, only trying to ensure that supervisors are covering the bases in meeting employees' needs. We fail, not for a lack of effort, but because we don't take time to think about our assumptions regarding the role of supervisors and what people are really seeking in the way of coaching, guidance, and development in this postmodern era.

Investing some time to unravel our assumptions about appraisal and coaching, we will quickly see why appraisal continues to take us down futile pathways. More importantly, this exercise enables us to clearly see what we need to do instead to help people perform at optimal levels.

Most variations of appraisal are predicated upon two fundamental assumptions about the capability of supervisors:

Assumptions

The supervisor has the attributes and skills to be an effective coach.

Supervisors have the knowledge to assess and guide improvement.

From inception, appraisal expects the supervisor to be the capable and knowledgeable "coach" who drives the process. True, in recent years, appraisal designs commonly incorporate feedback from nonsupervisor sources (e.g., 360-degree appraisals). In the end, however, nearly all of these designs make the supervisor the focal point in either the delivery or processing of collected feedback. Moreover, most of these "more progressive" designs of appraisal hold the supervisor accountable to oversee the learning, coaching, and improvement related to performance feedback.

Placing such responsibility upon the supervisor takes on faith that the supervisor has the *attributes* and *skills* of being a good coach—the people and communication skills, the ability to teach, the leadership skills, and the intuitive talent required to effectively counsel, guide, and coach employees. Such delegation further implies that the supervisor has the requisite *knowledge* to coach—knowledge of each employee's job performance and the causes of any deficiencies. It likewise assumes that the supervisor has the technical expertise and teaching skills to train and guide improvement efforts. In part, these assumptions are rational and reasonable—a supervisor who lacked all of these attributes would hardly be qualified. And while undoubtedly there are a few supervisors in every organization who can competently perform all these functions, most cannot. They lack either the necessary information (because of the broad span of supervision) or one or more of the skills needed to validate the above-listed assumptions.

Changes in the business world are making these assumptions *increasingly* invalid. Not many years ago, supervisors most commonly came from the ranks. They learned a job, did it well for a number of years, and were promoted to supervisor. As supervisors, they provided hands-on training and guidance to people essentially doing the same job they once did. Then came the economic cleansing of the 1980s and 1990s. Organizations were downsized, flattened, reconfigured, streamlined, right-sized, consolidated, and merged. At the same time, technology advancement expanded job duties and made jobs more complex. As a result of efficiency endeavors, supervisors previously responsible for 5 or 8 employees saw their number of direct reports increase to 10, 20, or more employees. And the trend toward flattening has perhaps not yet peaked. A supervisor at a General Motors plant in Lansing, Michigan tells us he has 61 direct reports and that the supervisors in his unit have 47 direct reports on average. A General Electric plant in Durham, North Carolina has 170 employees who make jet engines with ten thousand parts—the total number of supervisors? One woman, the plant manager. The plant runs smoothly with a network of self-managed teams.

These emerging structural trends and technology-driven changes have remolded the very essence of supervisory jobs, with further change on the horizon. Four tangible and significant changes are already evident:

- A sharp rise in the span of supervision (numbers supervised)

- Increasing number of people who are supervised from a remote geographic distance

- Supervisors more commonly managing people in jobs in which the supervisor has no or little experience or expertise (for example, in the collapsing of two departments, the supervisor may only have a background in one department; some supervisors are managing people in several different areas of expertise, even people in completely different professions)

- Supervisors more commonly having dual roles—working as a supervisor while concurrently holding another demanding job or handling significant administrative responsibilities that deplete time from supervision and coaching (see Figure 4.2).

Understandably, these structural realignments have dramatically diminished the supervisor's knowledge of how any particular subordinate is performing. These emerging trends signal the need to change the way we look at and serve people's coaching needs.

Despite the increasingly evident need for supervisors to take on new roles, purportedly more progressive designs of appraisal perpetuate invalid assumptions. Worse yet, some new appraisal designs saddle supervisors with yet *more* coaching chores. The "showcase" models of recent years expect the *super-coach* supervisor to synthesize 360-degree feedback, determine and measure competencies for every job, and provide sophisticated career counseling, all in addition to the past functions of providing direction, guidance, goal setting, and training.

The Past	→	Now and Emerging
Supervise few people	→	Supervise many people
Supervise at same location	→	Commonly supervise from afar
Experience and expertise in subordinates' work	→	Little or no experience or expertise in some subordinates' work
Primary role is supervisor	→	Primary role often is not supervision

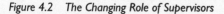

Figure 4.2   The Changing Role of Supervisors

We conjecture that the current popularity of the term *coaching* emerged from the sports world. After all, we think of the sports world as interesting, challenging, fun, and people working together in teams. While the analogy is tempting, the premises of the sports world are entirely different from those of the world of work. In the sports world, the coach is per se an expert in the tasks of the players. The sports coach observes firsthand every action and interaction of the players. The coach takes command and directs what happens, calling every play and instructing even as the play is executed—with hand signals, with shouts, or through headsets. Players who are insubordinate are either benched, fined, or traded. Right before their eyes, athletic coaches see all of the complex interactions affecting their players. They know what happened, why it happened, and see the results. They have ideas on how to deal with any deficiencies—right then and there (coaching from the sidelines) or prospectively in the next game or season.

Management conferences routinely bring coaches of the sports world as guest speakers, revealing their magical secrets of success for application in the business world. It may be fun to think of our work in the context of sports, but supervisors and people managers are not the same kind of coach. Work world coaches rarely have the expertise and knowledge of a sports coach. It also is not realistic for us to expect supervisors to see work systems as visibly as a playing field, nor is it desirable to expect them to call every shot. Perhaps if we discontinue the mental model of a sports coach, we would not create so many unrealistic expectations for our supervisors.

This superhero expectation we place on supervisors also clashes sharply with the way we seek out coaching in our personal lives. We don't look to a single person to fulfill every coaching need. If we need help with our diet, we see a nutritionist. If we need spiritual advice, we see our minister, priest, rabbi, a guru, or just someone we see as spiritually wise or advanced. If we need legal advice, we talk with an attorney, and so on. In the workplace, however, appraisal systems condition us to look for guidance from our boss, rather than looking for the best possible resource. Except for some relatively recent trends (mentoring, the use of Employee Assistance Plans, external coaches, etc.), most organizations heap *all* of the coaching and counseling tasks on the supervisor.

This overloading of coaching tasks makes less and less sense in the emerging business world. Supervisors are being called to take on radically different roles. Technical training and overseeing the work has given way to creating a sense of purpose and general direction and facilitating learning in a collegial environment. Appraisal, because of its underlying assumptions, matches poorly with the new brand of supervisors. We need alternatives to appraisal that do not assume that supervisors act in a superior role or portray them as the omniscient and omnipresent jack-of-all-trades. To design effective alternatives to appraisal, we must step back and discretely examine the assumptions that underlie each of the functions we associate with coaching, beginning with guidance and direction.

■ Guidance and Direction

Assumption

To get alignment and desired performance, people require formal and specific direction.

To perform effectively, employees require basic information. They need to understand the aim of the organization and understand how their work relates to the whole. Employee efforts must align and be in sync with the greater goals of their department and the organization as a whole. Employees must know whether their work efforts are sufficiently meeting the needs of their internal and external customers. They also need to know whether their skills and methods are effective. To effectively garner this type of information, most employees, in varying degrees, require some form of *guidance* and *direction*.

The particular form or method supervisors choose in providing guidance and direction stems from their fundamental beliefs about people and work. Usually these assorted beliefs all come from one end of the spectrum or the other. For example:

- Do we believe that direction and guidance are desired and sought? Or do we believe that they must be dispensed or imposed?

- Do we believe that people are naturally committed to organizational goals and achieving optimal performance? Or do we believe that dereliction and self-interest dominate people's perspective at work?

- Do we believe that people freely accept helpful guidance and direction? Or do we believe that people resist such direction, thereby requiring elements of control?

At least in name, many organizations subscribe to the healthier assumptions, what Douglas McGregor called *Theory* Y answers to these questions. Theory Y operates from the assumption that people like to work, care about organizational goals, and actively seek out and accept guidance that is helpful. (Theory X beliefs are diametrically the opposite.) Increasingly, organizations are earnestly striving to rebuild their work culture upon a foundation that reflects Theory Y and the good intentions of people. Everywhere, mission and value statements proclaim trust, teamwork, and empowerment. Organizations spend billions of dollars each year training supervisors to manage people in ways that reinforce these values.

Yet, these prodigious efforts have largely failed to transform our work cultures. Ironically, this failure has occurred despite an increasing number of managers and supervisors who espouse these emerging values and sincerely wish to make the shift. If their intentions are positive, why do their efforts fail to shift the culture? We fervently believe that the main culprit is the underlying assumptions of our work structures, policies, and practices. The prevailing people practices, foremost including appraisal, underscore conflicting messages—messages that unintentionally convey distrust rather than trust, skepticism rather than confidence, and messages that say "you the individual" rather than "we the team." This distrust is perhaps best evidenced by practices that, at their center, emphasize *control*.

■ Accountability or Control?

Assumption

All people will perform better if they are held accountable through a formal process.

In varying forms, appraisal processes strive to hold employees accountable against some type of measurable criteria. True, appraisal designers don't deliberately think about trying to control anyone—in their mind, they just want to help people to do their best. Though control is not intended, virtually every form of the appraisal bespeaks *control*. Simple appraisal plans retrospectively evaluate the employee on general behaviors, for example, productivity, efficiency, quality of work, attendance, communication skills. Other plans measure performance against specified duties and tasks, often taken right from the job description. In larger organizations, employees typically are measured against MBO or MBR objectives or other predetermined goals. More recently, many organizations are rating employees against a *competency model*. This approach attempts to determine the competencies required to perform a particular job (everything from tangible hands-on skills to intangible qualities such as leadership and communication) and then the individual employee's displayed competencies are measured. A growing number of organizations apply 360-feedback against measurable appraisal criteria, holding people accountable for targeted outcomes and improvement.

These various forms of appraisal are packaged as tools for "accountability" rather than *control*. We are comfortable with *accountability*, but not *control*—only monsters seek control. Our comfort with accountability is not misplaced. It's a worthy goal, at least to the extent that it means people should take responsibility for their work. The problem lies not in desiring accountability, but in the *means* of ensuring accountability. Rather than promoting accountability as a value, we try to *force* people to be responsible. We impose measurement and formal judgment to make sure that people are held accountable. This is precisely what appraisal does. With good intentions, we adorn appraisal with upbeat and friendly terminology, but the features of control are undeniably present and felt by every employee who undergoes the process. Peter Block's observations accurately depict the reality of appraisal.

When we talk to H.R. professionals about their appraisal practices

---

Peter Block's Observations on Appraisal

Performance appraisals are an instrument for social control. They are annual discussions, avoided more often than held, in which one adult identifies for another adult three improvement areas to work on over the next twelve months. You can soften them all you want, call them development discussions, have them on a regular basis, have the subordinate identify the improvement areas instead of the boss, and discuss values. None of this changes the basic transaction.... If the intent of appraisal is learning, it is not going to happen when the context of the dialogue is evaluation and judgment.[1]

implying *control*, we encounter expressions of disbelief. In their hearts, they *know* they have earnestly strived to create a supportive structure solely designed to *help* people perform, improve, and develop. We accept this as a true statement of their intent but then ask them to look at the features and packaging of conventional performance appraisal. In widely accepted forms of appraisal, we typically find that appraisal:

- is a mandatory procedure
- is documented in writing
- is administered by the boss
- holds people accountable for past goals and measures
- requires people to commit in writing to future goals and actions
- is placed and preserved for years in the employee's official personnel file
- mandates that the employee signs it
- is used to decide important decisions pertaining to pay, advancement, promotion, and layoff
- is tied to or used in conjunction with formal discipline and discharge.

Regardless of our good intentions, a common link implicit in all of the above design features is *control*.

The next important question is why would we intentionally or unintentionally rely on vehicles of control? Though consciously we may hold a positive outlook toward people, we commonly have unsurfaced beliefs and assumptions that run counter. If we dig them up and make them explicit, they might look something like this:

- Without control, people will withhold their best efforts.
- People will not, on their own volition, take responsibility to develop and improve their performance.
- Holding people accountable with a written formal process is an effective form of control.
- People will not improve without tangible and specific targets and goals.
- Documented processes, such as annual evaluation and structured performance feedback, will motivate people to improve their performance.

Sometimes when people first look at these assumptions, they say the list is somewhat cynical and doesn't emphasize the positive assumptions of appraisal. They say these negative assumptions really don't apply at their company because they employ enlightened managers. They then say something like this:

> In *our* organization, we don't have supervisors who get high on control—they just want to help people with legitimate needs. People want some evaluation of their work—they need to know how they are doing. People want feedback so they know what to work on. Those who are doing well need praise and encouragement or some sort of formal recognition from the organization that says they are doing a good job. Most of our people want direction and guidance on what's a priority, to know how their work ties to where the organization is headed, etc. We have caring supervisors, most of whom are sensitive and conscientious at appraisal time—their delivery is about guidance and goals, not control and coercion. Control is rarely used, and then, only as a means of last resort.

People erroneously assume that good intentions and well-meaning managers can effectively override the control message of appraisal. But again, the problem is not about intentions, it is about the design of appraisal and its attendant assumptions.

To test the existence of these assumptions, we often ask managers if they would be comfortable in letting their evaluations and feedback process be voluntary. They say no, explaining that people wouldn't do them or otherwise take responsibility for improvement. When we suggest that the employee be the sole keeper of the paperwork, they say people would not take the process seriously. These responses resonate unsurfaced beliefs that people are not interested in improvement and control devices are necessary.

Control may deliver results, but it brings unwanted effects. Softened approaches by sincere managers cannot override the blatantly coercive flavor of appraisal. Even though most supervisors do not consciously intend to manage by control, the features of appraisal (written judgment, employee's signature, placement in the personnel file, etc.) clearly rely on and are experienced as control.

When people feel as if they are being controlled, they are likely to resist, just for the sake of resisting. Ask married people, male and female, how they respond when they detect that their mate is trying to *make* them do something they have not freely chosen to do. Invariably, people respond to this question by saying they take a stand or actively or passively resist the control. In the workplace, it's no different. When people sense they are being controlled, even for good reasons, it triggers a response of resistance, outright hostility, or passive-aggressive behavior. Eminent psychologist Alfred Adler observed that overcoming feelings of inferiority is "an incessant striving of man and mankind."[2] He further observed that this natural and normal striving to overcome inferiority makes us sensitive and reactive to *control* and *coercion*, explaining:

> Human nature generally answers external coercion with a countercoercion. It seeks its satisfaction not in rewards for obedience and docility, but aims to prove that its own means of power are stronger.[3]

In the workplace, this natural, healthy, and human tendency to resist control commonly results in varying forms of passive resistance (because outspoken resisters do not survive). Worse yet, attempts at control leave in their wake "cynicism, grudges, mistrust, and de-motivation," cautions Peter Scholtes. Compliance may be achieved, but the relationship and employee commitment may be irreparably damaged.

■ Rating and Ranking as a Source of Guidance and Direction

Assumption

Rating and ranking are effective motivational and coaching tools.

Rating and ranking are widely accepted practices for coaching employees, even among organizations that do not tie pay to appraisal outcomes. The reason for this preference is unclear. Perhaps it's a carryover from grading in school. Maybe we believe that a precise number or rank communicates a very clear message. It also gives a ring of objectivity. As discussed earlier, people have an insatiable appetite to know where they stand—conceivably a precise number accomplishes this. Regardless of the specific reason, there must be an underlying belief that rating and ranking are helpful coaching tools. Otherwise, why would so many organizations, including those that do not use them for pay and promotion decisions, adopt the practices?

But are rating and ranking really helpful? With rare exceptions, we say they are not. We are not saying that evaluative information is never needed or of value. People need to know if they are performing well or

not. And for various reasons (training assessment, hiring method valida-
tion, new employees passing initial probation, career advancement, etc.),
the organization has a legitimate need to know how someone is doing.
Evaluation per se is not the problem—it is appraisal's multipurpose, an-
nual-event approach to evaluation that is the problem. In appraisal, all
people in the organization are systematically rated for *general* purposes—
this type of evaluative method does not render reliable measures (see
Chapter 3), nor is it an effective coaching tool in telling people how
they're doing. Worst of all, ratings invariably bring unintended, adverse
effects that are harmful to a productive atmosphere.

For starters, rating and ranking are inherently destructive of self-
esteem. Virtually all employees see themselves as excellent workers. Most
people are disappointed with their ratings and rankings unless they are at
the highest level. One study found that 98% of people saw themselves in
the top half of all performers.[4] Another study showed that 80% of people
saw themselves in the top quarter of all performers.[5] Other research indicates that 59% of workers across a variety of jobs disagreed or strongly disagreed with any rating that was not the highest on the scale.[6] People are
devastated when they see the great chasm between the actual and their
expected rating. As psychiatrist and author Dr. William Glasser has observed, "distrust, antagonism and anger" are "almost always generated by
being forced to submit to evaluation by others."[7]

Some contend that rude awakenings are helpful. We often hear,
"Every now and then people need a good dose of harsh reality." We see
little benefit in telling people that they are average or below average. This
type of information conveys little in the way of constructive or insightful
information. Even if it does serve some communication purpose, such information is needlessly de-motivating and destructive of confidence.
Overconfidence can be corrected without proclamations of inferiority
(for example, by helping employees discover and see for themselves performance deficiencies that are present, or by offering explicit suggestions
for better performance when the more experienced coach knows what
needs to be done). Qualitative information or statements about one's performance would be more helpful and less likely to destroy an individual's
psyche. Ratings also encourage superficial conversations. Instead of artic-
ulating the problem or opportunity, supervisors assume that a rating conveys clear and helpful information. Worse yet, in a coaching and feedback
conversation, the person rated is drawn to the rating (and its real mean-

ing relative to their standing, pay, or promotion), rather than gaining an understanding of the deficiency. A rating or ranking also contributes little to the ultimate objective of improving organizational performance. As Alfie Kohn astutely asks, What difference does it make if an individual is a top-ten-percent performer in an organization that is going down the toilet? And, conversely, why is it so important to know who is in the bottom 10% if the organization is doing a terrific job in meeting its customer needs and making a good profit?[8]

Another True Story

Dr. Bob and Appraisal

Dr. Bob, as his patients call him, is a general practice physician in a small central Wisconsin town. He is a partner in a medical practice that has grown from 3 to 18 physicians over the past two decades. In recent years, the staff and personnel duties grew to a level that a human resources manager was hired. The new H.R. manager requested that Dr. Bob do a performance evaluation on the three nurses with whom he worked. "I didn't like it and didn't see any need for it." Nonetheless, Dr. Bob complied. He gave them all outstanding ratings. The H.R. manager then called him and said his ratings could not be accurate, that they must have some deficiencies. "I told her they were all outstanding. They did a great job every day. If anything was not just right, we would discuss it that day. I worked with these nurses for eight years, we got along, and I was truly happy with everything they were doing." The H.R. manager pressed Dr. Bob again, saying they could not be that "outstanding" and surely he could think of some areas where they could improve. Dr. Bob succumbed to the pressure, reworked the evaluations, and wrote down some suggestions.

The impact of the appraisals was predictable. The nurses could not understand why they were not "outstanding" or why there would be documentation about them needing to improve, given the success of their practice and day-to-day relationship. Dr. Bob explained "It undermined our relationship and our trust with one another. They got the impression I was talking about them behind their back. I think they felt like there was some conspiracy against them of which I was part."

The whole notion of scales is problematic in yet another way. Jacqueline Cooney, H.R. Director for Central Research at Mead, says their research scientists and engineers have great difficulty in accepting a performance rating of 3 (on a scale of 1–5) as high-quality, solid performance. "No matter what words we put around it, they see a 3 as a C, and for people who were used to getting A's in school, this is unacceptable," she explains. A Big Ten university department chair confirmed a similar effect, noting that most professors spent eight or nine years in the university getting nearly straight A's. Because of this conditioning, they experience anything less than the highest rating as insulting and demoralizing.

■ One-Size-Fits-All Approaches to Guidance and Direction

Assumptions

A one-size-fits-all coaching structure works well for all employees.

Supervisors in each organization want or need to use the same approach to guide, develop, and manage people.

The inherent design features of systematic appraisal ignore the variability of people and situations, heaping upon every supervisor and manager a single, all-encompassing strategy for guiding and directing people. Such practice ignores the variability and diversity of people. It assumes that one method of coaching is effective for every employee, regardless of their personal traits or years of experience. Any of us who have spent time in organization life readily recognize that people's coaching and directional needs vary as to type, degree, frequency, and form of delivery. Appraisals discount this variability, prescribing one particular approach to be applied to every individual. While some organizations vary their appraisal format for employees in different occupational areas or at different levels (for example, executives may be evaluated under a special process), increasingly we see the growth of one-size-fits-all approaches, where the CEO and the custodian are coached and evaluated under the same plan. Despite the democratic and egalitarian appeal of adopting a common approach, it does not yield effective coaching.

Some would argue that a commonly shared approach is justified by the need for organizations to operate cohesively within a common culture, one in which the values, management styles, and approaches for working with people are in alignment. While there may be some benefit in seeking to weave a common culture, compelling everyone to subscribe to the same method of coaching and counseling goes far beyond this goal, needlessly depriving employees of guidance that is ideally suited to serve their particular individual needs.

Worse yet, a prescribed appraisal method strips supervisors of their individuality and unique preferences in managing people. It chains supervisors to a precisely structured method of coaching that is not of their choice. Supervisors are also unique individuals with their own brand and style of working with people. They each have their predilections and quirks; they know (or are searching for) what works for them and what does not. Some supervisors work well with informal styles, casually and effectively providing guidance and keeping people on track without formal meetings or imposing prescriptive goals. Other supervisors are comfortable and effective with a more structured approach, holding periodic meetings, developing and reviewing written goals. Their personality or style allows them to carry this off in ways that people do not see them as oppressive or control freaks. Managers will be most effective when they determine for themselves the tools and approaches for coaching and guiding people.

Earnest H.R. professionals often express concern that, without some prescribed form of coaching, feedback, and development, a good number of supervisors will ignore the needs of their employees. This assumption may be correct, but it seems unfair and ineffective to impose a specific practice on all supervisors as the solution. A more effective strategy would be to educate, train, and offer tools to those managers (more on this in *the instead* part of the chapter). If you question supervisors' interest and willingness to do the right things, then perhaps you have some bad fits and people need to be counseled out of the people management role, or to move on to a different work culture altogether. In transforming to a more supportive management culture, Preston Trucking encountered supervisors who just couldn't give up the idea of acting as the boss. Consequently, over a period of a few years, about 25% of their first-line supervisors left the company.[9]

Interestingly, gender and ethnicity significantly tend to predict one's preference for particular managerial styles. In an extensive study of leaders around the world, Judy Rosener found that men reported a preference of relying more on formal position power and the practice of "transactional" leadership, i.e., a view that job performance is "a series of transactions with subordinates—exchanging rewards for services rendered or punishment for inadequate performance." Conversely, she found that women were more likely to describe themselves as "transformational" leaders, i.e., "getting subordinates to transform their own self-interest into the interest of the group through concern for a broader goal."[10] When the organization chooses an appraisal method as the official people management tool, however, it deprives supervisors of the choice and freedom to find what works best for them.

Some may counter that an appraisal method does not necessarily deprive supervisors of choice. Perhaps this is correct in a sense, but a prescribed process nonetheless impinges on each supervisor's freedom and style. Consider, for example, a supervisor who enjoys using periodic goal discussions about the work itself and has been successful. Then his company adopts a competency-model appraisal, systematically prescribing elaborate development scales for every task and function each employee performs. The process further dictates evaluation on a 3-dimension scale, prescribing coaching methods right down to the forms to be used and scheduling the timing. While the directive to utilize competency modeling does not bar the supervisor from using his goal-method, it does plainly mandate a competing model for improving performance. Unquestionably, this dilutes and likely overshadows the supervisor's method of choice.

Systematic appraisal processes further ignore another variability—the *situation*, i.e., the nature of the work, the tasks, structure and environment, stressors, growth requirements, tolerance level for marginal work, and many other factors. As with people, some situations require more structure and some require more support. The degree of direction and structure would be high for a SWAT or surgical team in action. Conversely, the situation of a creative team at an advertising firm or a staff of high school guidance counselors typically would require support more than structure.

Another variability is the level of work experience. According to the Blanchard-Hersey model, a person with little maturity typically requires a great deal of *structure* and *direction* at first.[11] Once comfortable with the basics, this person may continue to have a substantial need for structure and direction but also may be more conscious of psychological issues, such as the pressure to perform, job stressors, peer and customer relationships, and the like. This triggers the need for the supervisor to provide more *support* in the forms of confidence-building, helping employees sort out the barriers, and getting people over the bumps without bruised egos. At some point, the employee matures and knows the job well enough that little structure or intervening support is required—the tasks merely need to be delegated through unambiguous communication.[12] Despite widespread acceptance of this and other situational models (they are routinely taught within business degree curriculums), the practice of appraisal seems to run clearly counter, prescribing a one-size-fits-all approach for coaching and guiding people in their work.

The greatest drawback to one-size-fits-all coaching tools is not its disregard of the variability of people, supervisor styles, or situations—it is the lack of choice and implied element of coercion. Josh Hammond and James Morrison, authors of *The Stuff Americans Are Made Of*, find that some cultures have greater needs for freedom and *choice* than do others. For example, the need for choice is greater in the United States and Norway than it is in Japan and Iran.[13] Hammond and Morrison conclude that, in cultures where freedom is highly valued, choice must be made explicit in all organizational endeavors, advising:

> (N)o new work process or procedure . . . should attempt to by-pass or short-change choice. Each step of the process should be screened for the presence of choice, explicitly expressed or implicitly implied. It has the power to unleash the imagination of a hamstrung work force, stimulate growth, foster creativity, enhance personal worth, fulfill dreams, or realize the things we hold to be self-evident. *Real choice builds and binds. It fosters respect and enhances loyalty. Choice guarantees engagement—the precondition for sustaining performance.*[14]

These pearls of wisdom underscore the power of choice. Where is the choice in appraisal? Managerial tools such as competency modeling, goal setting, or formal feedback can be useful coaching tools depending on the people involved and the situation. But by imposing on people a tool they have not freely chosen, we dim the possibility of meaningful growth and learning.

■ Goal Setting–A Good Strategy for Improvement?

Assumptions

Individual goal setting is an effective motivational tool and strategy for improving performance.

Having an annual conversation around improvement accomplishes improvement.

Conventional wisdom says that a good coach should use *goals*. People like goals. Goals motivate people. Goals get you good performance. Are these assumptions accurate? Yes, in the sense of reflecting on the potential of goals. Taken as gross generalizations, however, these assumptions are perilously misleading. As we shall discuss, individual goals have their benefits and drawbacks. The value and benefit of goal setting in any situation are every bit as complicated as are people.

Despite these limitations and complexities, many appraisal designs in recent decades push individual goal setting as the sure-fire cure-all for aligning and improving performance. In one way or another, most forms of appraisal focus on establishing and documenting specific individual goals as a means of getting improvement and increased motivation. In recent years, there seems to be a renaissance of individual goal setting in the context of neo-MBO. Even in the non-MBO behavioral or developmental appraisals, employees and the supervisor are expected to identify areas of performance weakness (often a minimum of three) and then write out specific goals to overcome those weaknesses. Developmental goals also are standard fare in most appraisal designs.

Organizations have oriented their appraisal processes toward goal setting because it is believed to generate more objective ratings. Over the years, organizations have struggled with the inaccuracies and unreliability of appraisal, as detailed in Chapter 3. The allure of measurable goals is the removal of the bias and subjectivity of human judgment, with thinking that goes like this:

> Goals are objective. There is a targeted number. The employee either makes the goal or doesn't. Goals remove personalities and biases from the process. You just get the straightforward, hard facts.

The logic is alluring because it does not articulate the attendant underlying assumptions. As a performance strategy, goal setting assumes, for example, that:

- Goal attainment represents good performance.

- Individual efforts have a dominant influence on the attainment of goals.

- Achievement of goals is always measurable.

- Measurements are accurate and free from human bias and distortion.

- The mere giving of goals motivates attainment.

In reality, these assumptions are not altogether true. Individual goals try to hold people accountable for performance outcomes that are gener-

---

Dogbert's Advice to Managers on Appraisal Strategy

Your objective is to convince each employee that his performance review is a measure of HIS performance ... if you don't explain it that way to employees, they will get all cynical instead of motivated. You must use your awesome powers of persuasion to make them think their environment is a predictable fixed point and only their performance is variable.[15]

---

ated by the system in which they work. For example, a production supervisor can only increase output if the machines and employees are able to work faster while preserving safety and keeping the final products within required specification. This is not a matter of leadership and supervision but may depend on the type and quality of the materials, the process and equipment, availability of engineers, technology, and capital investment, the local labor market, training resources, delivery and shipment schedules, and scores of other factors. As discussed in Chapter 2, individual performance is largely determined by the system in which one works. The improvement strategy of individual goal setting largely ignores this reality of organizational life.

We ignore systems theory, even when we received the training, because usually we *see* only the employee and the performance outcome, but we cannot see the system. We *can* see the salesperson who did not get the sale, but we cannot see the defective product, the lackluster promotional materials, the company's substandard warranty, or the late deliveries of that customer's last order. We *can* see the cashier whose drawer does not balance, but we cannot see the training she received, the glare on the computer screen, or the impact of being scheduled to work a 10½ hour day. Passing off the responsibility for performance outcomes to individuals is quite tempting. It's far easier to assign a goal than to try help an employee figure out the cause of the deficiency and what to do about it. A goal by itself does not tell a person what to do. If the supervisor merely gives the employee a higher target, without insights, explanation, or exploration of new methods, in effect that tells the employee that the supervisor thinks he's been goofing off. Otherwise the goals would already have been attained. Instead of pronouncing goals, the supervisor must take time to understand the origin of a performance deficiency. Is it a lack of skill or training? Is the employee uninterested or unmotivated? Answering these questions requires thought and open communication with the employee. Once the supervisor understands the probable cause, she must determine how she can help the employee overcome the deficiency. At this point, encouraging the employee to set a goal may or may not be helpful.

Is goal setting of value in motivating the employee? Just about every how-to book on managing people proclaims goal setting as an essential tool for individual coaching. Rarely, however, are the checkerboard results of goal-setting research acknowledged. Short of excavating the mountains of goal-setting research, let us focus on four important findings.

Acceptance and Commitment of Goals

While goals can be motivating when there is *acceptance* and *commitment*, little is known about how people decide to *accept* and *commit* to goals. Without acceptance and personal commitment, goals are largely ineffective. Participation in goal setting can increase *acceptance*,[16] but acceptance does not assure commitment (the person's level of desire or interest in reaching this goal). Acceptance cannot be forced—it must be genuinely voluntary to be effective. As Harry Levinson observed, people often are "told that they have opportunities to set their own objectives (but) in fact they merely are given a limited range of choices within those established by their superiors and often must modify their own objectives to meet the expectations of management."[17] While a seemingly friendly appraisal gives lip service to the employees' involvement in setting the goals, employees quickly sense what is really going on, dousing any opportunity for personal commitment.

Multiple and Complex Goals

While appraisals are designed around schemes of multiple goal setting, most of the favorable research on using goals is derived from *single* goals. The findings on multiple-goal situations is less conclusive in demonstrating the positive effects of goals. Goal setting is less effective when goals are complex and novel decision-making tasks and interdependent tasks are involved.[18] Most people also realize that the accomplishment of one goal adversely affects or sacrifices another goal.

Consider an example of how this plays out in the life of an Information Services (IS) manager who oversees the technical support for PCs. He is given the goals of decreasing the labor cost of his technical staff and at the same time commits to a "please-the-customer" goal of being more accommodating and tailoring service to better meet individual needs. He knows he can reduce labor costs by narrowing the software and equipment options. This strategy, however, invariably makes customers feel oppressed and handcuffed by the IS Department's lack of flexibility. If dollar amounts for labor costs are being measured, however, he may choose to narrow software options. Or, three months before the 360-degree feedback forms go out to his customers, he can say yes to please every customer, knowing it will drive up next year's labor costs. Though both goals are worthy, the formal measurement and time-bound context creates undue pressures and tends to promote quick or artificial solutions that drive the indicators, rather than finding more holistic solutions that can ameliorate both goals over a period of time.

Quantity Goals

To no one's surprise, studies demonstrate that *quality* suffers when employees are given *quantity* goals.[19] Most of us have been sold on the idea that giving individuals higher numeric targets is somehow motivating. Quantitative goals so often are pulled down from the sky, with no rationale but a better number. We readily adopt numeric goals because that's easier than planning *what* we will do. Sometimes these numeric targets, set solely for the sake of goal setting, are misleadingly *understated*. For example, an employee with an error rate of 5% is given a goal of reducing errors to 2%. This kind of goal can convey the wrong message—the error rate goal is 0%, not 2%. A preferable immediate goal would be to understand and eradicate *the causes* of errors—leading to improvement and employee satisfaction (that does not need to be hinged to an arbitrary number). When people take time to understand the causes, rather than focusing on an arbitrary number, they often find solutions that generate unforeseen, gargantuan levels of improvement.

Unintended Consequences

Like every other social intervention, individual goal setting brings unintended consequences. When individual performance goals are imposed on people through appraisal, invariably there are prescribed targets, measurements, deadlines, surveillance, and evaluation. These features undermine intrinsic motivation because they cause people to feel pressured and controlled.[20] *Individual* performance goals often impede cooperation and the natural sense of teamwork. They precipitate bureaucratic behavior where goals become an end in themselves. When people fail to meet established goals, their confidence and self-esteem are eroded—they become discouraged, disheartened, and cynical, especially when the achievement of goals is tied to compensation or continued employment. Goal shortcomings cause people to feel desperate or threatened, which tempts them to manipulate or distort data or act contrary to the customer's interest. For example, several years ago Sears was cited by California state authorities when its automotive service writers were found selling customers unneeded parts and service in order to meet commission quotas. Sears never intended this result, but this type of effect can always be expected when people are pressured to meet seemingly unreachable targets that are tied to pay and job retention.

Beyond the above drawbacks and limitations of individual goal setting, goals can unintentionally cause laxity on the part of supervisors. When a supervisor gives a goal, it often beguiles him into thinking that he has done his job—it becomes a point of *disconnecting* rather than connecting with the employee. Rather than taking joint responsibility (also known as teamwork) for the performance objective or deficiency by working it through *with* the employee, goals psychologically distance the supervisor from the employee. When the supervisor gives the employee a clear target, it fosters a false sense that he has done his part and the rest is up to the employee. In this age of "empowering employees," perhaps the supervisor tells himself that this is a progressive approach, empowering employees to figure things out for themselves. While such delegation of goals may be situationally appropriate, it hardly should be a stock strategy.

Despite the drawbacks and perils of individual goal setting, we do not condemn it. In many contexts and with particular individuals, goal setting can be useful. While goal setting is situationally appropriate, there is no justification to orchestrate multiple individual goals for everybody in the organization, through appraisal or otherwise. If we contrast what we know about individual goal setting, its strengths, weaknesses, and drawbacks, with the emerging and prevailing organizational trends, it increas-

The Mixed Blessing of Goals

Minnesota-based organizational consultant Mike Tveite relates a personal experience on the influences of goals. Though Mike was not a serious runner, he decided early one year that he would run a marathon in six months. He told everyone what he was going to do, believing this would make him accountable to his goal and spur him on. He came up with an extremely challenging training schedule and began the vigorous training. As the running got more intense, Mike suffered an injury. Because he had formally committed to the goal and told others, he kept running hurt. Though he had not completely recovered from his injury, he nonetheless ran in the marathon—his personal goal helped him persevere and finish. After reaching the finish line, he was in such pain and so exhausted that he could not participate in any of the customary post-marathon celebrations. He could not walk at all the next day. Nearly two weeks later, he was still too sore to play a round of golf, and he felt the effects for months afterward.

Yes, Mike said, the goal clearly motivated him. At the same time though, his myopic focus on the goal precluded him from thinking clearly. Mike observed, "While goals are helpful, they also cause you to do some stupid things." Mike further reflected that, had he evaluated his best interests when he first got hurt, he might have stopped running and postponed his goal for another time. The goal, however, blindsided his best judgment. "Goals work," Mike said, "but they are a mixed blessing, often prompting us to take actions that are not helpful."

ingly is an unwise wholesale improvement strategy. In workplaces today, we find the following emerging trends:

- Jobs and the work itself are becoming increasingly complex and interdependent.

- Technology and restructuring are augmenting the likelihood of individuals having multiple responsibilities, tasks, and priorities.

- The accelerating speed of change and resulting demand for quick responses have brought us to the point that some are suggesting that the concept of a *job*, no less annual goals, is obsolete. Rather than prescribed duties, people have a *function* that requires continual adaptation and responsiveness to meet the needs of the moment.

- Over the past two decades, the focus on the *quality* of work and products has equaled and probably surpassed the focus on *quantity*.

- Organizations more openly espouse the values of empowerment, autonomy, choice, and the use of collaborative teams in lieu of cultures based on top-down control.

- The emerging influence of chaos and complexity theories has begun to alter organizational structures toward more open, naturally evolving systems to accomplish the work.

When we view these trends against what we know about goal setting, our reliance on individual goal setting as the primary means of organizational improvement is an increasingly unwise strategy.

■ What to Do Instead—New Perspectives on Coaching

Coaching can never be effective within the context of a system-wide appraisal process. The faulty assumptions of appraisal doom the most well-intended efforts to a disappointing result. Alternative methods of coaching must begin with alternative assumptions (see summary of those assumptions at the end of the chapter). With new assumptions, the role of supervisors and methods of coaching and guiding undergo radical change. Accordingly, we make the following recommendations to effectively address those needs.

Drop Organization—Mandated Ratings and Evaluations

Due to their demoralizing effects, discontinue ratings and evaluations except in the cases where they are the best tool for the particular individual and situation or they are legally required. In such cases, use ratings and evaluations *only* as required and confine the extent of the judgment to the purpose *and* providing *useful* information. Don't apply arbitrary numeric judgments, when pass/fail or concrete statements will suffice. (See "Do Ratings and Appraisal Ever Make Sense?")

Foster New Roles for Supervisors

Rather than directing and monitoring the work, supervisors must unleash people to direct and monitor their own work. This transition is a major

Do Ratings and Appraisals Ever Make Sense?

Yes. Though we see no value in systematic, organization-wide appraisals, there are few instances where ratings (in effect, an appraisal) or other forms of structured evaluation may be necessary or useful:

Probationary Employees. Some rating of probationary employees or employees undergoing on-the-job training often *is* necessary. The purpose of the evaluation would be to ensure that newly hired or promoted individuals have the basic capability or aptitude to successfully perform the job. Has the person demonstrated the potential to be successful? Is the person a good fit for the job and the organization? Are the organization's hiring practices effective in bringing the right people to the job? Though some measurement or evaluation may be necessary, remember that probationary evaluations are subjective and suffer from the same maladies as ratings in general. Accordingly, if the determination needed is merely a gate-check on a pass/fail basis, there is little value (or reliability) in attempting to pinpoint on a scale the precise level of an individual's performance. That specific level of performance is probably unknowable, but, for most individuals, it will be plainly clear whether or not they are plausible prospects to continue in the position. Career advancement assessments are discussed in Chapter 7.

Required for Legal Reasons. Chapter 8 identifies the narrow circumstances (e.g., in healthcare and some government bodies) under which some type of evaluation of performance is required by law.

Particular Coaching or Counseling Needs. In some instances, written feedback that comprehensively addresses how an individual is doing with respect to all major duties is helpful. For example, an individual may ask her supervisor, a mentor, or a senior co-worker to provide this type of evaluative feedback. Similarly, a supervisor may observe a struggling employee who appears to be lost in his job, performing some duties well, and some not, without a clear focus on areas needing improvement. After reflection on the possible interventions, the supervisor may decide to sit down with the employee, review the job description, and provide oral or written evaluative feedback on each aspect of the job. Though this intervention reasonably could be called an *appraisal,* its use is warranted because it may be the most helpful tool for the particular situation and time.

departure from the prevailing mode in most workplaces. It cannot succeed without a whole new mindset and radically different approaches to managing people. It requires new H.R. practices and structures that foster a learning environment. In the emerging work world, the supervisor's primary goal will be to engender commitment and the proclivity for people to be productive, resourceful, and innovative. The organization must do everything possible to help supervisors and employees alike accept and understand that *the employee* is primarily responsible for his or her own growth and successful performance. This does not mean that supervisors become passive. It is not a negation of team and collaborative values. And it does not mean that the organization is abandoning efforts to support people and align their energies in a coherent way. It *is* a major shift in our fundamental beliefs about people. It means we see people as committed to the organization. It means we trust that, with education, appropriate training, and support, people will take responsibility to see that they perform well, grow, and improve. Shifting responsibility is not deserting employees—it is giving them the space to make choices and allowing their own spirit to direct their work.

After decades of conditioning employees to believe that someone else is responsible for their growth and welfare, this shift will be exceedingly difficult. It will feel awkward and uncomfortable for supervisors. Many employees will see this shift as a form of abandonment and neglect. Breaking old patterns is an arduous task. In an experiment with goldfish, a clear Plexiglas plate was placed in the middle of an aquarium, with goldfish on both sides. At first the goldfish bumped their noses on the invisible plate, but over time they learned to swim in circles without bumping the plate. After living in this environment for several weeks, the Plexiglas plate was removed. Though the whole tank was then open to them, the fish did not change their patterns, staying on one side or the other.[21] In our workplaces we long have imposed variations of Plexiglas constraints on employees. Removing the barrier by proclamation (*you are empowered!*) or a lofty vision statement cannot evoke meaningful change unless we help *everyone* transition to the new culture we desire. Hence, training supervisors will not suffice. Everyone will need to be oriented, educated, and assisted in seeing new roles and alternative assumptions. Ironically, the rank and file employees often subscribe to these unhealthy assumptions with greater fervency than do managers. Beyond education and enlightenment, the human resources practices, management styles, and structures of the organization must align with assumptions of a healthier nature as espoused throughout this book and elsewhere.

Create a Variety of Freely Chosen Delivery Systems

Move toward becoming a culture of *choice*. In place of appraisal, imaginatively consider an array of new resources and delivery modes in meeting coaching and development needs. Take out clean sheets of paper and decouple and examine each of the coaching functions (i.e., guidance, alignment, goal setting, feedback, and development) in the light of the work culture you desire. Drop from your design efforts the *a priori* assumption that supervisors are the focal point or prime mover of coaching and development. Design alternatives to appraisal that honor choice and recognize the variation of work situations, the variable needs of employees, and the divergent style preferences of supervisors.

One way to build confidence and encourage experimentation with various methods is to provide off-the-shelf coaching, guidance, and development tools that both employees and supervisors can easily access. Structured processes and formats that come with forms, software, CD-ROM, videos, and training materials can be quite useful and effective. These tools can shortcut learning, and choices in tools will accommodate the diverse needs of supervisors and employees alike. The range of possible off-the-shelf tools include tools and formats for goal setting, multi-source feedback, work style and personality inventories, strategic planning for work units, competency identification and assessment, employee development planning guides, and the like. There are literally hundreds of tools of this type, most of which are discoverable through the Internet and are displayed by vendors at all leading H. R. and organizational development conferences. Some of you may ask, don't most popular forms of appraisal include these types of tools? Isn't this what many forms of appraisal already do? Well, yes, but with some major differences in the context we are talking about. The tools would be *elected* rather than imposed as an organizational requirement (though the vendors will aggressively try to sell you that kind of package to optimize their sale). The resulting paperwork from these tools would not end up in personnel files—but would belong to the people that use them (possibly excepting a remedial intervention tool for an employee in serious difficulty).

Tools that are freely chosen by the employees and supervisors, based on their preference and unique needs, will result in an energy level never known in appraisal. Supervisors will apply and employees will accept tools more earnestly and enthusiastically if they have chosen it themselves. In some instances, the tool will be elected by the employee. In other instances, a supervisor or mentor may encourage or require a particular tool as part of a coaching strategy. Involuntary intervention with tools should be used sparingly and, as much as possible, work from collaboration with the affected employee. Elective tools are consistent with our professed value of empowerment. Moreover, if we are to hold supervisors accountable for the people they supervise, we must give them the freedom to choose the most situationally effective tool. For an example of an environment where employees and supervisors choose tools as appropriate, see the *University of Wisconsin Credit Union* case study and the *GM–Powertrain* case study in the next chapter.

Another way to encourage diverse approaches in coaching and guidance is to educate and train employees and supervisors about the many widely accepted contingent and situational leadership models discussed earlier. To promote effective situational leadership, educate everyone on the diversity of people (something we should be doing for lots of other reasons) and help everyone recognize that people have distinct individual preferences, needs, and outlooks that affect the way they learn, work, and want to be coached. In addition to conventional diversity training, training programs on Myers-Briggs personality types at work are readily available and serve the same goal. Commercial products, such as the Personal Profile DiSC® system, are quite friendly in helping people to see the great variation in work styles. Through these kinds of educational endeavors, people not only understand others better (a key ingredient for a team-oriented environment), they will better understand *themselves*, what works for them and what doesn't. From the strength of this knowledge, people will be better able to choose development and performance improvement tools that will be most helpful for themselves and others.

Case Study

University of Wisconsin Credit Union

The University of Wisconsin Credit Union (UWCU), located in Madison, Wisconsin, is a sophisticated financial institution managing nearly $400 million in assets and employing more than 200 employees. In an industry seldom known for being progressive, UWCU's people management practices incorporate a number of cutting-edge ideas. Its most recent employee satisfaction survey, completed by nearly 90% of all employees, achieved a median rating of 8 on a scale of 1–10, with nearly 85% ranking it at a 7 or higher. (The local area norm for job satisfaction was 6.74 for the same year.) Though financial institutions often are viewed unfavorably by employees due to the high number of low-paying, less-than-glamorous jobs, UWCU Vice President Maggie Hertz says UWCU enjoys an excellent reputation, adding "We have a reputation of being progressive, a good place to work. We have a lot of colleagues that come to work here willing to take a pay cut because they know our culture has been wonderful."

The story of UWCU's rapid transition to a "wonderful" culture is inspiring. Beginning around 1995, UWCU's leadership, most notably including its charismatic President, Don Percy, forged the vision of a new organizational culture. Foremost, it sought a culture that would foster a zealous commitment to high-quality service for its members and a work environment that embraced empowerment, collaboration, and caring about employees as human beings. The unofficial motto, Hertz said, became, "Members first, employees first." Both are important, she explained—members will only be treated well if employees are treated well.

With exuberance and a glimmer of excitement in her eyes, Hertz recounted the transition as both "challenging" and "fun." In a period of less than four years, UWCU has moved from a very traditional, top-down organization, with seven vice presidents (each ruling an empire), to a flattened, lean, and highly integrated organization of two vice presidents and ten directors, most of whom provide hands-on, in-the-trench leadership. The cornerstone of this transition was a new view of decision making. Decisions are no longer the fiat of a division vice president. Everyone in the organization was trained on the importance of research, systems, communication, and education as a means to change. Consequently, every change is considered an experiment and learning opportunity. In implementing any decision, leaders actively seek feedback with an open and nondefensive mind and a willingness to make adjustments or scrap an idea and start over. All important decisions, even those that pertain to a single function, such as human resources or marketing, now are processed by the Leadership Team, composed of thirteen formal leaders. In choosing the best course, they rely mainly on research and dialogue, not conjecture and whim.

A prime mover of this cultural transition was UWCU's desire to change its underlying assumptions about employees. The paramount shift, Hertz explained, was moving to the idea that "people *want* to come to work and contribute." Until 1995, the organization maintained an antiquated appraisal system, in which every supervisor filled out an endless form, writing a half page for each of many criteria. The bulky document was then typed, reviewed, and edited by the H.R. Department, and then revised by the supervisor before showdown time with the employee. Of course, the final product was kept in the personnel file "for legal reasons." Pay was loosely tied to the outcome, with a very small number of people literally getting nickeled and dimed because of a poor appraisal outcome. The process wasted a great deal of time, inspired no one, provided little useful feedback, and failed to serve as a reliable legal tool.

From this dissatisfaction and desire for a new employee culture, a design team formed to ditch performance appraisal altogether and develop a plan to replace it.

The design team, consisting of employees at all levels and a cross-spectrum of departments, worked for several months. Late in 1995, the design team's efforts resulted in an innovative and comprehensive alternative plan. The objective, according to Kathy Cooper, Project Manager and a design team leader, "was to get employees to take responsibility for their own development and feel it was *their* role and not the supervisors' (to accomplish this)." In the first step of the new plan, everyone in the organization attended classes and learned about the importance of research, systems, and process tools in attaining improvement. They also learned how to use an array of improvement, coaching, development, and counseling tools. "The training wasn't just training for the supervisors," Cooper explained, "It was training for the staff that said—*you are the one who is responsible.*"

The multifaceted training covered, among other topics and tools, the following:

- A quality management process strategy called PDCA (Plan-Do-Check-Act, a cyclical view of improving processes that promote learning) and other tools used to improve processes and systems.

- Collaborative, team, and meeting skills to facilitate meaningful and effective group discussions.

- A one-on-one worksheet to allow an employee and a supervisor to identify, work on, and follow up on desired goals.

- The use and development of competency matrixes (identifying the necessary skills for particular jobs, especially jobs with a large number of incumbents, such as tellers).

- A workplan grid that could be used to identify goals and priorities with suggested review procedures.

- Strategies and tools for assisting people with career and professional development needs and goals.

- A "performance improvement program" (PIP) that can be used for corrective action for people performing at an unsatisfactory level, including documentation of the intervention.

Though many organizations that practice appraisal use the above tools and strategies, what is different at UWCU is that none of the tools, except for necessary corrective actions, is required by anyone. The employee and supervisor are free to apply any or *none* of these tools or create something else, as appropriate. Hertz recalled how the transition was communicated:

> Nothing was dictated. Everyone was told that the whole goal of the training was frequent communication. We said, "You must figure out as a team how you best accomplish improvement. Use a combination of department meetings, one-on-ones, and whatever tools, and figure out how to get there."

Except for the rarely used, formal corrective process (PIP), the H.R. Department neither collects or places any of the paperwork from the various coaching and development tools in the personnel file. The only institution-wide practice is that all supervisors are asked to meet with each of their employees once a year to jointly plan any training required or desired in the forthcoming year (for budgeting and staff planning purposes)—no individual forms or written requirements are mandated by the organization relative to this planning.

Individual goal setting is not relied on as an organizational improvement strategy. The organization, however, develops a concise list of clearly stated organizational goals aimed at improving external and internal services over a three-year period. Extensive time is spent with formal leaders going over these goals. In turn, every functional area periodically holds meetings with all of its employees to reflect on these goals and look for ways to support them. About two dozen organizational strategic goals are divided into seven categories. Seven different cross-functional teams assume the leadership responsibility of devising strategies for and encouraging the attainment of the long-term goals. Research, process improvement, data, and education are consistently applied in the attainment of these goals.

As a result of these initiatives, Hertz reports, the UWCU Board and "everybody is working for the same goals, and everybody knows what is changing." The absence of appraisal, she thinks, has been most beneficial, but she went on to say that real challenge goes along with it, explaining:

> It's a continuing process of education. In fairness to our employees, we just need to make sure our supervisors realize the importance of ongoing, timely, and fair feedback, and taking time to sit down and talk about objectives and the use of the (coaching and process) tools. Sometimes supervisors don't do this, but it is our job to continue to educate them.

Congruent with a learning atmosphere, UWCU closes for one hour every Wednesday for "TeamTeach" sessions, aimed solely at learning and reflecting on changes, mostly at the department or unit level. "These are not supervisor led, for the most part," Hertz clarified, "No one from management stands up—it is *teams* of employees doing the presentations and sharing information with the groups." One internal team developed a method of collecting unsolicited feedback from customers (members) using the internal e-mail system and a database to promote learning. At the TeamTeach meetings, every work unit learns together how to use the tool in a hands-on, interactive way. Clyde LaFlash, Director of Project Services & Network Administration, explained that UWCU uses TeamTeach sessions to get everyone involved and reinforce the value of these kinds of systems and new practices.

Overall, UWCU has made great strides since embarking on this new course only five years ago. It has no intent to rest on its laurels, however. Further improvements in their people systems continue. For example, UWCU is working at ways to clarify its compensation, offer some form of gainsharing, and meet its goal of paying wages at a level 10% above the labor market (UWCU does not use any form of merit pay but applies some career ladder raises as discussed in chapter 7). It is also currently implementing a new self-learning, personal profile tool called the Predictive Index®. Despite many accomplishments, Hertz readily conceded that UWCU still has much work to do and many more mountains to climb. Reflecting further and smiling, she said, "But I am very proud of the way we have really worked on creating an experimental atmosphere—research, communication, education, and getting feedback on systems are truly emphasized in everything we do."

Use Goal Setting When It Is Effective

Goal setting may or may not be appropriate or helpful to the situation, depending on the type of work, the employee's need, the management style, and working environment. Help people managers understand that individual, multiple goal setting is not a surefire way to get performance, alignment, and motivation. Educate everyone in your organization on the benefits and drawbacks of individual, work unit, and organizational goal setting, perhaps with the emphasis described below.

Organizational Goals. Organizational goals are often necessary and beneficial. Organizations that adopt and communicate specific organizational goals perform better than organizations where people are merely encouraged to do their best.[22] Accordingly, in lieu of programmatic individual goals, adopt helpful organizational goals to improve the performance of the organization *and individuals*. Such goals are especially effective when coupled with a sense of common purpose, a clear mission, and genuinely espoused values. The UWCU case study is a tangible example of organizational goal setting. At the same time, recall that organizational goal setting, standing alone, is not sufficient for organizational improvement—redesigning systems and improving processes will generate genuine improvement. Everyone may be fired up by a passionate vision and clear organizational goals, but if the system remains unchanged, so will the outputs of that system.

Work Unit Goals. Between the individual and the organization lies the work unit. Setting goals at this level usually is a critical aspect of optimal performance. Work unit or department goals can create alignment and invigorate more cohesive efforts. Unit goals often motivate individuals because, when effectively communicated, they connect everyone in the department to each other and a common vision. Despite these advantages, keep in mind that unit goals can suffer from the same maladies as individual goals. Without plans or new work methods to achieve goals, little will be gained by merely establishing goals. For reasons discussed earlier, arbitrary numeric goals are neither inspirational nor helpful. For example, UWCU Vice President Maggie Hertz recounts that, like many financial institutions, it has been pressed to develop financial goals. Some goals are divvied up, with each branch getting a target as their share of the institution goal. Ms. Hertz, however, further reflected that the effects of such practice are not always positive:

> Parts of it (having a goal) are good because if they meet it, it is cause for celebration. But it goes back to your assumptions. When we compare the branches against each other, it also causes a whole bunch of negative things. When branches don't meet their goals, how does that make them feel? It may be something out of their control. It's not like they can go out on the street, pull people in, and sit down and write them a car loan.

Besides worrying about demoralization, remember that, to be helpful, unit or departmental goals must fully integrate with and benefit the organization *as a whole* (again, improved parts do not improve the whole). Though effective integration of unit goals is a daunting task, good communication, both within and outside the unit, is a step in the right direction.

As an example, consider Voyager Information Service, a fast-growing Midwestern Internet service company of 700 employees. It essentially eliminated its appraisal system, with only two individual feedback questions surviving a traditional scaled appraisal. Voyager, however, works very hard at the effective use of *unit* goals. Each operating unit, such as marketing, technical support, finance, and human resources, electronically posts all of its strategic goals for every employee to see. Every week, the executive for each area updates the posting with the specific progress made on each goal. Because the company operates subsidiary companies in several states, this form of communication has proven to be most beneficial.

Individual Goals. While a hyperfocus on individual goals can undermine the sense of working as a team, individual goal setting may be useful and effective in some situations. Some suggestions include:

- **Promote individual goal setting only where it is situationally effective.** Recall the lessons of situational leadership. Some jobs or situations require very specific goals. For example, for school teachers to be effective and ensure continuity from one grade to another, some clarity with respect to desired learning outcomes is needed. There

Dangers of Suboptimization

In setting departmental, work unit, or even individual goals, there's always a danger of *suboptimization,* i.e., when one part of a system aims at improving itself without determining the effect on the system as a whole. A change *within any part* of a system will affect other parts. For example, a department may make a change that brings measurable improvement, but if the interaction and effect of that change conflicts with the interests of other parts of the company, the change may be counterproductive for the system as a whole.

For example, each work unit of an auto company had a goal to reduce its costs. An employee in one division came up with an idea to save $80 per car—by investing $20 during one part of production, $100 would be saved in another part of production. The director of the division that needed to invest $20 per car, however, turned down the idea because it would have caused that division to overrun its cost goals, and the savings would only be reflected in another division's financial report. Unit and individual goals may be helpful in many respects, but the danger of suboptimization requires us to look beyond our immediate domain and consider the possible effects upon other components of the system and the system as a whole.

also is variability in employees' and supervisors' needs and preferences about structuring work. A person learning a job or on a career development path may need to have defined targets to ensure the learning of particular skills. Some people have a personal *preference* for individual goals, and some people *need* individual goals—they *should* adopt goals, and the organization and supervisors can support the process. Others neither need nor like goals—don't waste their time. Rather than systematically requiring individual goals through appraisal or otherwise, train *all* of your employees, not just supervisors, on the situationally effective use and benefits of goals. Provide them with helpful goal-setting tools and methods, such as off-the-shelf software geared for individual and group goal setting and planning. Organizations that drop appraisal usually do not altogether drop structured goal setting. In work settings where it seems necessary or greatly beneficial, proactively encourage goal setting. For an example of a rather flexible approach to individual goal setting, refer to the details in the *Madison Police Department* case study.

- **Avoid Arbitrary Quantitative Goals**. Target goals may be useful or necessary. If a desired percentage or number is absolutely needed to enable someone to keep his job, to sustain a product or service's viability in the market, or to ensure that the governmental inspectors will not shut the place down, then articulate that number or target. In such case, a precise numeric goal is significant and is reasonably useful in letting employees know that its attainment must be given the highest priority. Otherwise, discourage managers from using number goals merely for the sake of a "motivational" target.

- **Foster Individual Commitment**. To enhance commitment and acceptance, encourage goal setting where the individual, as much as possible, takes the initiative for setting goals. This requires patience and means giving people space and choices.

- **Have a Bias for Single Goals**. Remember that single goals for individuals are more effective than multiple goals. A few goals work better than many goals. Stick to single goals unless multiple goals are clearly called for. The *Madison Police Department* case study illustrates the effective use of single goals and other coaching principles of this chapter.

Case Study

Madison, Wisconsin, Police Department

The Madison Police Department (MPD) serves 200,000 city residents in a metropolitan area approaching one-half million people. MPD has 450 employees with fewer than 100 civilian employees. MPD has excelled for more than ten years without any form of performance appraisal under two different police chiefs and three different mayors. A 1999 U.S. Justice Department study of twelve metropolitan police departments found that 97% of Madison's residents were satisfied with the MPD, the highest level of any comparative city. Only one other city's satisfaction level exceeded 90% (San Diego, 93%).[23] The satisfaction level from African-American residents *equaled* this rate—no other city even came close. MPD enjoys an exceptionally low turnover rate and each year gets more than 1,000 applicants (most with 4-year degrees) to apply for less than two dozen openings for officers.

Where did this all begin? In 1989, MPD abolished a traditional 1–5 scaled appraisal practice in conjunction with a quality management initiative. Considering that police departments are paramilitary organizations, MPD's move to drop appraisals was daringly atypical. In place of appraisal, the Department aimed to develop systems and practices around one focal question: *What do enlightened leaders do?* The MPD wanted practices and approaches that fostered a learning organization, cooperation, and the spirit of community policing, i.e., where police departments proactively try to solve problems as *members* of the community, rather than just issuing citations and making arrests. This transition meant training every officer on systems theory, quality tools such as the Plan-Do-Check-Act (PDCA), a seven-step quality management method, and a police assessment model called SARA (an acronym for Scan, Analyze, Respond, and Assess).[24]

In place of appraisal, MPD did not adopt any kind of mandatory reporting of feedback, development, or formal performance assessment, except in the case of probationary officers. During the first twelve weeks on the job, newly hired officers (post–training academy) receive evaluations everyday from everyone with whom they work. During their first 24 months, officers receive a monthly paper, summarizing feedback and performance suggestions. Probation ends with a formal review on a seven-point scale. Once probation has ended, however, officers no longer receive any kind of performance appraisal. What did MPD do instead? It decoupled the functions of appraisal, developing more useful tools consistent with its espoused values and philosophy.

Guidance and Direction: Overall guidance and direction are emphasized through a clearly conveyed mission, vision, values, operating philosophy, and common goal of community policing. These are intensely inculcated in the training academy, leadership training, and day-to-day work.

Feedback: Feedback and related coaching are the continual responsibility of all sergeants and officers who supervise. Coaching and development are determined individually, based on the style of the leader and the officer. According to Joe Balles, MPD Sergeant, "The sergeants are encouraged to create their own method of feedback and figure out what works in their district."

Goal Setting: When appraisals were first abolished, the Department asked officers to follow a model called the "Four-Way Check" in which the line officers and supervisors gathered viewpoints from a peer, a subordinate, a supervisor, and themselves, and then distilled the information to arrive at an improvement plan. According to MPD Captain Noble Wray, this practice "went okay" for a few years, but it failed to encourage reflection on work or get everyone to look at systems as a learning organization would. Officers with less progressive supervisors seemed to get little benefit. This dissatisfaction, according to Captain Wray, led to a search for something that better fit the organization's new perspective of leadership and focus on system improvement. "Our organization owed employees some discussion and dialogue about how they were doing in terms of the bigger picture and their beats," Wray explained. What evolved was a relatively elegant tool with an unpresumptuous name: the "Problem Solving/Goal Setting Process." With this practice, every officer each year is required to look for an opportunity to solve a problem or work at a goal outside of doing day-to-day duties. Wray clarified the process:

> Goal setting is not a performance evaluation system—it was designed to encourage people to sit down and work on a goal ... to get an individual officer in a geographic

area to get a beat profile, to take a look at what is going on, and identify problems to work on. This may be problem solving or setting goals on what you want to accomplish. Usually the sergeant will sit down and do this with the line officer.

The process is not MBO or making a list of goals, but choosing *one* goal, such as cleaning up the drug dealers off a particular street or developing ways to improve communication between officers and dispatch. The officer may undertake the goal alone or jointly choose a goal with other officers. The goal should take a "systems perspective," Wray emphasized, using the SARA model and other process improvement tools. "If we hadn't gone through systems training and tools, we would just get quick solutions. Instead, our people are studious, they look at data, seek input, use PDCA, and look for system causes," Wray noted. The problem or goal is entirely up to the officer. "It comes from the officer, not the supervisor. We do everything we can to get the goal to come from the officer because everybody's beat is different," Wray explained.

What if an officer didn't have a goal? "In that case," Wray answered, "the supervisor would ask the officer: Is there proper scanning of information and data? Have you been to community meetings? What are the opportunities?" Officers write their goals in a notebook kept at the precinct or district station. Each goal has its own notebook. Anyone can look at it. On a daily basis, officers are asked to make entries in the book, reflecting their observations, actions taken, and so on. The notebook gives officers who have chosen joint goals an opportunity to continually communicate with each other, even if they work on different shifts. It also provides ongoing communication to the supervising sergeant. On a quarterly basis, the sergeant sits down and holds a meeting with the officer or officers who selected the goal to talk about how the plan is going and offer insights or assistance. No paperwork associated with the Problem Solving/Goal Setting Process goes into the personnel file. It is simply a measure to encourage officers to take a longer view of their job and deal with problems at the root cause level.

Culture: MPD fully understands that appraisal alternatives are not very helpful without a positive people culture. Consistent with its goal toward community policing, the Department engages in a number of practices that decidedly depart from the usual command-and-control law enforcement style. "We can't expect our officers to treat people in the community any better than we treat them," cautions Captain Masterson, Human Resource Team Leader. Each year at MPD every officer, sergeant, and lieutenant picks his or her own assignment, shift, *and boss* (a good solution for chemistry and bad-fit problems!). Selection is done in the order of seniority. A Management Team, consisting of all captains, the Assistant Chief, and President of the police officers' union, collaboratively and through consensus address management issues, adopt personnel policies, review command staff reports, and make important departmental decisions. Over the past ten years, three different union presidents have sat on this team, contributing to a cooperative milieu and fostering a genuine partnership approach. Problem solving in small teams of line officers and command staff is a routine part of the management practice. Line officers routinely are involved in decisions affecting the whole department, such as choosing the type of squad cars the Department will purchase. The promotion career advancement method also is very open, progressive, and consistent with the espoused culture (detailed in Chapter 7).

Conclusion

In this chapter we have demonstrated that healthier assumptions can lead to new roles for supervisors and more effective ways of providing coaching and guidance. In the next chapter, we look at another critical aspect of coaching, *feedback,* in light of similar assumptions. Before moving on, take a minute to think about alternatives to the underlying assumptions raised in this chapter and summarized below.

Review of Chapter Assumptions

Conventional Assumptions

The supervisor has the attributes and skills to be an effective coach.

Supervisors have the knowledge to assess and guide improvement.

Alternative Assumptions

- Depending on the situation, people, and particular need, an employee's supervisor may or may not be an effective coach.
- To fulfill their coaching needs, most people will require an array of coaching resources, including, but not necessarily predominantly, the supervisor.

Conventional Assumption

To get alignment and desired performance, people require formal and specific direction.

Alternative Assumptions

- Alignment and desired performance are enhanced by a shared sense of purpose and common vision for the future.
- If people have the right information and opportunities, they usually will perform their work in alignment with the organization's needs and pressing priorities.
- Alignment is advanced by effective leadership, which may include both informal and formal direction.

All people will perform better if they are held accountable through a formal process.

Rating and ranking are effective motivational and coaching tools.

Alternative Assumptions

• People will perform better if they have adequate direction and guidance.

• Under the right conditions, people will hold themselves accountable to do the work that is required.

• People are intrinsically motivated to do a good job.

• People will perform better when they feel trusted.

• People will use good information to improve their performance, if given the training and opportunity.

Conventional Assumption

A one-size-fits-all coaching structure works well for all employees.

Alternative Assumption

• Employees' preferences and needs for coaching, direction, and support vary with the individual and the situation, and change over time.

Conventional Assumption

Supervisors in each organization want or need to use the same approach to guide, develop, and manage people.

Alternative Assumption

• Supervisors' preferences and needs in supporting and managing people vary with the individual and the situation, and change over time.

Conventional Assumption

Having an annual conversation around improvement accomplishes improvement.

Alternative Assumptions

• Improvement results from identifying the cause of a problem or specific opportunity for improvement and developing a plan to act on such information.

• Open conversations about performance issues, problems, and opportunities may lead to the development of helpful plans to achieve improvement.

• Improving processes and systems generates improvement.

Conventional Assumption

Individual goal setting is an effective motivational tool and strategy for improving performance.

Alternative Assumptions

- When individuals freely accept and commit to a goal, it can be an effective motivator.

- A group of people, as a work unit or organization, will perform and align better with common goals.

Conventional Assumption

The organization and the supervisor are responsible for individual employees' morale, performance, and development (repeat from Chapter 1).

Alternative Assumption

- As healthy adults, people need to be responsible for their own morale, performance, and development, with and without support from the organization.

Conventional Assumption

Improving individuals' performance improves organizational performance (repeat from Chapter 2).

Alternative Assumption

- Improving systems and processes improves the performance of the organization.

5

Feedback That Makes a Difference

Ultimately, managers aren't responsible for their people's performance. People are responsible for their own performance. There's feedback all around you—if you pay attention. If you're not getting enough feedback, ask for it.

Anne Saunier, *Fast Company*

In any well-functioning organization, anyone ought to feel free to give anyone else feedback.

Peter Quarry, *Feedback Solutions*

Giving good feedback. Everyone thinks it is important. It's what supervisors are supposed to do. If supervisors were organized like Boy Scouts, "to give good feedback" would be the first item of the official oath. And while everyone acknowledges its value and importance, timely and helpful feedback is conspicuously *absent* for most people in organizational life. The "art" of feedback is seldom practiced by many, and when practiced, it is practiced badly. In large part, the culprit is the prevailing practice of appraisal, which engenders many false notions about the nature of feedback. Beyond appraisal, many of us fail at giving and receiving feedback because we do not understand its true dynamics. Our expectations of feedback are unrealistic, and we fail to see the barricades that obstruct and distort the flow of communication and openness to change.

Here at the onset, we must clarify what we mean by *feedback* because of its many connotations in the business world. To organizational communication scholars, *feedback* is not communication about someone's performance but is a technical term for the message that the *receiver* of a communication *gives back* to the sender, i.e., conveying that the message was understood or achieved the desired impact. Systems theorists, such as Peter Senge, use *feedback* to describe the reciprocal or loopback effect of a system's outputs upon the inputs.[1] In this book, however, *feedback* is used to convey its day-to-day, vernacular meaning in the workplace, i.e., the evaluative information one person gives to another person about how he or she has performed on the job, a project, and so on.

Beyond the basic definition, it may be helpful to understand the differences between positive and negative feedback. *Positive feedback* occurs when one is told he has done something well or correctly. *Negative feedback* does *not* refer to criticism handled in a harsh or inappropriate manner—it's simply conveying information that something was done incorrectly or inadequately. Some people associate giving performance feedback to be a part of coaching, giving redirection, and guidance on how to improve. While this more expansive view of feedback is commonly recognized, our focus here primarily deals with the communication of evaluative information.

In this chapter, we examine feedback in the context of appraisal, exposing some of the faulty notions that shape our thinking. We clarify the dynamics of feedback and demonstrate why appraisal is not an effective vehicle for feedback. In place of appraisal, we advocate a totally new type of work environment built on radically different assumptions, i.e., a work culture where *employees* are primarily responsible for getting their own feedback, and feedback is not an annual event, but a seamless aspect of day-to-day human interactions and learning.

■ Starting with a Story

Departing from "we" the authors, one of us (M.J.) has a personal story that is insightful for our journey into the realm of feedback:

I was privileged to be assigned by General Motors (GM) to work at Saturn Corporation and serve on the design team for its start-up human resources system. Part of my assignment was to help convene a group of

H.R. professionals, hired from various GM divisions and elsewhere, in designing several H.R. systems and practices that would be needed for the new Spring Hill facility and corporate offices. It was an exciting venture to say the least. One day I was facilitating our design group when my senior colleague, George Francis, a highly experienced H.R. executive, was present. In bouncing ideas around, I frequently referred back to my experience with Oldsmobile. Several times, I said, "*At Oldsmobile,* what we did was . . ." or, "When we faced this problem *at Oldsmobile,* we . . ." Actually, I was not even aware that I was referencing Oldsmobile, but I did have a vague sense that I was not connecting with the group on some of my ideas.

At the break, George inconspicuously took me out to the hallway. He told me that I was repeatedly initiating ideas with the "Back at Oldsmobile, we . . ." George said all of my ideas were helpful and worthwhile suggestions. Then he said, in words that I can painstakingly remember, "Your ideas would be so much better received if you didn't say 'at Oldsmobile.'" He went on to explain why. "When you start out with 'Oldsmobile,' your ideas immediately lose merit because people have all sorts of notions about Oldsmobile and traditional GM approaches." George said he could observe some of the group seemingly shutting down as soon as I said "Oldsmobile." Though I was not consciously trying to push Oldsmobile ideas, with George's insight, it was immediately clear to me why Oldsmobile references might be a turn-off. In the Saturn start-up, we were trying to create "a different kind of car company," inside and out—it was an experiment in departing from traditional GM methods of managing a car company. I felt a little embarrassed and stupid, but George's sentiment was only to be supportive and helpful. He was just trying to help me see myself through another lens. George concluded our discussion with a pearl of wisdom. He said, "If your ideas are good, they will have more power if they stand on their own." His words instantly rang true with me. He illuminated for me a blind spot that was undermining my best efforts. I got the message. Walking back in the room, I was grateful for the powerful, yet wonderfully simple, insight.

Stepping back and looking at this story, what can we learn? It seems clear that feedback was given and *heard*. The feedback was not part of a formal review process but was timely to the event. It was personal and interactive. The feedback was given in a specific and nonjudgmental way in which George seemed to have Mary's best interests at heart. George's extensive H.R. background and visible skills made him a credible source. Valuable and useful information was conveyed. As we shall explain, these circumstances demonstrate many of the critical conditions necessary to successfully convey feedback.

■ Conditions for Effective Feedback

In helping our audiences understand the circumstances and conditions that enhance the reception of feedback, we always start with a question that helps them personalize the learning. You can do this exercise right now. Take a moment to think back on your life—your working life, when you were in school, or elsewhere—and recall a time when someone gave you feedback that was useful and helpful, that caused you to make a change for the better. It should be a situation where you really *heard* the message, it registered, you got it, and took it to heart. Recall the circumstances and conditions, how you felt, what you saw, what you heard. For example, consider: *What was the context? What were your thoughts and mindset? How did the giver of the feedback relate to you? How did you feel about him or her? What did you hear?* Now, jot down what you recall about the circumstances of the feedback.

Now look over your list. We ask audiences to reflect on the same experience, and then we chart their responses. Amazingly, in asking this question to thousands of people, we consistently get the same set of answers, with only slight variations in wording. Examples of typical answers are listed in the box.

The list of common responses, as well as M.J.'s story, gives us a checklist of the most essential conditions that are necessary or significantly contribute to feedback having genuine impact. We can condense the list to seven elements, most of which will need to be present to allow feedback and learning to occur for the recipient:

1. **The feedback giver is a credible source.** The giver has expertise, knowledge, or otherwise is known to the receiver to be a source of valid information.

2. **The feedback giver is trustworthy.** The giver is sincere and can be trusted and respected.

3. **The feedback is conveyed with good intentions.** The giver either has the receiver's best interests at heart, or it's otherwise apparent that

---

Typical Responses to "When I Really Heard Feedback . . ."

- I saw that the information could benefit me.
- The giver of feedback had my best interests at heart.
- I was open to listening at the time.
- I respected the person giving the feedback.
- The giver knew what she was talking about—I valued her opinion.
- I didn't feel like I was being judged.
- The feedback was heartfelt—it was sincere.
- I trusted the person who gave me the feedback.
- Their advice was specific with examples and clear advice.
- The giver chose a time when I was listening.
- There was information I needed to hear—it showed me a blind spot.
- It was personal and interactive—I was able to clarify the message and ask questions.
- I was ready to hear it and make a change.
- The issue was important to me—I had a desire to improve.

---

the feedback is intended to serve a worthy purpose (i.e., is not solely self-serving to the giver's interests).

4. **The timing and circumstances of the feedback are appropriate.** Feedback is effective when it's timely and conveyed under conditions that are conducive for learning. For example, it's conveyed at a time that the receiver is open to feedback. Also, most people prefer to receive negative feedback privately.

5. **The feedback is given in a personal and interactive manner.** The feedback is given in person—the receiver can hear the giver's intonation, observe the giver's facial expression and body language. There is an opportunity for the receiver to ask questions and clarify the message.

6. **The feedback message is clear.** The feedback successfully communicates a clear message or new information about something the receiver has done, not done, or needs to do.

7. **The feedback is helpful to the receiver.** The message contains good information or new insights that are useful or enlightening. Well-intended, accompanying advice may or may not be useful, but the information conveyed is considered valid and allows the receiver to learn.

When we ask audiences to describe what was impactful about successful feedback experiences, 85 to 90% of the responses can be linked to the above list. We rarely have people tell us that meaningful feedback had come to them during the formal structure of appraisal feedback. When we share the above points with audiences, they uniformly affirm that they cover the circumstances in which feedback works for them.

■ Feedback Assumptions Within Appraisal

Appraisal is intended to facilitate feedback and communication. Communication, in its simplest form, is commonly illustrated by the graphic shown in Figure 5.1. To be successful, feedback, like any other form of communication, requires that the sender convey the message *and* that the receiver receives the message—communication does not occur unless there is reception. To improve the quality of feedback, during appraisal and otherwise, we spend lots of hours and money training the supervisors on how to *give* feedback, but we rarely train employees on how to *receive* feedback.

Many of us do not contemplate the idea that the receiver of feedback must possess skills to gain any meaningful benefit from the process. For example, a receiver needs to know how to go out and ask for feedback, whom to ask, and when to seek it. A receiver must know how to display

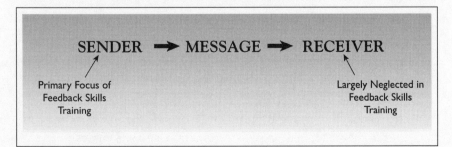

Figure 5.1   Conventional Feedback Training

an openness to feedback. A receiver needs to have the skill of asking questions to ensure that the feedback is specific. (For example, "How am I doing?" is usually too vague to elicit useful information.) A receiver should further understand the value of repeating and rephrasing the message to the giver in order to confirm that the message was clearly understood. Part of the skill of receiving feedback is knowing what to do with it, and how to sort out what is useful and what is not (for example, recognizing that some criticism must be taken with a grain of salt).

While the art and technique of feedback must be applied at both ends, the lion's share of organizations provide no training on the receiver end. The failure to train receivers greatly diminishes the opportunity for successful feedback. Worse yet, it indirectly underscores a passive, dependent role for the employee. A person who is unskilled and untrained in the intricacies of the feedback process can only take a backseat role in the process, and she certainly doesn't feel a sense of responsibility. Dependency is unintentionally promoted within appraisal feedback schemes because the entire process is initiated by organizational directives and the supervisor's actions—little or nothing is derived from the employee's initiative. Organizations often try to combat this gross imbalance by allowing the employee to make his own performance assessment as a preliminary or collaborative step, or by giving employees a place to put their comments on the final appraisal documents. Though arguably helpful, such measures do not shift responsibility to the employee, nor do they elevate the process to the level of co-ownership.

■ Unhealthy Feedback Assumptions

As we have seen with the other functions, appraisal promotes a number of unhealthy assumptions about the nature of feedback. Among many, let us consider five assumptions that are commonly implied within the design of conventional appraisal.

Assumption

It's the supervisor's job to ensure that feedback is given.

Every supervisor should provide necessary and useful feedback. The assumption as written, however, places the *responsibility* for ensuring the flow of feedback upon the supervisor. In traditional appraisal, this assumption fosters the expectation that the employee should look to the supervisor as the sole initiator and provider of feedback. In 360-degree appraisal processes, often the supervisor is the primary compiler, gatekeeper, or interpretative counselor of feedback information. All of these processes place the employee in a dependent role. A more helpful assumption would be: *It's everyone's job to give and receive feedback.* Feedback can be effective only if the receivers are at the *least* jointly responsible to initiate, seek, and gather the feedback they desire and need.

Recall that feedback is effective when the feedback is given in a timely manner, when the information is helpful, and the message is clear. If the employee is taking responsibility to initiate and gather her own feedback, it's more likely that the feedback will be timely and helpful and the employee will attempt to understand the message. Moreover, when employees rely on the supervisor to initiate feedback, they miss ideal opportunities for powerful learning.

An unintended consequence of appraisal is that it causes employees to narrow-mindedly associate feedback with the *process* of appraisal, a *formal* conversation, or an annual event. This myopic focus keeps employees from thinking more resourcefully about the many opportunities for feedback. Consequently, they fail to seek out valuable information that is available to them *all the time*. When we ask audiences—*How many of you have received feedback in the past year?*—we find only a few hands going up. Invariably, someone raises his hand and says, "I haven't had any feedback in eight months!" Upon further discussion, we find most of them *have* gotten some feedback, but because it wasn't formal or tied to appraisal, they assumed feedback had not occurred.

Upon further inquiry, we find that most people in the audience have never straightforwardly *asked* for the feedback they felt they were missing. The problem here can be blamed neither on the supervisor or on the employee, but on our conditioned and constrictive perceptions of feedback and the underlying assumption—*It's the supervisor's job to initiate and give the feedback.* Appraisal promotes this assumption, but reshaping our work environments will require more than discarding appraisal—it will require *education* for everyone, and the adoption of an alternative assumption: *Feedback is readily accessible all the time and can be more effectively obtained when it is sought out by the individuals themselves.* A nurse can ask for and give feedback to the physician immediately after the surgery. A grounds custodian can ask superiors and customers for feedback at the end of a week's work of shaping up the corporate lawn. A programmer asks users for feedback when the design is completed and a month after implementation to find out how it's working.

When people are trained in feedback skills and seek out the information they need, they get timely and useful feedback, *and* there's a bonus benefit for the supervisor or feedback giver. We all realize how difficult it is to give someone negative feedback—we fear damage to the relationship or the receiver's self-esteem, it's difficult to find the right words, and by nature, most of us try to be positive. Another barrier is the difficulty in initiating the discussion. Because of these challenges, many supervisors delay and avoid giving criticism, and perhaps this is also why supervisors procrastinate or are derelict in turning in appraisals. However, when a person *asks for* feedback, many of these barriers melt away. For whatever reason, it's easier to provide negative feedback and constructive advice to someone when it has been requested. This is particularly true when the question is specific. Think about how open you could be if someone came to you and said, "I feel a bit uneasy about the way I handled some things on our last project—I was wondering if you could give me some feedback or insights based on what you saw?" Yet another bonus comes on the receiving end. When you have asked for critical feedback, it's somehow much easier to accept the criticism than when it's dropped on you involuntarily.

Assumption

Feedback from the supervisor is a critical aspect of improvement for all people in all jobs.

While supervisory feedback is important for most of us, it s not always accurate. Because supervisors' span of control is becoming broader and more complex, feedback from the supervisor is increasingly less important. The *best* source of feedback depends on the nature of the information required. For example, a manager fumbling with the budget process might obtain better direction from the CFO (or someone in the finance department who deals with budget snafus) rather than a boss. Similarly, a marketing manager who reports to a product vice president may be in greater need of feedback from another marketing professional than from a boss (yes, the boss may view the marketing as poor and the employee must hear this, but that feedback gives little insight as to the source of the problem and does nothing to help the marketing manager figure out how the problem can be rectified). Likewise, when supervisors want to learn about their effectiveness as *people* managers, they may be in greater need of feedback from subordinates than a boss (while a boss may give helpful feedback about people management skills that appear to be lacking, employees probably will be the best source of feedback in getting at the deeper causes of what is not working and why). One positive influence of the 360-degree feedback movement has been greater awareness of the multitude of people who can offer critical and useful information. While supervisory feedback is beneficial, it makes little sense to design a feedback process that facilitates feedback exclusively or predominantly from the supervisor.

Another drawback to over-reliance on supervisory feedback, even when well intended and well executed, is that it often is unreliable and inaccurate. Supervisors unknowingly bring lenses and biases that distort their perceptions of individual performance. Moreover, a supervisor cannot always see the interactions and dynamic effects of the *system* upon an individual's performance. For example, over a period of several months, an insurance adjuster may experience a sharp increase in the amount of the average claim he authorizes. During his performance review, the supervisor tells him that he is too lenient. This feedback may be inaccurate, however. The cause actually may be driven by some type of external change (e.g., new medical treatments, a change in the type of materials used on auto bodies), or the inflated pattern may be merely an odd variation of justifiably higher claims randomly landing in this particular adjuster's lap. Inaccurate feedback not only misses the point, but it compounds performance problems. In this example, the adjuster may respond to the faulty feedback by getting tougher on the claimants and their lawyers. The result is a higher rate of litigation of claims, ultimately *increasing* the company's total costs and claim payout.

The problem with this and similar examples is not an inept supervisor. Supervisors have been conditioned by appraisal to see performance deficiencies as something that they are supposed to link to the *employee's* actions or inaction. Consequently, they believe it's their job to correct individual deficiencies through feedback and redirection. (In the insurance adjuster example, we would predict that, in his next performance review, the employee will be criticized for poor judgment in denying claims that should have been settled!) In the prevailing business culture, the myopic, one-on-one focus of supervisory feedback as the key driver of improvement deprives the supervisor and employee, or a team of employees, the opportunity to look at causes and learn together.

The goal of feedback is to get information to help us improve, including encouragement when performance is on track. Good feedback contains helpful *information*. Our obsession with linking feedback to supervisors impairs the quality and depth of information. The trend toward using multi-rater or 360-degree system as a feedback tool (*not* 360-degree appraisal) is only one step toward a more expansive view of feedback. Getting good information, the right information, begins with considering the nature of the work and the particular issue of concern. For example, in many jobs, process and system data are the most objective, accurate, and helpful source of feedback for improvement. In ways that people feedback cannot, *data* feedback provides insightful information that illuminates the need and opportunities for improvement. For example, by tracking submission times, a pharmacist can learn how long walk-ins are kept waiting. The data may indicate peak times and suggest that better staffing patterns could reduce customers' long waits. A loan officer who reviews the patterns of loan rejections may find ways to shortcut the process in the future, thereby increasing her productivity and wasting less of her customers' time in the future. Processes and systems emit endless amounts of extremely helpful information. If we are to develop powerful systems of feedback, we must teach people to tap into these sources and recognize when they may be more helpful than *people* feedback. When multiple sources of feedback are viewed together, they are *more* insightful and enriching than any single source, including a conscientious and knowledgeable supervisor.

Assumption

Formal feedback should be given on a periodic basis (annually, quarterly, etc.) to help people continuously improve.

While there is potential benefit to holding feedback or improvement discussions at periodic intervals, this strategy is not effective when it is relied upon as the primary driver of feedback. This is true for several reasons. Foremost, it engenders the wrong mindset toward feedback. Rather than being viewed as continual, interactive, ongoing, and situationally driven, it conditions supervisors to think that feedback should be doled out in bushel baskets at predetermined intervals. Consultant Anne Saunier puts it in another perspective, "Doing annual appraisals is like dieting only on your birthday and wondering why you are not losing weight."[2]

Feedback scheduled at time intervals further has the unintended effect of *discouraging* timely feedback. For example, an employee poorly handles a project during October and early November. The supervisor has observed this, and, at the end of the project, she considers setting up a meeting, but then realizes—*it's near that time of year!* and the following month she will be working on appraisals (for issuance in January). She thinks, "Oh, good, that will give us something constructive to talk about." (She is happy because appraisals expect supervisors to find performance problems—when they can't think of something negative, appraisal has conditioned them to believe they are somehow failing in their job!) Then comes the second week of January. She brings up the poorly executed project in a sensitive and caring way. Despite her good intentions, the employee experiences it quite differently—it feels more like WHAM! Surprise attack. Then the mental state of shock quickly slips into seething anger, not because the message is critical or incorrect, but because, he thinks, "The timing stinks!" Instead of listening, he's thinking, "If she had a problem with that project, she should have told me then." He feels sabotaged and betrayed, and the relationship is irreparably ruptured. Moreover, his recollection of the details has faded, impairing the opportunity for learning. Some would say the supervisor's delay in giving the feedback is not caused by appraisal, but by her bad judgment in waiting. But the mindset generated by appraisal must share the blame.

For feedback to be effective, it must be timely. Timely most often means integrating feedback into our day-to-day work. As we discussed, many supervisors find it unpleasant to give unfavorable feedback—the fact that appraisal time is not here yet gives them an excellent excuse to postpone the task. The resulting delay: (1) usually decreases the quality of information; (2) allows needless continuation of deficiencies; and (3) greatly increases the likelihood of the employee feeling surprise and betrayal. "The Mistake That Won't Go Away" illustrates yet a different problem when annual feedback is *not* a surprise.

The Mistake That Won't Go Away

Heather works as a human resources analyst at a large manufacturing plant. Part of her job is to track and project for costing purposes the labor costs associated with each product. Over time Heather has proven to be very reliable and competent in all of her duties. One year, during the month of May, Heather applies the wrong algorithm and understates labor costs by a significant margin. Relying on Heather's figures, the company runs the final costs and pricing. When it appears that something is wrong, Heather's boss, Mark, the plant H.R. Director, rolls up his sleeves and works with Heather to identify the sources of the error. The damage is done, however, and the error has caused the costs to be egregiously understated. Consequently, losses on the project are incurred, and plant management is put in a poor light with the parent company.

Mark is a conscientious and caring supervisor. Of course, Heather's error is serious enough to warrant a discussion. Mark sits down with Heather, and she tearfully and sincerely takes full responsibility for her unintended mental mistake and its dreadful consequences. Together they have a thorough and thoughtful discussion, talking about how the error occurred and ways to prevent it in the future. By the close of the meeting, it is clear to Mark that Heather realizes the significance of the mistake, and she is committed to measures that will prevent its recurrence.

Six months pass and, with the arrival of January, it's time for Heather's annual review. Mark, as an H.R. professional, understands that the appraisal is designed to reflect Heather's performance for the *entire* year prior. He is required to rate Heather with respect to all of her key responsibilities, including, "Accurately and timely provides data and estimates on labor costs."

Given the magnitude of the error, Mark grades her down on that point, and good soldier that he is, he follows the form and spells out what Heather had done, the action taken, and so on. Since the incident and their sit-down six months before, Heather has performed well in all job responsibilities, and everything's been running smoothly. Heather considers the fiasco of the prior May behind her.

Upon sitting down with Mark, however, she sees the glaringly inferior rating. Following procedure, he addresses her calculation error again, explaining the sub-par rating and its effect in lowering her overall rating. The whole thing rings wrong with Heather—she feels that the issue *was* presented and dealt with months ago. Though intellectually she understands the appraisal process, at the level of her emotions, she asks herself, "Why are we going over this again?" Her eyes well up, and being forced to revisit the biggest mistake of her career, she becomes shaken and distressed. An endless pause follows.

Mark sees how shaken Heather is, and, feeling regretful, small, and apologetic, says, "I'm just doing my job, you know, Heather. This is a mandated process, and it's nothing personal against you." Nonetheless, Heather experiences the besmirching rating as if someone has branded a scarlet letter on her for a past sin. Although she had reckoned with and worked through the error months before, the appraisal depresses Heather all over again, deflating her confidence and enthusiasm for several weeks after.

In this story, we see how appraisal can force feedback on events that were already dealt with in a timely manner. Some might say that the error needed to be documented in the event of future errors, but certainly there was ample evidence of the error, and, if that were insufficient, Mark could have documented when it was first uncovered inclusive of any counseling provided. Mark was right when he told Heather that the review process was *nothing personal,* and that is precisely the problem with performance appraisal.

In other aspects of our lives we know the value of timely feedback. Though the sports metaphor is not always analogous, good coaches, at the youth and professional levels, give timely feedback. After every game, win or lose, even when the players are exhausted, depressed, or anxious to celebrate, the coach calls the players together to point out observations, talk about what went well and what didn't. They would never think of waiting until Monday. Even the U.S. Army Special Forces now takes time for this type of group reflection after every training exercise.

Granted, there's a call for the kind of feedback that takes a longer and reflective view of the work or how an individual is doing. Appraisal feedback perhaps is so intended, but, when provided annually, it is arbitrarily timed to the placement of the earth's rotation around the sun, (whether we schedule it every January or on the employee's anniversary date), rather than a time tied to the work. Longer-view feedback more logically should be timed with the flow and cycle of the work. Some jobs are more *project-based* in which the work flows in a cycle. The cycle time may or may not be annual. For an in-house accountant, an annual cycle, occurring sometime after the fiscal year wrap-up is done, may be a good time for reflective feedback. Other projects, however, have different or variable cycles. For example, an account executive at an advertising firm may spend four and one-half months developing a product campaign, from the date of inception to acceptance by the client. The end of the campaign may be the most ideal time for feedback from contributors and customers about the flow and efficiency of the project. Aside from work cycles, the need for well-timed reflective feedback may be clearly necessary in the case of employees who are going through a training cycle, facing a probationary window, or attempting to meet career track advancement based on the achievement of skills and competencies.

On Coaching Generation X

Dr. Hank Karp, Dr. Danilo Sirias, and Kristen Arnold have observed that the supervisory needs of Generation X are different than that of other generations. They offer the following advice:
The majority of Xers had two parents working during their formative years. To make up for this lack of attention, Xers have a need for closer personalized contact from those above them. Younger workers expect—no, demand—feedback, frequently and quickly. Formal, sporadic performance reviews are not timely enough to provide guidance just when they need it. Create a dialogue among team members and enable the delegation process of assignment, review, and revision to occur more frequently. Encourage individual relationships on and off the job.[3]

Individual personal preferences regarding the timing, style, and format of feedback vary significantly. Feedback is intended to *help* people, and its timing should be comfortable for the people involved. Depending on the nature of the work, the supervisor's particular methods and style of coaching, and the needs and preference of each employee, calendar-driven sit-downs (monthly, quarterly, or annual feedback) may work fine. Some people may like the formal meeting approach, and others may definitely prefer feedback to be simple and timely (for example, see "On Coaching Generation X").

Assumption

Feedback motivates people to do a good job and improve.

Feedback in and of itself does *not* motivate people to improve. In fact, both positive *and* negative feedback have the potential to de-motivate employees. Let us examine each separately.

Positive Feedback and Motivation

Many people assume that positive feedback is always motivating, but human motivation is complicated. We are not sure that positive feedback gets people to work *more* diligently, but it seems to encourage people to *continue* their good efforts. If people are led to expect positive feedback, and they fail to receive it, it also seems that such disappointment would be de-motivating.

Researchers are still unraveling the dynamics of feedback and motivation. One finding that dumbfounds people is that positive feedback can be *de*-motivating. Research by Professors Richard M. Ryan, Edward L. Deci, and others indicate that positive feedback is de-motivating when it feels controlling and destroys people's feelings of autonomy. This even includes praise. Surprisingly, in a number of experiments, Professor Ryan found that positive feedback or praise was more likely to undermine the intrinsic motivation of women than men. The reasons are not clear, but the studies further indicate that women are more likely than men to perceive praise as controlling.[4] Alfie Kohn's *Punished by Rewards* also recounts a number of studies that have shown how praise backfires when it's used as a motivational tool.[5] Psychologist Richard Farson, co-author with Carl Rogers of the 1955 classic, *Active Listening*, offers some fascinating perceptions on praise.

If praise and positive feedback are de-motivating when they feel controlling, consider the context of appraisal. As detailed in the last chapter, it's steeped in control features (involuntary, given by the boss, signed by the employee, placed in the personnel file, connected to discipline). Positive feedback packaged in appraisal earmarks it as judgment and control, not the intended sincere appreciation for the work done. On a more subtle level, whenever someone else is assigned to judge our work, we feel disempowered. To foster a climate of autonomous adults, we must allow and enable people to be primarily responsible for judging the success of their own work.

Positive feedback can bounce yet another way. Consider how the good feeling of positive feedback is quickly diminished when it is contrasted with other feedback. For example, you receive a good appraisal rating in one year with your boss singing great praises. The next year you again receive a high rating, but with lackluster comments. It's easy to experience this as a negative or a downer. (Praise may also be akin to illicit drugs—you need higher and higher doses to get the motivational high.) Similarly, assume you get a performance review that feels pretty good, especially in light of your supervisor's encouraging comments. You walk out feeling good, only to find out later that a co-worker, who seemingly is performing at the same level as you, was rated higher (perhaps given the unattainable, esteemed rating of 5) or was nominated for a special raise or

---

Surprising Drawbacks of Praise

Richard Farson, author of **Management of the Absurd**, *says praise often is not helpful for several reasons.*

1. Praise is an *evaluation* and *judgment*; therefore, it usually makes people feel uncomfortable and sometimes threatened.

2. Rather than reassuring people of their worth, praise is in effect a form of gaining status over another person. The giving of praise implies one is in a position to sit in judgment. This sometimes makes a person feel diminished.

3. When people are conditioned to look for praise in their work, it *constricts* rather than encourages creativity because the employee is focused on praise rather than the task. Similarly, praise is an easy out that can discourage supervisors from getting *involved* in people's work, its problems, and possibilities.

4. Praise is associated with criticism because so often it's used to sugarcoat blame or be a part of the "sandwich" technique, in which harsh criticism is preceded and followed by praise.

5. Rather than bridging people, praise sometimes puts distance between people. ("See for yourself," Dr. Farson says, "if praise doesn't tend to hold off, to separate, while other behaviors—like listening—tend to include, to embrace.")

6. Praise tends to terminate rather than encourage communication. In human communication, an evaluative statement in a conversation usually means it has ended (e.g., "You're doing fine. Keep up the good work" and people go back to what they were doing).[6]

---

bonus, not included in your review. The once-positive rating now becomes demoralizing.

Our point is not to downplay the value of sincerely given praise or appreciation for work. As you consider alternatives to appraisal, however, we are waving a yellow flag that positive feedback is not a panacea for motivation.

Negative Feedback and De-Motivation

Negative feedback tells people that they're doing something incorrectly or insufficiently. Negative feedback is a critical part of growth and development. Sometimes it's necessary, and sometimes it is not. In any case, how does it affect motivation? If positive feedback can destroy one's natural motivation, what does *negative* feedback do? Professor Deci answers:

> It is far more disastrous. Experiments have showed that, too. When people were told that they did not perform well, they felt incompetent and controlled, and all their intrinsic motivation was drained away.[7]

People more readily understand that negative feedback can be de-motivating. Though, for lots of other reasons, recipients of negative feedback may be motivated to try harder, their *natural joy* or *desire* to do the task is lessened by negative feedback. A personal recount (see box on next page) illustrates this de-motivating effect.

The personal example demonstrates the powerful de-motivating effect of any form of negative feedback. This is not to say that negative feedback is not necessary or useful—quite frequently it must be dispensed for good reasons. We further recognize that negative feedback can often be indirectly motivating if the receiver cares about the *consequence* of negative feedback. For example, if one has a strong drive for perfection, whether healthy or neurotic, being told of a deficiency may propel efforts to improve. If advancing one's career to the next level is vitally important to an individual (because of pride or the desire for greater income), receivers of negative feedback may redouble their efforts.

The problem with appraisal, however, is that its design preempts the supervisor's discretion about the benefit or necessity of negative feedback—it assumes that it is an ideal strategy for improvement when, in fact, the complexities of human nature often make it less than ideal. There often are alternatives to negative feedback, as we discuss in our *Insteads* ahead.

Assumption

Feedback on performance strengths and weaknesses improves individual performance.

Typically, appraisal aims to get improvement by focusing on strengths and weaknesses. While feedback on strengths and weaknesses is *sometimes* useful, it's generally not an effective individual and organizational improvement strategy for several reasons:

- As discussed, negative and positive feedback for many reasons is often de-motivating.

Personal Recount of Negative Feedback as De-Motivator

Co-writing a book requires a great deal of communication and feedback. This is a perspective from T.C.

Initially writing one of the chapters in this book was particularly exhilarating for me. It contained issues for which I had great passion. Once I started writing it, I took every available moment to exuberantly do the writing, sort out the research, and get out the ideas. I sent an advanced draft to my co-author (M.J.), and we sat down together at a local coffeehouse so I could get her feedback on the chapter. Though, up until this point, most feedback on my writing had been positive, it quickly became evident that Mary was disappointed. She told me that it was far too academic for our intended audience, with too much on research and studies, and little that would connect well with the typical H.R. person or people manager who is trying to understand our message. She repeatedly said the flow was choppy and hard to follow. She patiently and kindly gave specific examples and made suggestions on different approaches and possible deletions and additions.

Though the voice inside of me acknowledged that Mary was absolutely right in her counsel, it nonetheless was disheartening and painful after I had put in so many hours in trying to write a good chapter. All of the conditions for effective feedback were present. I respected the giver of the feedback as a person and for her knowledge. I knew all of her comments were driven by the best intentions. The timing and circumstances were appropriate. Her messages were clear, and all of the information was extremely helpful.

While the conditions for feedback were right, and it was offered in a kind and effective manner, it nonetheless diminished my *intrinsic* desire to write that chapter. After receiving the feedback, I needed to get back to the revisions right away, yet it took me a couple of days before I could get myself to pull out the chapter and begin the rewrite. My desire to finish the book motivated me to revise the chapter, but it took me nearly two weeks to finish the revisions. Much of the joy I initially experienced in writing the chapter had vanished. Upon finishing the chapter, I could see that it read and flowed ten times better than my earlier draft. Even though I was exceedingly grateful for the feedback, and it was clearly beneficial, it nevertheless curtailed my intrinsic motivation to finish that chapter.

- As covered in Chapter 2, the faults, weaknesses, and dereliction of individuals is not the primary door for improvement—improving processes and systems is the highest yield strategy.

- While appraisal, by design, is intended to focus on *both* strengths and weaknesses, the process, as experienced, dwells on the latter. In part, this is because the receiver's focus will be drawn to the negative for two reasons: (1) people will be disappointed in any inferior rating—as mentioned earlier, one study found that 59% of the time, people disagree with anything less than the highest rating;[8] and (2) people will be drawn to the negative—research indicates that people's mental filing systems are biased to pay less attention to the good than the bad, and that negative words grab the brain's attention more than positive ones.[9] We have also found that supervisors tend to focus more on the negative because they associate appraisal with finding faults people need to work on. Accordingly, while the process is intended to focus on *strengths* and weaknesses, the effect (and often the discussion) spotlights the negative.

- There is nothing magical about encouraging improvement by having a conversation with people about their weaknesses. True, all people, in some form or another, need feedback to improve, grow, and develop, but conveyance alone scarcely improves performance. As Paul Squires and Seymour Adler have observed:

  (F)eedback may indicate the need to improve performance, but not provide a sufficiently clear and detailed path to improvement. If reviewers fail to specify in detail particular developmental needs and action to be taken in pursuit of them, employees may be left more frustrated and confused than they were prior to feedback.[10]

  Rather than through feedback, improvement can be better attained through more information, training, education, support, encouragement, a development plan, modeling, or new methods, many of which will need to come from someone other than the supervisor. True, often appraisals tie into these things, but so often the expectation is that providing the feedback or having a conversation around improvement magically leads to better performance, with only lip service given to these more meaningful interventions.

- The underlying assumption of the "strength and weakness" approach is that we can pluck out weaknesses and get people to work on them. Sometimes this approach puts blinders on the possibility of building *strengths* and getting weak areas out of the *job* altogether. Many organization development (O.D.) experts, such as Peter Block, believe that *building on strengths* is a far more fruitful strategy than trying to correct weaknesses. Discussion of strengths may open the conversation about "fit" and the search for a different job, within the organization or elsewhere. The idea that we can re-mold people comes from mechanistic thinking that people are malleable like things. In fact, however, it is exceedingly difficult to change people's innate predisposition and patterns, even when they have a good attitude about trying to improve. To a certain degree, people are what they are. If organizations would focus more on leveraging people's strengths, they might get greater gains in productivity and contribution than they would from focusing on their weaknesses.

■ Noise Effect of Feedback

Beyond the undermining effects of its assumptions, appraisal impedes feedback in another significant way—*noise* in the communication process. Noise refers to factors that distort the conveyance or clarity of a message being communicated. In a commonly accepted communication model, *noise* is more than physical noise that might keep one from hearing. Noise is anything that disturbs or impedes the effective conveyance of the message—it may disturb the sender's ability to communicate the message (*encoding* the message) or the receiver's capability of listening, cognitively and otherwise (*decoding*) (see Figure 5.2). If you are fretfully watching your three-year old caper around while you are on the telephone, this distraction creates *noise*, impeding your ability to listen effectively. If you meet with your CEO, and her reputation or higher-level status causes you to be in awe, nervous, or in fear, this mental state is a form of noise. If your employees are angry with you because of mandatory overtime associated with a project, that anger will create noise when you speak with them about the project, affecting the quality of their listening.

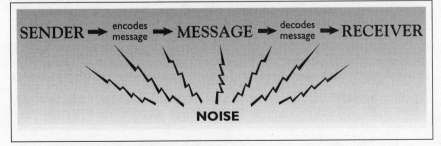

Figure 5.2 Communication Model with Noise

Understanding a little bit about *noise*, let's look at noise and the communication vehicle of appraisal. The design of conventional appraisal incorporates a number of noise emitters that undermine the opportunity for meaningful communication. Consider the multiple functions of appraisal:

- Connected formally or informally to discipline and termination

- A determinant of pay raises and bonuses

- An indicator that explicitly or implicitly affects or measures employees' opportunities for career advancement and promotions

- An accountability tool where goals are set and measured, the success of which, or lack thereof, will trigger favorable and unfavorable consequences

- A planning tool for development, training, and growth

- A "report card" that signals to employees their level of self-worth in the form of a rating, ranking, or descriptive terms.

This list is incomplete, but it is readily apparent that these issues are vitally important to a person's worklife. In fact, the issues could hardly be more serious, putting one's self-esteem, livelihood, and future on the line. For most organizations, a key goal in mandating appraisals is to ensure that employees get useful and necessary feedback, i.e., to encourage reflective listening about performance deficiencies and opportunities for improvement. Given the baggage of all the other critical drivers (pay, status, discipline, etc.) associated with appraisal, is it reasonable to expect that deep listening and meaningful conversation can occur? The appendages of appraisal emit blaring noises and irreparably damage the quality of listening. For example, it may be difficult to listen if someone must contemporaneously accept the fact that he is a 2.50 on a scale of 1 to 5, especially considering that the vast majority of people see themselves as top performers. Further, appraisal's link to pay, status, and discipline in particular precipitates "defensive listening." Defensive listening shuts down the employee's ability to earnestly listen—the employee will never be able to truly hear and accept any well-intended feedback, no less be open to change. If you have ever participated in an appraisal discussion, as a giver or receiver, you know what this defensive listening looks like.

Common design features of appraisal also create noise:

- The employee knows that the feedback outcome will be placed in his or her personnel file in perpetuity.

> ## Consultant Kelly Allan on Feedback and Money
>
> A raise is a transaction about how much *money* you or I can get. Feedback is a conversation about how much meaning you and I can create. Feedback is about success for your people and your customers. Pay is about marketplace economics and skills. Pay and feedback are not related.[11]

- The employee is required to sign the document, which, when adverse, feels as if one is confessing to a crime! (It's very common for employees getting bad appraisals to refuse to sign them, even when the signature lines says signing only signifies "receipt.")
- The feedback is conveyed by a person holding formal position power, the supervisor or manager, a person who has great influence over every aspect of one's work—assignments, training opportunities, advancement, and continued employment. This creates a "walking-on-eggshells" environment that extinguishes the opportunity for open and honest conversation.

If we were deliberately trying to design a process that would ensure distortion and an absence of communication, we could hardly do better than appraisal.

Case Study

Wheaton Franciscan Services

Wheaton Franciscan Services, Inc. (WFSI), based in Wheaton, Illinois, is a $1.5 billion healthcare conglomerate with nearly 16,000 employees and hospital and healthcare subsidiaries in several Midwestern states. Through the early 1990s, it embarked on a course of abolishing appraisal (traditional ratings linked to merit pay) and developed wholly new strategies based on the quality management philosophy of Dr. Deming and its mission, vision, and values as a religiously sponsored organization. Its H.R. vision calls for all leaders to continually develop good communication skills so they will be "able to provide and receive effective feedback and communication." Across the organization they have dropped performance ratings in varying degrees and merit pay altogether, granting pay increases in accordance with the market (the pay range is tied to a minimum of the 60th percentile in the market).

In place of appraisal, the corporate office requires at least one annual sit-down conversation each year to provide an opportunity for the supervisor and employee to look together at the work and their working relationship. A simple form provides a context for the conversation, focusing on objectives, changing roles, long-term aspirations, a personal learning plan, and eliminating barriers. "The aim is not related to assessment of performance," says WFSI Senior Vice President Bob Strickland, "The objective is improvement." Strickland said that the gist of conversation is: "What can I do to help you? What is going well in the relationship? How can we work together better? What are the barriers you are facing in your work? What are your learning goals for the next year?"

WFSI initially required the resulting form to be placed in the personnel file of the employee. Strickland reported that, for some employees, this practice perpetuated the stigma of the former appraisal process. "It made employees nervous. Some feared that, with the document going in the personnel file, it somehow could be used against them, so we stopped doing that," Strickland said. In 1998, WFSI made use of the form optional. Strickland said this change was received very favorably by employees, noting that it seemed to help employees relax and get into the flow of the conversation. Strickland further reported that, more than anything else, the disconnection from pay has been the most powerful factor in promoting learning conversations. WFSI's experience illustrates the potential benefit of disconnecting the *noise* factors associated with appraisal from communication processes.

■ Drawbacks of Feedback as an Improvement Strategy

Appraisal by design places overreliance on feedback as an effective organizational improvement strategy. While every organization should foster avenues and vehicles for feedback, it should not be relied on as a primary improvement driver, especially in the context of appraisal. Consider three critical reasons.

Low-Yield Strategy

Individual improvement is a low-yield strategy. Appraisal is a plan based on the idea of getting every employee to improve by giving them performance feedback. The unsurfaced assumption is that improving *individual* performance creates *organizational* improvement. As we discussed in earlier chapters, if there is no change in the methods, materials, equipment, structure, and other components of the *system*, the unspoken message to the employee is that the deficiencies are the product of his dereliction, laziness, indifference, or incompetence. An organizational strategy centering upon *individual* feedback suggests that improving the parts improves the whole, an inherently incorrect perception.

Promoting an Unhealthy Employee Culture

If we truly espouse an adult, empowered, and team-oriented work culture, we must send consistent messages. Improvement initiatives based on giving individuals feedback about their strengths and weaknesses is diametrically incongruent with this type of culture. It sends the *wrong* messages. It perpetuates the disempowering belief that *the supervisor is responsible for feedback, growth, and improvement.* It creates a dependent mindset that negates the employee's obligation to go out and seek feedback as it is needed. To help people see weaknesses and strengths, we must foster and instill opportunities for collaborative learning as the centerpiece of improvement.

Negative Impact on Performance

Feedback is sometimes not the best coaching tool. Because feedback can feel controlling and therefore de-motivating, it should not be encouraged as a stock supervisory tool for every situation. A comprehensive study (meta-analysis) that looked at hundreds of research studies on feedback involving more than 23,000 subjects observed that in one-third of the studies, the feedback actually had a negative impact on subsequent performance.[12] While feedback is often necessary, supervisors should always be mindful of *non*-feedback approaches to coaching errant employees. For example, in lieu of giving negative feedback, a supervisor could simply ask the employee to offer her perception about an assignment or regular task. While people can have inflated views of themselves, when questions are specific to the day-to-day work, they often are more critical of themselves than the supervisor. If the employee identifies the deficiency, it alleviates the necessity of negative feedback and allows the supervisor to proceed in helping the employee talk through options for getting better results. Another way to avoid negative feedback is simply to suggest that the employee try a different approach ("Next time, why don't you try . . . "). Though this may imply negative feedback, it is more gentle, and may enable the employee to find success without dwelling on the negative.

■ Mandated Feedback–Alternatives with Too Many Drawbacks

Fed up with the frailties of appraisal, many organizations try to craft systematic feedback systems in their place. People typically and understandably conclude that a structured and periodic feedback process can eliminate the drawbacks of appraisal if: (1) ratings and rankings are dropped; and (2) the functions of pay and discipline are disconnected. While these steps *immeasurably* improve conventional appraisal, the resulting feedback process nonetheless sends unhealthy and misleading messages about the nature of feedback and improvement (It's the supervisor's job to give it. It's a once-a-year event. Its timing is not driven by events. The receiver is not responsible to initiate it. Improving the parts improves the whole.). A periodic, structured feedback process may be an excellent transitional strategy for organizations abolishing conventional appraisal, but it will impede the evolution of a truly healthy employee culture in the long run.

The ubiquitous dissatisfaction with conventional appraisal has generated a major movement toward multi-rater or 360-degree feedback as a new form of appraisal. In 1992 alone, employers invested an estimated $152 million on multisource feedback processes.[13] Hopes of greater objectivity, no doubt, ignited this popularity. The 360-degree appraisal attempts to provide the receiver with feedback from everyone he or she works with—direct reports, peers, superiors, co-workers, internal and external customers, suppliers, and others. As Peter Scholtes says, it is like putting yourself in the middle of a lazy Susan and spinning yourself around. The underlying belief is that conventional appraisal has failed because the supervisor, as a rater, is not objective or sufficiently knowledgeable to give accurate feedback. If others are involved, the 360-theory goes, the feedback will be more objective and provide a broader base of information.

It's also believed that, because most people feel uncomfortable in conveying negative feedback, the anonymity of 360 will promote more honest feedback. These assumptions are not entirely faulty (e.g., 360-degree feedback does indicate a higher rate of reliability of ratings[14]), but 360-degree feedback does not serve as an effective *appraisal* system nor can it be relied upon as the most ideal conveyer of feedback because it has several drawbacks.

Drawback 1: No Employee Choice

The use of mandated 360-degree feedback systems, as commonly practiced, perpetuates unhealthy assumptions. For example, if a supervisor or person other than the employee is primarily responsible for initiating, assembling, or interpreting, or other joint effort is imposed (rather than letting the employee choose to involve others at his own discretion), it promotes the notion that someone else is responsible for the employee's growth and improvement.

Drawback 2: Not Effective Feedback

Assuming that 360-degree feedback is disconnected from all appraisal functions and the information is funneled to the employee for her to use and share at her discretion, 360-degree feedback should not be touted as the predominant feature of a feedback initiative. Recall our learning at the beginning of this chapter as to when feedback is effective. The *receiver* of the feedback must respect the source for sincerity, knowledge, and expertise. With the usual anonymity afforded in 360-degree feedback, people can seldom recognize whether these characteristics are applicable. The limited communication (often relying on checked boxes and scales) and lack of interaction between the giver and receiver further does not foster a personal experience or clear and helpful communication. In most designs, there is little or no opportunity for the receiver to clarify the message, or for the parties, together, to reach a greater understanding about any feedback issue. To illustrate this point, if someone were unclear about feedback, there would be no way to ask the giver to provide some specific examples. This lack of interpersonal exchange reduces the opportunity for learning. When people receive negative feedback, there is a natural temptation to rationalize it as insignificant or decide that the perceptions are biased or invalid. While anonymity offers advantages, not knowing the source makes it easier for people to adopt a defensive mode and reject the feedback.

Because 360-degree feedback is often periodically scheduled, usually annually, the feedback also is not particularly timely. As our recommendations below detail, we do not condemn 360-degree feedback. For some purposes, it may offer some advantages. For example, it's useful in situations where people may be particularly uncomfortable or reluctant to provide straightforward, face-to-face feedback (e.g., subordinates giving negative feedback to their boss).

Drawback 3: Connection to Pay and Promotion

If an organization uses 360-degree feedback as *appraisal*, the broad source of feedback arguably is more objective, but the assumptions and problems of appraisal are otherwise perpetuated. For example, the conveyance of feedback will be distorted by its connection to pay and advancement outcomes, placement in the personnel file, etc. As discussed earlier, research shows that the quality of anonymous, multi-rater feedback suffers if the raters know that the outcomes will be used in personnel decisions.[15] There are some indications, thankfully, that organizations originally intending 360 for evaluation and pay decisions are backing away from this and limiting its use to development.[16]

Whatever its virtues, 360-degree feedback is not a magic potion for facilitating helpful feedback, optimizing communication, or fostering a more supportive, team atmosphere. Peter Senge, drawing from the work of Chris Argyris, notes that 360-degree feedback provides anonymous ways for people to tell management what is wrong without accepting any responsibility for improving the situation. "The feedback process thereby subtly reinforces the view that management is the source of problems and only management has the power to fix them," Senge observes.[18]

Moving From Structured Feedback to Learning

Columbia University Professor W. Warner Burke defines three stages of organizational training and development. The *first wave*, he says, was the T-group, beginning in the late 1940s. Dr. Burke defines the *second wave* as "structured feedback," which began in the late 1950s, was strengthened in the 1970s, and now has culminated with 360-degree structured feedback. The *third wave* of innovation in training and development, he says, calls for *action learning*, a clear break from structured feedback mechanisms. *Action learning* is "learning about learning." It involves, "combining the solving of actual problems in real time in the organization with learning about how to work together better, how to solve problems more effectively, and how to improve the learning process in general."[17]

■ Feedback Without Appraisal–What to Do Instead

In developing a good feedback strategy in lieu of appraisal, begin with a good perspective. Understand at the outset that this feedback strategy is not an effective *centerpiece* for an organizational improvement effort. Yes, feedback is important. And, in lieu of appraisal, you want to foster a work environment where feedback is valued and practiced. Timely, useful, and accepted feedback can enable individuals to make great strides toward optimal performance. But encouraging effective feedback is only one substrategy among many key elements in transforming a work culture that values improvement—other aspects are covered in Chapter 6. Assuming your organization has sorted this all out and wants to promote and bolster feedback without appraisal, where does it begin?

The people of your organization will effectively use feedback when they recognize, understand, and genuinely *value* the importance of good communication and information sharing. This cannot be achieved by merely abolishing appraisals. It cannot be accomplished by some alternative feedback form or structure. It requires an orchestrated effort on many fronts to collectively spark a cultural shift, one that will transform people's perceptions and thinking about feedback at the deepest level. This shift can be achieved through four measures: Creating a clear vision of the culture your organization desires, training everyone about useful feedback, providing structures that encourage individual feedback, and using non-feedback communication tools, discussed below.

Create a Clear Vision of the Culture Your Organization Desires

Utilizing the organizational change approaches discussed in the book's last two chapters, help everyone in the organization understand what you are trying to achieve. Through awareness and education, foster a *shared vision* in which people see the importance of good communication and commit to sharing information. Help them understand that communication and feedback must become an integral part of the day-to-day work for everyone in the organization. This means adopting a common belief that it is *everyone's* responsibility to continually share and seek out helpful information. Help people see that they will be truly empowered when each one of them, not the supervisor or organization, is responsible to seek the feedback each requires.

This shift will not come overnight, but organizations can make great strides by having the leadership espousing *and practicing* values that support the effective dissemination of information that leads to improvement—values such as candor and openness, freedom of expression, and a prevailing assumption that people have good intentions in giving feedback. People must see the benefit of the continual flow of information that connects and enables us to be more effective. It's also important to help people realize that with the broad span of supervision in today's flat organizations, it is increasingly unrealistic for a supervisor to be the primary source of employee feedback.

Perhaps what is most important is recognizing that the purpose and function of information is *learning*, a concept that is given little more than lip service in most organizations. We will have greater success in designing initiatives and systems to support and encourage feedback if we see it as a subpart of an information and learning system. The emphasis on learning must be talked about and emphasized as appraisal alternatives and feedback initiatives are developed and implemented.

Enlighten, Educate, and Train People About Useful Feedback

Part of the task is to help people understand what feedback is, how communication really works, when feedback is most useful, and the value it brings. A key component is helping people understand that the receiver of feedback has at least as much responsibility, and probably more, than the giver of feedback. This requires education that expands people's thinking about feedback, for example, teaching people ways to get and use feedback on processes and systems or how to get feedback from internal and external customers.

The organization also must help people develop the basic skills around giving *and receiving* feedback. Though most feedback training materials overlook or minimize *receiver* training, we found a superb feedback training video set, called *Feedback Solutions*, that gives *equal* balance to giving and receiving feedback (additional information on this in *Further Reading and Resources*). The series provides extremely practical, down-to-earth insights on feedback and teaches people how to ask for feedback, when to ask for it, and the skills they need to get the information they need and want. After people learn receiver feedback skills, they understand that any time they're not getting feedback, it's mostly their own fault. Feedback is continually available to them—they just need to go out and ask for it in the right way.

Employee training ideally should also include education on various feedback tools, such as questionnaires, surveys, and the pluses and minuses of using multisource feedback systems, including 360-degree feedback. Expand people's awareness that valuable information and feedback also come in nonverbal forms, including system and process data and the patterns and responses indicated by customers.

People managers will need special help in adjusting to this new culture. If employees are expected to seek their own feedback, managers need to understand that the culture shift does not alleviate the obligation to initiate good, timely feedback when it is beneficial. Understanding how this all works is not about learning *techniques*—it's learning a new art and increasing awareness about the dynamics of information, learning, good timing, and the like. Train your people managers to recognize that, when corrective measures are necessary, there are options outside of negative feedback (as discussed earlier), as well as formal measures when the performance situations become serious (covered in Chapter 8).

Provide Structures That Encourage and Support Individual Feedback

Fostering an environment where informal feedback is woven into the day-to-day work should be the primary goal of any feedback improvement initiative. One study finds that 64% of people prefer informal, on-the-job conversations with their supervisor over formal interviews with their supervisor.[19] This does not mean, however, that *elective* feedback tools and structured formats should not be used. They can be helpful, especially as people transition from a world of formal, once-a-year feedback to continuous, informal feedback. Ideally, your organization should offer an array of feedback formats, tools, and processes, and offer related training to givers and receivers alike. For example, you could provide a list of prepared questions on forms and templates that are helpful in particular occupational areas. You can offer software that enables people to easily gather, track, and display feedback from work processes and systems. You also may wish to design an *elective* 360-degree feedback system as a developmental tool, offering employees the training and administrative resources to help them. Finally, to encourage use of feedback methods and processes, provide forums through department meetings, employee newsletters, and elsewhere

---

Other Alternatives to Appraisal Feedback Systems

More than a dozen leading business authors, scholars, and consultants have condemned and discouraged the use of performance appraisals, including Peter Block, Philip Crosby, Steven Covey, and the late W. Edwards Deming. Some of them do not prescribe specific alternatives.

Steven Covey has said that "Performance appraisals are the 'bloodletting' of today's management."[20] Instead, Covey urges managers to develop win-win agreements with their employees over performance issues. Unfortunately, some employers have stretched Covey's recommendation into a new variation of MBO appraisal, placing elaborate performance agreement documents in the personnel file (rather than encouraging, on a personal level, the development of win-win understandings based on trust and communication within a *relational* context, as Covey counsels).[21]

Deming encouraged all people managers to have a spontaneous, unplanned, and unhurried 3–4 hour annual conversation with each of their employees at least once a year, with a primary goal of *listening*. The purpose would not be for criticism or performance feedback but to take a broader view of the work and "for help and understanding on the part of everybody."[22] The Wheaton Franciscan model, referenced in the case study, was, in part, derived from Deming's recommendations.

---

for employees and managers to share their learning on feedback endeavors. Organizations exemplifying open, variable, elective or more flexible approaches include many of the case studies in this book: University of Wisconsin Credit Union and the Madison Police Department (Chapter 4), WFSI and GM–Powertrain (in this chapter), Glenroy, Inc., Gallery Furniture, and Entré (Chapter 6), Memorial Hospital (Chapter 7), Michigan State University (Chapter 8), and EDS (Chapter 10).

As discussed earlier, do not replace appraisal by developing a structured feedback process and imposing it on everyone in the organization, unless such is legally required or the structure is intended as an interim, transitional process in moving away from appraisal.

Raise Awareness and Use Non-Feedback Communication Tools

So often we tend to focus on feedback as a way to enhance communication and get improvement while missing other powerful opportunities.

How Much Time Will Dropping Appraisals Free Up?

Consultant Del Nelson has artfully described all of the savings from abolishing appraisals:

It will free all the resources of all the people who make the appraisals, justify the appraisals, log the appraisals, get de-motivated by the appraisals, compare the appraisals, study the appraisals, write . . . and maintain regulations on appraisal, develop a procedure to appeal the appraisal, appeal the appraisal, adjudicate the appeals of the appraisal, develop new appraisal systems (the life span of which seems to be three to five years, maximum), print the appraisal forms, stock and issue the appraisal forms, review the appraisals, approve the reviewed appraisals, type the appraisals . . . it will free up a 'whole heap of folks' who will be available for real work.[23]

We spend endless hours conducting quarterly or annual individual feedback sessions. That time could be better utilized in department or team meetings that can more substantively deal with improvement issues. Over the past two decades, exciting, new, and highly useful group communication tools have proliferated, and they consistently seem to yield new insights and higher commitment. The practice of *dialogue* has justifiably garnered great attention in the business press, and, if it is properly conducted, yields powerful results. A tool called *open space*, most popularly crafted by Harrison Owen, has demonstrated incredible power to energize a small or gigantic group of people to commit to multiple improvement initiatives. Another tool, proven over four decades, is *future search*, which, in two or two and one-half days, a group of diverse stakeholders reflect on critical trends and devise guideposts for organizational strategic improvement. All three of these communication approaches align extremely well with, and actually emerge from, the more open, organic organizational models we discussed in Chapter 2. For each of the three communication approaches, we have provided references in *Further Reading and Resources*.

Finally, the best insight on what to do instead may come from another case study, GM–Powertrain, which in moving away from appraisal, placed its initial focus on creating a culture where feedback was valued and integrated in the day-to-day work.

General Motors–Powertrain Division

In the mid-1980s, GM–Powertrain, a Division of General Motors with more than 26,000 employees, was struggling as was GM in general and the rest of the American automotive industry. GM's market share was declining at an accelerating rate, and the automobile market was beginning to see GM products as inferior in quality to those of their Japanese competitors. In this same time period, Dr. W. Edwards Deming, an 86-year-old visionary of quality management, was gaining increasing attention as a driving force behind Japan's emergence as a world-class economic power. GM, and other industrial giants such as Ford, Xerox, Procter & Gamble, and Eastman Kodak, turned to Dr. Deming, hoping he would be the elixir for their economic woes.

Given the gargantuan size of GM, early on its leaders decided to narrow Dr. Deming's intervention to focus on only a few subsidiaries, including GM–Powertrain. GM–Powertrain's continual problems with its engines, as measured by warranty claims, ratios of engine problems, fuel economy, and emission measurements, made it an ideal candidate for quality improvement. The upper level leadership at GM–Powertrain was open and receptive to the idea of working with Dr. Deming in moving to a new philosophy.

Under Dr. Deming's guidance, GM–Powertrain instituted a rigorous educational program for its highest levels of leadership, affecting every functional area of the company. After working closely with Dr. Deming for one year, GM–Powertrain's H.R. staff began to look at its functions and role in the transformation. They examined the company's performance appraisal practices by looking at its functions and purposes. Up to that time, the company had imposed a conventional form of performance appraisal, utilizing a 6-point scale with the outcomes connected to merit pay raises. Predictably, the ratings were skewed by their connection to pay and 75% of the company's employees were rated in the top two categories, superior and outstanding.

Recognizing feedback and communication as critical components, this area seemed like a logical focal point in moving away from appraisal. Under Dr. Deming's tutelage, the H.R. staff began to probe the untested, underlying assumptions connected to feedback. This exploration revealed that feedback, as it had been practiced in the appraisal system, carried assumptions that conflicted with the overall direction of the company. These assumptions suggested that *the supervisor knew and the employees did not* and otherwise implied dependency on the supervisor as the primary source for learning and growth.

First Design. Working from a set of healthier assumptions, over 18 months a design team created a new feedback process. The resulting process was disconnected from pay (more on that in the next chapter), and the employee receiver was required to choose feedback givers from a designated group that included supervisors, co-workers, and subordinates. After the employee made his or her choices, feedback forms were distributed and returned to the receiving employee's immediate supervisor. The supervisor synthesized the information and prepared a summary in narrative form, without any ratings or scales, highlighting the employee's strengths and opportunities for improvement along with developmental suggestions. With the assistance of Dr. Gipsie Ranney, a chief statistician appointed by Dr. Deming for the GM quality management transformation, the H.R. staff then studied the effects of the new feedback system.

Learning occurs when you find out that you are wrong about something, and that was exactly the design team's experience. After two years, it seemed clear that nearly everyone liked the new system better, especially the idea of getting feedback from peers and subordinates. However, the usage rate (a perennial problem of appraisal practice) was dropping—from 75% the first year to 60% in the second year. This finding was a mystery. Going into the process, everyone had said that they *must have* feedback. In fact, they *demanded* it. People said they liked the new system better. The team assumed that the problem with old system was the abominable ratings system and the tie to pay, but both of those were gone. So, why was usage going down? This created a learning opportunity and breakthrough.

In scraping to get an answer, the design team looked for deeper knowledge. An organizational development Ph.D. researched the academic literature and reported that, for feedback to be heard and internalized, the *receiver* needs to feel that the giver is competent, knows what he or she is talking about, and has the best interests of the receiver at heart. The survey of the research further revealed that the timing of the feedback was critical—to have a positive impact, feedback must be given close to when the work is done. To the surprise of the design team, the critical elements of successful feedback did not have a lot to do with the feedback skill level of the giver. Another important finding of the research was that helpful feedback was not contained to formal moments and was available in the work environment *all the time* and that a good many people were not adept at noticing or taking advantage of this. These insights about feedback created an "aha" moment for the design team and opened the door for an entirely different design.

Design After Learning. The new design first of all took on a sharpened focus. Since the organization had undertaken a major improvement initiative based on looking at systems and improving processes, improving job performance was not the primary goal of the feedback system. Rather, it was trying to address the personal growth and development needs of people. From this foundation and the research findings, the team decided to make the *receiver* the driving component of the process. This shift first required education—to help receivers develop feedback skills, and perhaps more importantly, give them the knowledge that feedback is continually available to them in their day-to-day work. To allow access to broader views of feedback, the company provided multi-rater forms that the employee could send out to peers, superiors, subordinates, and customers, totally at each employee's option. By making it elective, the designers believed that the process would yield more acceptance. In making this decision, the team asked itself—*What benefit would GM get in forcing an unwilling employee and/or unwilling supervisor to give feedback?* Their conclusion: *not much.*

Accordingly, the new feedback process called for people to learn how to gather feedback on a continual basis. It gave each employee the power to decide *if* and *when* feedback would be requested and *who* would be asked. The freedom of triggering their own feedback gave employees unlimited options. For example, they could seek feedback four months into a new job, once a year, or at the end of a project or extended assignment. What the employee did with the information was also left to the employee's discretion. The employee could take it to a supervisor or mentor or anyone who he or she thought could be helpful. To support feedback, growth, and development, designers established the *GM Individual Growth Strategies,* which provided *optional* modules around a particular set of needs:

- **Job Clarification and Feedback.** This module provides people with the tools and skills for self-initiated feedback. The educational piece helped people understand the role of feedback and personal development—why feedback should be the responsibility of the individual, and the basic skills necessary to be a *receiver* of feedback. It offered an array of feedback and analytical tools for employees to use, including task grids, process suggestions, interview tips, template correspondence, forms, and surveys for gathering feedback.

- **Self-Assessment and Alignment.** This module aims at helping people assess their skills, interests, and values to assist them in job and career choices. It also tries to help participants understand the importance of "fit." The module offered several tools, including a value certification process, a self-directed search instrument, and off-the-shelf products such as Career Anchors (developed by Edgar Schein).

- **Connecting Strategies.** This module educates people on the influence of formal and informal systems that affect career paths. To enhance skills in working in informal systems, the module offers a personal style assessment tool (MBTI).

A special module for the development of managerial skills was also offered.

Overall, the new initiatives were very well received. The voluntary usage of the elective feedback module proved to be 50%, a percentage that may appear modest but exceeds what some companies get with a *mandatory* appraisal process. The *Master Learning Plan,* used to determine the effectiveness of the new systems, revealed that people were using feedback skills in their day-to-day work, and a sizable percentage of employees, especially those in need, were using the career assessment and strategy tools. This system is now being used throughout much of General Motors, and variations have been adopted by other organizations, such as at parts of Daimler Chrysler.

Conclusion

Abolishing appraisal does not mean abolishing feedback. In its most advantageous form, it means transferring the responsibility for feedback to the person who can benefit the most—the employee. Taking on a new view of feedback, information, and communication requires a whole new mindset. This is accomplished by consciously discarding our unhealthy assumptions about feedback and, through enlightenment and learning, enabling everyone in the organization to embrace a healthier perspective of its benefits and limitations, as well as the possibility of alternative communication vehicles.

Review of Chapter Assumptions

Conventional Assumptions

It's the supervisor's job to ensure that feedback is given.

Feedback from the supervisor is a critical aspect of improvement for all people in all jobs.

Alternative Assumptions

- It's everyone's job to seek out the feedback they need to grow and improve performance.
- When the skills for "receiving feedback" are learned and applied, useful information will be conveyed.
- Supervisory feedback in many contexts is necessary and useful.
- Supervisory feedback is not always accurate.
- Feedback is readily accessible to us all of the time, in various forms, from a variety of resources.
- Feedback can be enriched when it comes from multiple sources and people.
- In helping employees improve, giving feedback is only one option among many.

Conventional Assumption

Formal feedback should be given on a periodic basis (annually, quarterly, etc.) to help people continuously improve.

Alternative Assumptions

- Feedback must be timely to facilitate improvement.

- People's needs and preferences for feedback are highly variable in terms of format, frequency, and content.

Feedback motivates people to do a good job and improve.

Alternative Assumptions

- People intrinsically desire to do a good job and improve.
- The motivational benefit from feedback, if any, varies with the situation, the method, and individuals who give and receive the feedback.
- Positive and negative feedback in many contexts can be de-motivating.
- Feedback is most effective when solicited by the receiver (the employee).

Feedback on performance strengths and weaknesses improves individual performance.

Alternative Assumptions

- People need feedback to improve, grow, and develop.
- Feedback on weaknesses without other measures does little to improve performance.
- Leveraging strengths often is a more effective individual improvement strategy than identifying and correcting weaknesses.
- Helping individuals to learn and improve systems and processes improves performance.

6

How Do We
Pay People
Without Appraisals?

The answer to the question managers so often ask of behavioral scientists—"How do you motivate people?"—is, "You don't."
Douglas McGregor, *The Human Side of the Enterprise*

Human beings are more alike than unalike. Whether in Paris, Texas or Paris, France, we all want to have good jobs where we are needed and respected and paid just a little more than we deserve.
Maya Angelou

Many organizations use appraisal to drive pay decisions, or at least this is the common belief. They use appraisal because they want to tie contribution to pay. They do this because they believe this will motivate people to do their best. They further believe that paying according to contribution is only fair, it's the right thing to do.

In this chapter we try to sort out the way all of us think about pay, motivation, and work. We attempt to bring into plain view our accepted notions and personal beliefs about pay and stack them up against our experiences and how they play out in the real world. More important, we invite you to discover, within yourself, intuitively known truths that do not reconcile well with the "givens" we take for granted relative to pay and motivation.

These unchallenged beliefs, for many organizations,

are the propelling force behind our relentless pursuit of appraisal. If we take time to examine our unsurfaced beliefs about pay and motivation, we can get really clear about what we want to do instead. We can sort out what we truly hold as near and dear and valid and what we reject. From there, we can create genuinely new approaches to pay, pay without appraisal, and pay systems that better serve our interests in maintaining a highly motivated workforce. All of this does not culminate in a prescriptive answer on what to do about pay. We do, however, offer an array of tangible alternatives for the separate, but intertwined, functions of fair pay and motivation. We ask only that you bring an open mind.

■ The Complexities of Money, Motivation, and Work

Money is important to just about every person who holds a job. Nearly everyone wants to be paid fairly and paid well. But because pay is important, does this mean that you can motivate people with money? Or that people work only to get money? Some of the behaviors we see in the workplace would suggest that the answer is yes to both questions. For example, we know that people will refuse a job offer if the money is inadequate. Every day we see people leaving jobs in which they are very happy solely to get a higher salary somewhere else. We also know that, when people realize they are being underpaid relative to others in the organization for the same kind of effort and talent, they feel unappreciated and quickly become less motivated and discouraged—they may even quit. These and other illustrations demonstrate that money can be a powerful force in "motivating" us to do certain things.

But money and work are complicated issues. While money is a powerful force, this does not mean that we work only for money or that money motivates us everyday to put forth our best efforts.

Our inherent desire to work for something other than money can be demonstrated by a hypothetical scenario and question we often ask audiences. Assume your boss hands you and your colleagues a project at 8 A.M. You and your colleagues roll up your sleeves and work on this all morning, coming up with ideas and putting it together. By afternoon, the project is really shaping up, but your boss walks in and says, "About that project I gave you this morning, I gave you the wrong proposal. I was distracted in catching the ball scores as I picked it up off my desk and mistakenly handed you the one engineering rejected. Throw that one away along with what you've been doing, and start over on this one. Sorry about that," and the boss walks out. What is your reaction? Without exception, people tell us they would be upset and angry. Some say they could be forgiving if this were an isolated incident, but that they would nonetheless be upset. If work really was only about money, however, this type of incident would not be an issue. After all, in the scenario, you would be paid in full for all the time you spent on the bogus project. You may not suffer the need to put in extra hours or an increased workload, but you would still be upset. This is because, regardless of money, *each of us has a deep desire to do meaningful work*. After going through this scenario, many people tell about how they took a pay loss to quit jobs that did not allow them to contribute, that seemed like a waste of their time and talent. All of this does not mean money isn't a motivator. It does, however, begin to show us the depth of complexity in sorting pay, motivation, and work. As we have said throughout this book, human beings are complicated creatures.

■ Incentive Pay–Does It Get People to Do Their Best?

Having acknowledged the unsolvable riddle of people and pay, let us briefly explore the connection between pay and motivating people to do their best. Typically, pay systems tied to appraisal operate with the idea of rewarding people with increases or bonuses based on the "merit" of their work. The implied assumption may be stated this way:

> ### Assumption
>
> **People will withhold their best efforts if they are not extrinsically rewarded, i.e., money motivates better performance.**

The assumption of pay-for-performance is that, unless people can see some kind of reward for their best efforts, they will slack off and be derelict in their duties. This assumption commonly emerges from two underlying beliefs:

- If people can't see a reward (something extra for their efforts), they will not be motivated.

- If people aren't rewarded, they will feel unappreciated and become de-motivated.

Both of these statements raise important issues that need to be examined separately.

With respect to people needing a reward to be motivated, let us go out on a very unpopular limb and say that, while people work for money, most people are *not* motivated by money in *doing* their jobs. Assess your own views of money and work. If you negotiate a very fair rate of pay from your employer, will you do your best even if no bonus or future adjustment is promised? Most people say they would not hold back anything, and they would do their best. Even though people can say this is true for them, they nevertheless have a difficult time letting go of the belief that incentives need to be offered to get the best from people, or at least for other people, they say.

The research around pay is most interesting. It's surprising for most of us to learn that scientific research does *not* decidedly affirm that incentives motivate people to perform better. Let's sort out some of the pertinent findings, pro and con. First, research does demonstrate that pay incentives *can* motivate improved performance under the following circumstances:

- in the short run
- in doing simple, mindless tasks or work
- when the work is *quantity* driven
- when the quality of the work is not particularly important.[1]

Accordingly, when these conditions apply, you can expect money to motivate. For easy tasks when the *volume* of work, rather than quality, is particularly important, incentives may be a good choice. If the work is really boring, you may need incentives to get decent production. For example, if you have a strawberry farm and a ten-day harvest season, paying pickers by the quart will probably work well in getting high productivity.

In looking at typical jobs we find in today's global market, however, they are not mindless, and quality is very important. Despite decades of intensive research, there's little or no evidence that pay incentives can improve the *quality* of work performed in complex, managerial, or professional positions. Alfie Kohn is perhaps the world's staunchest and most outspoken advocate against merit pay. In his book, *Punished by Rewards*, he draws upon several hundred studies on incentive pay, posting more than 100 pages of research citations. His overall assessment of the research is:

> (N)o controlled study has ever found a long-term enhancement in the quality of people's work as a result of any kind of reward or incentive program.[2]

Kohn subsequently made this claim in a *Harvard Business Review* article, and it attracted a flood of angry letters from proponents of merit pay. We found it interesting, however, that none of the detractors cited controlled studies that disputed Kohn's interpretation of the literature. Recently, an extensive study (meta-analysis) on incentive pay was published in the *American Compensation Journal,* and those researchers, making a case *in favor of* the use and benefit of using financial incentives, conceded from their review of the evidence that "financial incentives may not necessarily improve performance quality."[3]

Despite the lack of supporting research, you may still hold onto the belief that the promise of pay increases and bonuses will get better performance. Even if you are correct, we would caution you to proceed carefully. Most people's experience and volumes of research reveal that pay-for-performance schemes bring unintended, unhealthy side effects that severely undermine performance and organizational objectives (see "The Unintended Consequences of Incentives"). In assessing the impact of these side effects and the weakness of incentives, Kohn concludes "The bottom line is that *any* approach that offers a reward for better performance is destined to be ineffective."[4]

The Unintended Consequences of Incentives

Alfie Kohn's best-selling, highly controversial book, *Punished by Rewards—The Trouble with Gold Stars, Incentive Plans, A's, Praise, and Other Bribes,* amasses the outcomes of decades of research on the effectiveness of incentives and extrinsic rewards. Perhaps more interesting than the discussion of the power of rewards as motivators is his recount of the research on the unintended consequences of using incentives:

Incentives kill intrinsic motivation and interest in work. Rewards can feel controlling and hence are de-motivating. When you say, "Do this and you get that," it sends an un-surfaced message that the task is not of value in and of itself because you must give something in exchange for it. When Kohn told Oprah Winfrey on her TV show that rewards destroy intrinsic motivation, it set her back so much that she asked her producers to replicate one of the experiments Kohn had cited. Before hidden TV cameras, ten children were offered a $5 reward to test puzzles for a supposed toy company. Ten other children were asked to try them without any offer of reward. Afterwards, the children were asked to wait in the room while toy company representatives left. The children were told that they could play with the puzzles or do whatever they wanted. While left alone, they were secretly videotaped. The out-come? All ten kids who were not offered a reward continued to play with the puz-zles. Among the ten offered a reward, nine of them did not touch the puzzle at all. This experiment, designed by Edward Deci, is just one example of the ways rewards can undermine intrinsic motivation.

Rewards Punish and Cause Fear. Someone may get pumped up about getting a perfor-mance bonus or hefty increase, but if they fail to get the reward, often they feel pun-ished. Fear of losing the reward causes undue stress and may interfere with performance.

Rewards Rupture Relationships. When people think about their work getting them a pay raise, it causes people to see their bosses as a goody-dispensing machine rather than a person. The conversations often become more about getting credit and avoiding blame rather than learning. Merit pay schemes create competition with co-workers for scarce dollars from the pay-increase budget. One worker's success di-minishes the other.

Rewards precipitate actions that do not serve the best interests of the organization. Incentives may cause people to do things *that damage* the best interests of the orga-nization. Marketing people may ship before the customer wants it just to hit the MBO target. A person who has made a mistake or needs help with a problem will conceal it to avoid being rated as less competent.

Rewards discourage risk taking, creativity, and problem solving. When rewards are at stake, people focus on the target and don't think creatively. They also avoid the risk of trying something novel because of the possible penalty of losing out on the re-ward. The focus on getting the reward detracts people from thinking about the deeper causes and roots of problems. Creative sparks are lost when people fail to challenge their bosses for fear of retribution at appraisal and salary-increase time.[5]

With all the stock organizations put into pay-for-performance and in-centives worldwide, it's rather amazing to see that the research does not clearly demonstrate that it is beneficial. On the other hand, if we take a moment and introspectively reflect on our personal experiences with in-centive pay, perhaps these findings are not so surprising. With the rise of Taylorism after the beginning of the twentieth century, piece rate plans initially were widely adopted in American manufacturing. Over a few decades, however, these plans seemed to all but fade away, even in non-union shops. For sales people, straight commission in theory is a perfect incentive plan—people get paid only for what they produce. Nonetheless, high turnover and unmotivated sales people are pandemic complaints of sales directors who are forever scheming with contests and bonuses to somehow make incentives work better. Interestingly, a good number of businesses have eliminated commission and performance incentives for sales people, yet they've experienced substantial *improvement* in sales since elimination. Companies have found non-incentive approaches successful with auto sales people, manufacturer representatives, and other traditional commission jobs. An excellent recount of this type of transition is reported by the Marshall Industries CEO, Robert Rodin, in his book, *Free, Perfect and Now*, the company dropped commissions and incentive bonuses for hundreds of sales people and managers, increasing sales from one-half billion to over 1.7 billion dollars in just a few years.[6] (See also other case studies in this book, including *Gallery Furniture* and *Entre' Computer Service* in particular.)

■ De-Motivation and Motivation

What about the other belief attendant for using pay-for-performance— *people will be de-motivated if they're not rewarded?* In a sense, this belief is valid. Frederick Herzberg concluded that money is not a motivator, but it is a powerful *de-motivator*. If pay is not adequate or appears unfair, it will de-motivate most of us. Just because money *de-motivates* us, however, does not mean that money *motivates*. Herzberg distinguishes motivation and de-motivation by asking: If your pay were cut in half, would you work just as hard? Nearly everyone answers this question no. But if your pay were doubled, would you work twice as hard? Some people tell us they might work harder for a few weeks, but in the long run, they would not work any harder. When speaking, Kohn uses the metaphor of heating and air conditioning in a workplace. If the temperature is too hot or too cold, performance will decline. It does not follow, however, that, if you can find *the perfect* temperature, people will be performing off the chart.

Organizational theorists have postulated and found evidence to support that we will adjust our efforts based on *the equity* of what we put in (inputs) and what we get (outputs).[7] We also compare the inputs and outputs of other people similarly situated. In theory, inequitable ratios of outputs (rewards received) will be de-motivating. For example, if a person gets good results for an organization by working harder or longer hours, but over an extended period of time receives no pay increase, equity theory (or perhaps the unfairness of it, in the view of Herzberg) suggests that the person will become de-motivated. Similarly, if an employee learns that another employee, doing the same job with the same or lesser qualifications, is earning more money, there will be de-motivation. In either situation, however, the *de-motivation* caused by perceived unfair pay does not demonstrate that the person was *motivated* by pay to begin with.

■ Our Expectation to Be Paid According to Our Contribution

Assumptions

Pay is not fair unless it is linked to performance level (i.e., better performers of a job expect to be paid better than poorer performers in the same job).

People want to be paid based on their individual contribution.

Regardless of what the research shows, most people are predisposed to believe and expect that they should be paid in accordance with their individual contribution. If you survey your employees on their agreement with the above assumptions, most of them will solidly endorse them. In Western society, and particularly in the U.S. with its heightened focus on individualism, people are conditioned by the conventional practices and culture to accept these principles.

While the notion of being paid for one's contributions expresses a legitimate, widely accepted value, its implications are difficult to unravel. Most of us swallow the belief whole in a simplistic way without really examining our expectations. By making the underpinnings of our beliefs explicit, we can better understand what we hold as true, and then decide if we are being realistic. In Figure 6.1, we try to do this. Column one of the table lists what most people believe about themselves and others, while the second column lifts some of the fog.

When one contrasts the first column with the second, it's easy to understand why people readily embrace the overriding assumption that people should be paid according to contribution. People's assumptions, however, are *not* valid. We know that systems largely drive organizational performance, and that it's too difficult to precisely discern an individual's contribution (with the possible exception of people who truly stand out at both ends—see Chapter 3). We further recognize that much of the differ-

Individual Beliefs Regarding Pay-for-Performance	Reality Check
I am a much better performer than others.	Studies show that the vast majority of people perceive themselves as top performers when compared with others.
When I get the job done well, it's the result of my hard work and excellent skills.	Attribution bias distorts our interpretation of events and causes us to believe that positive work outcomes are the result of our individual efforts and skills.
Others do not work as hard or as well as I do.	Attribution bias causes us to believe that others' positive performance is due to luck or favorable conditions, and their bad performance is the result of their laziness or lack of ability.
My employer can recognize and distinguish the contributions of my performance versus what is caused by the system or others.	The system largely drives individual performance—it is very difficult to discern with any precision individual contribution to performance, especially in the case of complex and managerial jobs.
Based upon months or a year of performance, an employer can distinguish good workers from the mediocre and subpar.	Except possibly for workers who truly stand out at the very high and low ends of the spectrum, it often takes years to distinguish the approximate level of an individual's performance.
The difference in performance between one employee and another is largely attributable to greater effort, skill, and commitment.	Differences in individual performance largely arise from the variations and complexities of the work situation and environment.

Figure 6.1 Underlying Beliefs in People's Wish to Be Paid Based on Their Individual Contribution

ence in performance levels between individuals arises from random variation or causes that have little to do with an individual's effort and skills. Finally, we know that most people's belief about their performance, even if there were a method of pinpointing its value, is *absolutely* biased. It's a mathematical impossibility that 80% of the people could be ranked in the top quarter of all performers, as people believe. If the underlying beliefs in Figure 6.1 were true, then people's expectation could arguably be reasonable. The reality (in column two) cannot be changed, but through education, expectations can change.

■ Designing Pay Structures with Different Objectives

If pay is not a not a true motivator of performance, at least in jobs with any measure of responsibility or complexity, then what are the main objectives of a pay system? Setting aside the ethical obligations of an organization, there are two key objectives:

1. Pay people well enough to recruit and retain those who can best contribute. Mostly, this is accomplished by paying the market value and keeping wages current with market changes and inflation. Another key aspect of this objective is creating systems that enable people's pay to increase as people grow, improve their skills, and make greater contributions. This need not be approached *as a reward for merit* but may be more about an organization paying an individual more because his or her market value has increased.

2. Adopt pay practices that avoid *de-motivation*. De-motivation stems from pay practices when they are unfair or when there is excessive focus on pay and extrinsic motivation.

    A. *Pay people fairly*. This minimally means paying people a decent, livable wage and a wage that is relatively in keeping with what others are paid for doing similar work, both within the organization and in the external market.

    B. *Take people's focus away from pay*. If people are paid fairly, there will be less focus on pay. People tend to think about what they don't have. If we stop trying to use pay as a motivator (do that and you get this), we will not suffer the de-motivating effects triggered by extrinsic motivators, as discussed earlier.

Discontinuing pay practices that try to motivate people does not necessarily mean that merit and contribution cannot be a factor in your pay system. It only means that you are not using pay to get people's attention and get them to act differently in order to get a reward.

To avoid an unhealthy focus on pay, develop within your organization a commonly shared set of beliefs about motivation and the ways money can be important. People should have some understanding as to how your compensation philosophy and plan relate to those beliefs. For example, if your new plan calls for the wage market to drive increases, they should understand what that means—who is "the market" for your company and how it affects salaries. Does your company want to be at the top, 80th percentile, or the middle of the market, and so on. If there are career steps that tie to increases or some type of special case "merit" adjustment plan, then everyone should understand how that works. The goal is to end up with an environment where people are not wasting time walking around wondering—*where do I stand?* Mysteries are unnecessary and destructive. As Kohn advises: *Do everything in your power to help them put money out of their minds.* If the pay system is understandable and within some bounds of fairness, then people can focus on their work and not waste emotional energy on pay issues.

■ Pay Without Appraisal

Before talking about specific pay alternatives, with or without a "merit" concept, we must clarify some of the dynamics and loose terminology associated with pay practices. There is much ambiguity and misinformation about the nature of market adjustments, cost-of-living adjustments, and *merit* pay. Businesses love to call pay adjustments "merit pay" or "pay-for-performance" and consequently use these terms indiscriminately. The words sound so positive. People would rather be told they're getting *a merit raise* or recognition pay than that they survived another year. But merit is not always *merit*—it means different things in different organizations.

In some organizations *merit* is just as the word implies. The contribution of each individual's performance is purportedly measured, and pay or bonuses are adjusted accordingly. Some of these organizations give widely varying differentials, and others only tweak pay within very narrow limits, but in either case, the intent is to tie pay to the specific level of an individual's performance.

In other organizations, however, they talk about *merit pay,* but what they really do has little to do with individual performance levels. *Merit* is simply a way of saying that no one gets *an automatic raise,* but in fact, nearly everyone gets a raise on the same formula. Variance occurs only for a tiny fraction of people who are below an acceptable level (and likely get no increase) and a few individuals who receive larger increases for various compelling reasons (not so much a reflection of good performance, but for other pressing reasons, such as to recognize a critical skill shortage or encourage a key person to stay).

If this approach is not really tied to individual performance levels, then what drives the increases? It's usually a combination of cost-of-living adjustment (COLA), an across-the-board increase (in good financial times), and market adjustment. Commonly, it is just a blur of all three. (Compensation administration uses many scientific and technical words, but in practice, there's more "winging it" than science).

Market value sounds like a definite, precise, and objective figure, but it's not. First, the market rate is not a number, but *a range*—it has a high, a low, a median, and an average rate, and different organizations target different points as a goal. Second, a person within a given job often has a different market value depending on the number of years of experience. As a way of measuring such fluctuation, professional and some managerial jobs are often paid on what's called a *maturity curve*. The curve is a calculation on a graph, in which years of experience are plotted against pay, as Figure 6.2 shows. There is a curve instead of a straight diagonal line because often the first two to three years are for learning and seasoning—productivity is relatively low. Until professionals, such as engineers or attorneys, get some solid experience and can work more independently, their market value is lower. As they approach proficiency, pay rises rapidly. Once they are seasoned, the size of their increase begins to diminish. In some professions, the skill of someone with ten or twenty years versus four years of experience is relatively insignificant and accordingly so is the difference in their pay. Sometimes by calculated measures, sometimes by intuition and the influence of turnover, people are moved along this curve.

Because of the popularity of the word *merit* (*you deserve it!*), organizations that move people along a maturity curve or other pay progression

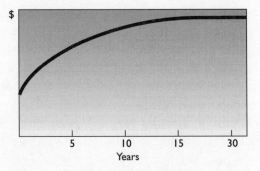

Figure 6.2   *Professional Maturity Curve*

call it *merit*. This is more illusion than truth. To the degree that it reflects a person's professional growth, the term is not completely a misnomer, but this definition is different from the more sweeping notion of paying according to individual contribution and performance.

By distinguishing these different *merit* philosophies, we are trying to help you understand where you have been. Some of you have applied a system that aimed at the *merit* of individual contribution, and moving away from this approach will be a major adjustment. In other organizations, you've used the term *merit* to describe market and experience-based adjustments, but *merit* in the sense of *individual performance* has had little effect on pay adjustments. In the latter case, the transition away from appraisal-connected pay may be more a matter of dropping appraisal than actually changing your pay practice.

■ Non-Merit Pay Approaches

By moving away from conventional merit pay, an organization can create an understandable and relatively objective system of compensation. This will eliminate a great deal of wasted time and energy that managers, supervisors, and H.R. staff spend explaining and justifying why someone gets 1 or 2% less than someone else or what they expected. Best of all, a system that does not purport to measure individual merit eliminates the de-motivation, erosion of commitment, and other unintended effects of having *mediocre* stamped on one's forehead. While a good pay raise and recognition may feel inspiring for some of your employees, the negative effects on the also-rans and losers more than offset the gain, if any, associated with the winners.

How do organizations make pay adjustments in the absence of appraisal and individual measurements of contribution? Typically pay is advanced in accordance with general COLA and market changes relative to each occupation and level of experience. The organization may also explicitly or implicitly tie pay to length of time in a job or profession. This type of practice does not negate altogether the underlying principle of merit or that people should be paid in accordance with their contribution. Outstanding individuals can progress in pay in a number of ways that do not involve typical merit pay practices. For one, people can advance on what is called a "career ladder," where clearly identified skills,

Learning from Organizations Dropping Pay for Performance

"Carrot and stick" is so deeply ingrained in our culture that organizations that drop incentive pay should expect a perpetual obligation to educate their managers and employees. For example, we have learned from organizations such as Glenroy, Inc. and Wheaton Franciscan Services (WFSI) that if you abolish merit pay or move away from the traditional form of merit (as discussed below), new people coming into your organization believing that they are excellent performers will be looking for special increases to reward their superior performance. Only through continual education will people understand the faulty assumptions that give rise to their beliefs.

Robert Strickland, Senior Vice President at WFSI tells us that when they are competing with other organizations in trying to hire the scarce talents of a software engineer or certain medical professionals, merit pay has become an adverse negotiation issue. The offeree of a position tells WFSI that she has another offer of the same amount *and,* she's been told, she will get merit pay adjustments. "When you are trying to attract candidates in a competitive market," Strickland explained, "the lack of an incentive or bonus plan will be seen by prospective candidates as a negative." Strickland further explained that this is an issue of misconception or mislabeling, not substance. WFSI works very hard at trying to stay at the 60th percentile of the market, inclusive of what is called incentive pay in other organizations. Competing organizations give raises driven by professional advancement, longevity, market increase, and cost of living, but call them *merit.* The *merit* aspect is illusory, because when market data are gathered, the so-called merit portions of pay are not extracted.

In the case of WFSI, their nonmerit approach *does* ensure that pay is above average of market level regardless of how other organizations choose to earmark their pay increases—a dollar is a dollar. Reflecting on WFSI's five-year experience without incentive pay, Strickland said:

> The theory behind not offering merit pay is not easy for people to understand. It seems our people who are in critical roles understand, but others do not. The empirical research also does not make a slam dunk for our case—moving away from merit pay can be challenged by extrinsic motivation theory.

Strickland has observed that people's belief in merit pay driving performance is so strong that when there is any dip in the financial performance of the organization, the naysayers will quickly emerge to say, "This wouldn't be happening if we had pay for performance," though there could be 150 different causes.

accomplishments, and educational measures allow a person to move to a higher pay grade. Yes, these systems sometimes include subjective judgments that can bring rating problems similar to appraisal. However, in some instances, the human evaluation and subjectivity can be reduced or completely eliminated, as described in the next chapter.

Outstanding performers can also be advanced in compensation through promotion. This occurs in two ways. One is the traditional competitive promotion. The other is a backdoor method but is nonetheless legitimate. For example, within a work group, one individual may truly stand out with exceptional skills that are plainly visible. Typically that person's assignment changes over time because the manager wants to get optimal use of unique talents. Perhaps this person has exceptional analytical skills and ends up getting the most difficult and complex assignments or is heavily relied upon as a trainer or "lead worker." When these special assignments or roles extend indefinitely in time, most organizations follow a procedure called *reclassification* to generate a pay adjustment. The person's evolved job (not the person in the job) is evaluated relative to other jobs in the organization or the external market, is reclassified to a higher grade or level, and a pay adjustment results. Under traditional *job* evaluation methods (again not evaluation of the individual, but the job), significant, ongoing differences in responsibilities or higher skilled work will warrant an adjustment to a higher pay grade. Within the emergent fluid and organic organizational structures today, this backdoor method is an increasingly common way of handling promotions. More and more, we hear about the "the end of the job" because the fast pace of change allows no one a fixed set of tasks and pay must evolve as the person evolves.

Case Study

Glenroy, Inc.

Off the Interstate, in Menominee Falls, Wisconsin, a suburb of Milwaukee, sit two modest industrial buildings. Inside those buildings, a small-scale, but monumentally important revolution in human resources practices has taken place. Glenroy, Inc. is a manufacturing company that makes flexible packaging materials and thermal laminating films used in pharmaceutical, food, and home products. In an era when many smaller manufacturing companies have folded or been bought, Glenroy has thrived, quadrupling its gross income over the past fifteen years. In the same period, its workforce has grown from 43 employees to 136 employees producing more than $40 million in goods each year.

How did all these good things come to be? In the late 1980s the company real-ized that the top-down, quantity-driven, rely-on-inspection method of manufacturing would not enable the company to remain competitive. It also could not achieve founding President Roy Jablonka's dream of building a firm "destined to be different" with a "legendary reputation for quality" in packaging products. Like Procter & Gamble, Xerox, and other manufacturers, Glenroy's leadership took note of the quality management movement and began to explore ways to fundamentally change the company. Reflecting back, Executive Vice President Mike Dean said Glenroy was pretty typical, relying on what he calls "supervision" or "push" management. To work more effectively, Dean said, they needed to shift to "leadership" or "pull" manage-ment in which, rather than pushing people, they pull and lead them with leadership skills, "guiding people and helping to bring people along by asking them what is the right thing to do, not telling people."

As Glenroy leaders studied ways to transform the company, they recognized that human resources practices were just as important as the manufacturing processes. After all the leaders attended extensive training on quality management, they con-cluded that the old way had to go, *literally*. In a highly spirited, but inauspicious begin-ning, Glenroy scheduled a tailgate party in its employee parking lot before a Greenbay Packers game and burned all of the company's personnel manuals in a 55-gallon drum to cheers and applause. "We knew that what we had was not what we wanted," Dean explained. "Our employee manuals were for no better purpose than *scorekeeping*—keeping track of sick days, discipline, and a number of things that only irritated employees." Dean said, in lieu of the old manual, "We shifted the responsi-bility for people to be at work back to the people, using training and education."

These actions led Glenroy to think about appraisal. Up to that time, everyone but the President at Glenroy received an annual appraisal. It was a multi-page form that listed behaviors on which people were rated from 1 to 10. The outcome was tied to pay raises, and there was supposed to be coaching and goals. Dean said the supervi-sor ratings were pretty "subjective," and feedback was an "illusion."

In lieu of appraisal, the company recognized that improvement did not come from formal feedback sessions but came from educating people on improving pro-cesses and systems. It also recognized that good performance was mostly a product of "good fit," getting the right person for the job *and* the company. Glenroy goes to great lengths to screen new hires. "We look for *we* and *us* kinds of people, not *I* and *me* people" and people who can be committed in a collaborative culture (but not a *yes* person), Dean explained.

In abolishing appraisal, the company shifted responsibility for education and growth to the employees. Employees are trained in process improvement, tools, and methodology. The company also practices open-book management. Each month, every employee attends a small group (20–25 people) meeting with the President, the CFO, and other leaders, to get reports first hand on finance, sales, and other changes, with an opportunity to ask questions.

In place of appraisal, no formalized feedback process was created. That responsi-bility rests with people involved on a day-to-day basis. The biggest challenge in discarding appraisal was converting to a new pay system. After much reflection, the company decided to abolish all incentives, including commission for its sales representatives and merit pay for all employees, including the President. Glenroy leaders saw merit pay as an obstacle to getting people to cooperate and collaborate with one another. "A key part of our culture then became helping people understand the impact of a competitive environment and why it was important for us to have a noncompetitive environment," Dean recalled.

In place of incentives, the company established pay grades tied to the external market, with a commitment to pay no less than the 60th percentile. In that system, still in effect a decade later, everyone starts at a beginning rate somewhat below the market goal. At the end of one year, they are moved to an interim rate (halfway between the start and established rate). After two years, they are moved to the established market rate. These are automatic adjustments and no one at any point receives merit-based adjustments. Increases are based on market adjustment of pay ranges. Higher pay only comes with promotion. With rare exceptions, Glenroy promotes from within, posting all jobs and using committees to screen candidates. It also takes time to identify and develop people who exhibit natural leadership skills.

The company offers a company-wide "smartness" award called the Glenroy Performance Award or GPA. GPA is a quarterly noncompetitive bonus. Everybody gets it, or no one does. Based on a rather intricate and discretionary assessment, the company looks at its overall performance: in lowering scrap, gaining in the market, costs, returns and credits, budget impact, and other factors. "It's about how smart we were," says Glenroy CFO Jim Daugherty. In quarters where "smartness" is shown (which happens more often than not) a bonus is distributed to every employee on the payroll. Each employee receives a payment equal to the ratio of their pay to the total payroll for the quarter preceding. When the bonus is paid, it usually equates to 5–7% of a person's quarterly pay. The payout is not considered a reward or incentive, but a benefit for contributions made. Jim Daugherty said he didn't think the money had anything to do with *motivating* good work. "If you want people to act to make the company run better," Daugherty explained, "then give them a stake in it *and* let them know what *they* can do to make a difference. That's what the GPA is about."

After more than a decade without appraisals and merit pay, the company and its workforce seems quite pleased. Dean says, "You couldn't get appraisals in here with a bulldozer." Daugherty says sometimes people tell him they should get merit pay or that they can make more money elsewhere. He talks to them about how merit pay issues divide employees and says, "We have enough to compete with the world as a company, but that doesn't mean that we have to beat each other up on the way." Despite the occasional questions about performance differentials, turnover at Glenroy has been extremely low over the past decade.

The drawback to advancing people through reclassification is that it can result in an unfair, good ol' boy advancement system with serious EEO implications. These problems can be minimized, however, by adopting diversity values through diversity training, mentoring, and educating everyone on career development, feedback, and political skills (*political* in the positive senses of that word—see Peter Block's *The Empowered Manager*).

Also in lieu of merit pay, organizations may want to consider adopting some sort of profit-sharing, gain-sharing, or ESOP cash or deferred benefit plan. The goal is NOT to give people an incentive or motivate them (years of studies on this do not seem to clearly indicate motivational power with these kinds of practices). Rather, it's to give the employee a greater sense of ownership and a psychological and tangible stake in the organization. From a fairness perspective, such a plan arguably may help to avoid *de-motivation*. When the company does well, everyone shares, and this makes compensation more fair. Nearly every organization we have spoken with that dropped appraisal has implemented or is working toward this type of measure.

Case Study

Gallery Furniture Company

In Houston, Texas, a beautiful, warehouse-sized retail furniture store has departed from business as usual. Gallery Furniture has embarked on a cultural transformation, abandoning conventional retail personnel practices. Gallery employs more than 200 people in sales, warehouse, delivery, data entry, office, and custodial jobs. Jim McIngvale is the owner-President, but refers to his job title as "willing worker."

Beginning in the late 1980s, Jim attended Dr. W. Edwards Deming's four-day workshops ten times. At that time, many organizations got the quality bug but let it fizzle when the flavor of the month changed. This is not the case at Gallery, however, where years later they are still at work with the same philosophy. How has all this affected the company? Since 1991, Gallery has experienced a dramatic increase in sales and profits. "Customer satisfaction," McIngvale says, "is off the chart." He said everyone at Gallery works very hard to try to please the customer—that is the focus. Since 1991, sales have risen from $25 million to $100 million a year. More important to McIngvale is the appreciation of customers. "They tell us we're the best—no place else treats us like your store does," he proudly exclaimed.

Changes in compensation and personnel practices have been key to the company's decade of success. In 1991, McIngvale stopped paying commissions, bonuses, and incentives to his sales staff. "Dr. Deming told me to take my sales people off commission, and I took a leap of faith," McIngvale recalled. "He was right, and it has worked in taking better care of the customers." In place of incentives, all sales people became salaried. And all employees receive an equal share of 20% of the profits each quarter—with 10% paid in wages after the quarter and the other 10% deferred into a 401(k) qualified distribution. Some sales people, perhaps "prima donna" types, McIngvale noted, left when commissions were discontinued. Most stayed, and the turnover in sales has dramatically dropped. The company also did away with incentives previously paid to drivers to sell additional services during delivery.

The organization *officially* dropped performance appraisals in 1991. (Appraisal was never really practiced at Gallery, but some prior personnel managers had unsuccessfully tried to initiate it, McIngvale reported.) In 1991, the Company told its employees that it would not have appraisal as part of its work environment. "It's giving people report cards in school, and that has never done any good," McIngvale observed. "Appraisals are mostly a personality contest, and we didn't want them." He explained why appraisals are unnecessary at Gallery:

> We appraise people every day as they need it. We talk to people and listen to them. We try to give people jobs and tasks they like to do. We help them if they need it, but mostly we try to make work fun. Work is supposed to be fun. Appraisals get in the way of this. We're in the customer business, not the appraisal business! Ninety percent of people will be disappointed with appraisals because they all expect top ratings.

Along with abolishing incentives and performance appraisals, the company eliminated merit pay. People get longevity raises (seniority) based on a predetermined scale at the end of each year of employment for their first ten years at which point the pay range caps off. Adjustments to pay ranges are made as dictated by the market. As detailed in the next chapter, employees advance themselves by applying for higher level jobs, and getting to the right "fit."

Unlike some organizations that have dropped appraisal, Gallery has not elected to institute any form of annual conversations or formal feedback system. Explaining the lack of a formal conversation, with heartfelt passion, McIngvale said "We talk to people every day and try to help them—I look into people's souls, and they look in mine every day. We both know where we're at and don't need that (a formal system)."

■ What About Abolishing Appraisal WITH Merit Pay?

If you must have some sort of *merit* principle in connecting pay to individual contribution, you *can* do this and nix appraisal. While this course of action will necessitate human judgment and evaluation, subject to all of the bias and frailties we've discussed, there are ways to do this with fewer destructive effects than appraisal. We'll discuss two different paths.

Negative Merit

The negative merit concept is easy and often overlooked. If a person is in counseling or in some level of formal discipline for unsatisfactory or unacceptable performance, you may deny, withhold, or defer pay increases, whether or not they are based on COLA, market adjustments, career ladder, or otherwise. Withholding increases for a person in trouble is a very common form of corrective action. In essence, this is a *lack of merit* situation.

If you wish to consider this option, two important caveats apply. First, be sure that your employee policies and labor agreements do not prohibit this kind of measure. Better yet, within your corrective action or disciplinary policy, specifically state that individuals whose performance is unsatisfactory are *ineligible* for increases (or reserve it as a discretionary option). Some organizations dropping appraisal require supervisors each year to sign off that a person is at least performing at the minimum level (see *Michigan State University* case study). If your organization elects such a mechanism, it could bar increases for people who fail to get the sign-off.

Second, you must think about unintended effects of denying an individual an across-the-board adjustment or COLA. If you are sincerely trying to bring someone around in a corrective action system (and a good many organizations do succeed at this), the denial of this kind of pay adjustment will feel like *punishment* and may put salt in the wound, perhaps pushing the employee, in terms of decline in attitude and commitment, beyond reparation. If your corrective action is really trying to help someone, withholding an increase may not be a smart strategy. On the other hand, for legal considerations and otherwise, there are times you need to send a message that may make this the right choice.

Merit by Exception for the Truly Outstanding Performer

Another approach is to award merit pay only to the truly outstanding— those whose performance *clearly* stands out as *exceptional* in spite of the system. The underlying premise of this approach is that the system largely drives people's performance and, for most people, there is no reliable way to pinpoint their level of contribution. At the same time, there usually are a tiny fraction of people whose performance clearly and unmistakably stands out above the rest. These are so easily recognizable that they are viewed as "outside the system."

Any process that identifies outstanding individuals, of course, involves subjective judgments and can suffer from bias and abuse similar to that of appraisal-driven merit pay. Looking for someone *exceptional*, however, involves a different kind of judgment and, because of that, it can be more reliable than appraisal. In appraisal, the aim is to determine the precise rating or ranking of one individual versus others. In *merit pay by exception*, however, there is a strong presumption that the vast majority of people are not outstanding (outstanding = *to stand out*). Thus, it works better than appraisal because its aim is to merely identify the very few who are the truly *exceptional* or *outstanding*. Harvard Business Professor Michael Beer concurs that this should be the focus of merit pay and notes "there are lots of ways to do this without orchestrating tons of paper and asking people to fill out forms."[8] Merit pay by exception, as commonly practiced, can be effectively accomplished with a consensus of judgment from a large number of people. As an example, Dr. Beer said that, if a group of managers takes some time to meet and engage in a "powerful, skilled discussion," using inquiry and reflection, they could reliably identify people who stood out at either end. He mentioned Hewlett-Packard as one company that has successfully used this type of discussion.

As GM–Powertrain abolished appraisal, it spent many months developing a merit pay by exception practice. In the beginning it tried to endorse the concept of merit pay but had great difficulty in finding a way to decide—*who is an exceptional performer?* (Agreeing on the principle of rewarding the exceptional performer was the easy part, the tough challenge was—*how do we decide who is exceptional?*) In deciding what to do, they considered three approaches:

- *Free Expression*. Under this approach, managers individually selected people from their own workgroup. A pilot was tested at one facility with abysmal results—the managers identified 25% of the work population as *exceptional*. The huge percentage plainly signaled that this method would not work.

- *Control by a numerical target or limit*. This idea was to establish an upper limit target of not more than 5% of the population. This concept was quickly discarded, mainly due to an experience that occurred just a few years before. (GM Corporate had issued a directive that every department was to identify its top 10% for a hefty raise, the next 25% for a good raise, and the bottom 10% for no raise and career counseling—the middle 55% were only to receive a very modest adjustment. Every division experienced an ocean of problems with this carrot-and-stick approach.) The design team foresaw that a target or 5% approach would largely replicate the fiasco of the earlier GM dictate.

- *Clearly defined process.* In this approach, a large group of managers would employ an elaborate process to gather input and then meet. Through multiple input and assessment, extensive sifting, discussion, collaboration, and dialogue, the golden nuggets would eventually become evident to everyone. When a large group of managers (sometimes as many as 20) were brought together for discussion, the rule was that *everyone* would need to agree for a person to be proclaimed as *exceptional* or *outstanding*. When people disagreed about the *exceptional* status of a particular individual, that meant, at face value, the person was not exceptional. If someone truly stands out, they believed, everyone should be able to see that.

This third method was chosen as the most practical and seemingly reliable method of choosing exceptional performers. The designers of this approach recognized that their "theory" was not verifiable science or immune to mistakes, but they nonetheless had confidence that interactive discussion and inquiry would result in people's best judgments. To increase consistency and the likelihood that every manager was coming from the same place, they wrote a definition of *exceptional* (see Figure 6.3). In applying this method to a group of approximately 1,400 managerial employees, in one year, 4 people received an adjustment for exceptional contribution, in another year it was 10, and in another, it was 14, demonstrating that the process has kept *exceptional* within the vicinity of their initial goal.

A slightly more liberal and broader approach to merit by exception is illustrated at Entré Computer Service and Michigan State University (see case studies below). For organizations that cannot bear to part with the presence of more traditional merit pay, the University case study demonstrates that an organization can preserve a viable merit pay approach without the annual agony of appraisal.

Definition of an *Exceptional* Employee (GM–Powertrain)

- Has inarguably stood out from the rest of the work team for a sustained period of time in contribution as evidenced by commitment to organizational beliefs and values (methods) and system optimization (results).

- Is easily declared so by those that know him or her. . . It's a consensus by acclamation; no debate.

- *Exceptional,* given its most elementary definition, is rare. To identify more than a few individuals as such negates the *exceptional* label and makes it an intolerable contradiction.

- It is more likely that a given work team will have NONE rather than ONE exceptional team member.

Figure 6.3

If your organization wishes to keep a broader-based form of merit pay, we would make the following recommendations:

- Use well-defined criteria and collaborative input and assessment to contain some of the bias and distortion that you will experience.

- If you believe that merit differentials must be awarded to a larger degree than a small fraction of the workforce, at least refrain from using wholesale merit pay. Don't label COLA and market adjustments as merit. Merit should be reserved for distinguishing contributions against specified criteria.

- Whatever process you use to assess or rate merit, detach it from all other functions, including coaching, feedback, employee development counseling, and promotion decisions.

- Contrary to commonly conveyed Skinnerian advice, do everything you can to get merit pay out of the minds of your employees as they do their day-to-day work.

- Don't fall into the trap of believing you will necessarily get *fairer* merit pay decisions by measuring people against established performance goals. As discussed earlier, goal-based incentives are nonetheless fraught with rating errors and damaging side effects.

Entré Computer Services

Entré Computer Service, in Lansing, Michigan, designs and implements information systems networks. The company was founded by Ed Souders in 1983. Souders had worked at IBM for 25 years and brought to Entré many of IBM's practices, including appraisal, pay-for-performance, and sales incentives. In the emerging computer market of the 1980s, the company fared well early on, but by 1991, it had a ratio of debt to equity of ten to one and was courting bankruptcy.

In 1991, Souders attempted to re-invent Entré, shifting it from being sales-driven to having a passionate customer focus. Key to this transition was moving from a "me-me" culture to a team culture, aligned with the Deming philosophy. Toward that end, it abolished appraisal and revamped its pay practices, discarding pay-for-performance, commissions, and bonuses.

"In place of appraisal," Souders explained, "we substituted the *engaged manager*." The whole company of 60 employees convenes every Monday morning for 60–90 minutes to talk about what is going on and together assess how everyone can better cooperate. The company annually reserves an amount equal to 10% of each person's salary for training and development initiatives. Totally on an elective basis, people meet with their managers once a year to talk about development and plan how that person's training dollars will be utilized. Realizing the value of continuous skill development, most people choose to participate in the process.

Borrowing an idea from an Ohio firm, PQ Systems, everyone at Entré receives a bonus based on company profits—35% of the company's annual profits are shared with all employees. Sixty percent is distributed based on seniority and forty percent relative to each individual salary as a percentage of the whole. This annual distribution is not promoted as an incentive: "It's just a way we give people a piece of the pie," Souders explained.

Salaries and increases are set according to the wage market. An increase in skill level may also generate a pay increase in tune with the market. Entré has not altogether abolished the notion of merit or recognizing extraordinary contribution. Souders explained that, in a smaller company, there are times when people are pushed to give far more than what had been expected going into the next year. An important project with a pressing deadline may require months of extra-long days and weekend work. A person may cover two jobs for an extended period because someone's out on medical leave. Each year, the key managers of the company meet and reflect to see if an unusual situation justifies extra compensation. The differential is paid in the form of a lump sum, usually several thousand dollars. The lump-sum bonus typically is given to only one or two people each year. The differential bonus is given without fanfare or announcement because it is not intended as formal recognition or a motivator. Souders explained, "It's just our way of trying to be fair with people who have made an extraordinary contribution." Since the special contribution is for work done in the year prior, no salary increase is attached to the bonus.

Sales people are also paid on a salary and market rate basis. When the company dropped commissions, seven sales people, previously paid on commission, were offered a salary equal to 5% more than their best year, inclusive of commissions and all earnings. Chasing the rainbow, three sales people declined to stay when incentives were canceled. Reportedly, all three then earned less money, and one has since come back. An anonymous survey, taken four years later, asked sales people if they would like to go back to a commission basis. The answer: a unanimous no. The sales people commented in their survey that the salary approach was instrumental in maintaining a team-oriented, customer-driven atmosphere.

Tom Shewchuk, Vice President of Technical Services, directly supervises twenty-five people who provide technical support to clients of the Company. His primary job, he says, is to provide support to the technicians to enable them to do their jobs. He manages to meet with all twenty-five employees at least once a week. At each meeting, he works from an agenda of his four goals as leader, asking various questions that elicit the information needed:

Leadership Goal 1: *Ensure maximum productivity of the Support Team.* Do you understand your current job responsibilities and how they are evolving?

Leadership Goal 2: *Ensure the Personal Development of the Support Team.* Are you getting the personal training you planned for and need right now?

Leadership Goal 3: *Ensure that Support Team members understand what their job responsibilities are.* Do you have enough work to do? Do you have a good sense of what is the priority right now?

Leadership Goal 4: *Ensure employees are as happy as they could possibly be while at work.* Is everything okay? Are you happy in your job? Are you stressed? Are you having any problems here at work that we need to solve?

Shewchuk further clarified his leadership role, "I'm not a baby-sitter. It's all based on trust. They have no time clock. They do their jobs. When performance issues arise, I investigate—more than 90% of the time I can link it to a problem of the system." Regarding the annual development meeting with his employees, Shewchuk does not see it as a performance feedback session. "They get feedback everyday from me and the customers," Shewchuk explained, "The annual meeting is about personal development. We just try to have a good conversation about what they want from their jobs, where they would like to go with their job, and what training they think they need." Shewchuk noted that development is *the employee's* responsibility, both at the annual meeting and throughout the year. "I make suggestions sometimes, but usually we're already on the same wavelength," Shewchuk added. By the end of the meeting, a training plan for the following year is decided.

What is the effect of this culture shift? Since 1991, Entré has increased its sales by nearly ten times and has earned a much better margin on every dollar—in fact, the company ranks in the top 10% for profitability in comparison to other companies in the same industry. In 1998, Entré built a beautiful, state-of the-art building with facilities that emphasize team and collaboration. Only two people have private offices. Everyone else has open cubicles. Even Souders works in an open-space cubicle like everyone else. Turnover has remained consistently low, even though the computer field endured a highly competitive job market throughout the 1990s. Nine years after transition, the company still requires all new hires to undergo extensive training on systems theory, customer focus, and the underlying philosophy that drove the company away from appraisal and incentives.

■ A Little Advice About Changing Pay Practices

If you are looking to change your pay practices in conjunction with abolishing appraisal or otherwise, here are two points of preliminary advice.

Start with education. If your organization currently has some form of merit pay, or at least what is called "merit pay" or "pay-for-performance," it's absolutely essential that you start with *education*. As we already discussed, people have all sorts of illusions about their own performance, the performance of others, and the employer's ability to measure performance. Using the model we describe in Chapter 9, start the education process with a work team. Help them understand how the system drives performance, how appraisals are unreliable in evaluating performance, and what we really know about money, motivation, and de-motivation. These ideas truly come from another world—they will sound like a foreign language to the work team. The ideas must be worked through based on experience, logic, and what we know from the research. Many people will need time with the issue before it is truly internalized. To fully understand how difficult it is to internalize this kind of learning, see "Boo in the Zoo," a personal account from one of your authors.

Once the work team has a firm grasp of the pay and motivation issues, *develop a plan to educate upper management.* It's absolutely imperative that all key executives of your organization fully understand and support any new compensation direction. Without this commitment, you may doom yourself to fail in the most frustrating and bitter way. Education for the rest of the organization is also a must. If you fail to take time to educate and engage in the practices derived from what is called "change theory," we can almost assure you that the transition will be a total fiasco. If you are dropping merit pay or going to a new model of merit pay, and people do not fully understand what is going on, suspicion and rumors will undercut your initiative. People associate pay practices with measures to save money by lowering people's compensation. This knee-jerk paranoia comes from past salary and benefit initiatives in many organizations that indeed were detrimental to employees.

Boo in the Zoo

As discussed earlier in the case study of GM–Powertrain, in 1986, I (M.J.) was assigned to work with Dr. Deming in transforming our H.R. practices. Early on, Dr. Deming encouraged us to think about underlying assumptions, why we did this, and why we did that. He tried to help us understand that people are intrinsically motivated and that the carrot of merit pay was *overjustification*. He got us to think about the harmful, unintended effects of competition, merit systems, and recognition awards. I listened and did the mental work, but in many ways, I didn't really get it—this was entirely new thinking for me.

A year later, I was still struggling. I couldn't see what was wrong with rewards or why recognition would really bring harmful effects. Like many people in American society, I was conditioned to believe that rewards and awards were positive instruments. After all, I had been the beneficiary of these systems in the past—they must be right!

Then on a beautiful fall day just before Halloween, I took my daughter, Katie, then age 5, to the local Potter Park Zoo. Unbeknown to me, the Zoo was holding a Halloween event for kids called the Boo in the Zoo. As we approached the zoo grounds, we saw a large circle of people gathered. We walked over and saw about 30 preschool children parading around in Halloween costumes. They were being judged for the "best costume." Nearly every costume was adorable—no one was better than another. They were funny, original, imaginative, and beautiful, and many were homemade. All of the children walked around wearing a beaming smile from ear to ear—it was evident that they were quite proud of their little outfits.

Then a man said it was time to announce the winners. Parents and children held their breath fixating on the announcer's lips, "…and third place goes to Jamie Anderson, second place to Aaron Jones, and first place to Maggie Muldoon." Polite applause followed each announcement, but after the last winner was called, I looked around and saw the disheartened faces in the circle of 3-, 4-, and 5-year-olds. They were all losers, though we are taught not to say or think that. They came proud and excited about their costume, but now, somehow it was judged and it became nothing. I further noted the winning selections appeared arbitrary, and I would not have made the same choices. Some kids cried, and I saw probably seventeen parents trying to comfort their kids, telling them they looked great and all the reasons they should not feel bad as a loser.

As I took all this in, it finally hit me. My year-long struggle with Dr. Deming's ideas suddenly vanished in observing this one painful event. In the flash of that moment, I could see precisely what Dr. Deming was talking about in terms of unintended effects. Making some people winners always makes other people losers. Dr. Deming did not feel all competition, such as competition between businesses, was wrong. But I think he was saying that much of it is not necessary, including the unnecessary competition we create within organizations for pay increases, bonuses, and employee awards.

A Quasi-Merit System Without Appraisal

Michigan State University, highlighted as a case study in Chapter 8, maintains a system with merit pay principles, even though it has discarded performance ratings for its clerical, technical, administrative, professional, and supervisory employees. Having moved away from a purely traditional merit pay and appraisal plan, the university grants special adjustments on a limited, case-by-case basis. Each year, employees receive a general (cost-of-living) increase. In addition, employees are given progression increases based on time in the job. Special merit pay adjustments are available in exceptional situations. The process for implementing these special adjustments is simple and straightforward. The supervisor writes a memo to the H.R. department, describing the employee's accomplishments and the reasons a special increase is warranted. The process also provides a means of informally dealing with labor-market pressures. If the software engineer market heats up and people are being tantalized with external offers, the department can expeditiously get adjustments by documenting the situation in a memo.

Certainly an unstructured process of this type could be subject to political bias, EEO issues, and abuse. Lauren Marinez, Assistant Director of Human Resources, however, says several practices curtail the likelihood of these kinds of problems. Unlike the private sector, all pay decisions are open and subject to review by unions, colleagues, and regulatory agencies, both inside and outside of the university. The H.R. department also works hard at continually training supervisors and bringing them together from different departments to deal with H.R. practices, improvement, EEO, and diversity. Departments are inclined to be very conservative in awarding special increases because all pay adjustments must come out of the budget of the department requesting the raise.

Special adjustments, based on merit, market factors, or a combination, are granted to about 5% of employees per year (270 of 5,275 in the most recent year). This reasonably low percentage of special adjustments, it would appear, demonstrates that supervisors are exercising restraint in the special discretion granted their department.

Some might say that this open, write-a-memo approach could result in highly arbitrary and subjective pay decisions. While this is true, there is no reason to believe that the abuse would be less common than that found with appraisal-driven merit systems. To its credit, this system does not make pretense of objectivity with boxes, numbers, and criteria (that so often are tainted with bias and politics anyway). The majority of employees are represented by unions that take their roles seriously, and there has been no indication from them that the system is creating widespread inequities or problems. Moreover, the university maintains a very accessible, completely independent, internal EEO office that accepts complaints and investigates inequitable practices. Since dropping appraisal, however, it has not experienced any noticeable rise in complaints concerning pay issues, and the H.R. department spends a lot less time refereeing disputed appraisals.

■ What to Do Instead–Motivation

Having addressed de-motivation and getting pay out of the way, a remaining function of appraisal still needs to be addressed, i.e, without appraisal—*How can we foster a highly motivated workforce?* Start by keeping in mind McGregor's advice that "you don't" motivate people. Motivation is the desire someone has to do something, and no one can create that desire in another human being. Though you can't really motivate another human being, organizations *can do* a great deal to foster conditions that bring out the best opportunities for people to be motivated. In a nutshell, motivation is fostered through one overall strategy: *Enable employees to find meaning in their work.* This goal may sound idealistic and difficult to apply, but because people are drawn to finding meaning, many doors are open to any employer who takes time to think this through.

The best way to find these doors is to first understand that *meaning* is the driving force for all human motivation. We cannot create meaning for a person. What is meaningful for one person versus another varies as much as our fingerprints. In Figure 6.4, we offer a model of motivation that we have loosely drawn from the work of Maslow, McGregor, Carl Jung, Viktor Frankl, and others. It reflects the healthier assumptions and principles discussed throughout this book. Figure 6.4 operates from the premise that *meaning* is the only true intrinsic motivator. When people find meaning, the result is *joy*. While people are naturally drawn toward meaning, the absence of certain *conditions* (column one in Figure 6.4) will preclude people from finding meaning and thereby undermine motivation.

Recognizing the power of *meaning* as a motivator, we present a sequence of three approaches to developing a highly motivated workforce: create a compelling vision, promote and provide interesting work, and create a climate of teamwork.

Create a Compelling Vision

All human beings possess an innate drive to learn, to serve, to contribute, and to connect to a purpose larger than themselves. Accordingly, foster a *compelling* vision that enables people to understand why they are there, what the organization is trying to do, and where it is headed.

To find meaning, people need to connect to the *service* or *product* of

NECESSARY CONDITIONS FOR SELF-MOTIVATION	THE SOURCE OF SELF-MOTIVATION	OUTCOME OF FULFILLED MOTIVATION
Individual Emotional and Mental Health	calling service purpose connectedness	
Safety and Trust	interesting work working with others	
Dignity and Self-Esteem	**MEANING** challenge excelling	**JOY**
Autonomy and Freedom	creating learning beauty	
Perspective	love	

Figure 6.4 Human Motivation

the organization, not the financial statement, though certainly that is important. Companies such as Saturn and Southwest Airlines have garnered remarkable success by fostering cultures with a clear sense of purpose, a distinguishable mission, and defined values. "A different kind of car company" was a great deal more than clever advertising—it has been an intense experiment to get an entire workforce to think from a different set of perspectives and values. At Disney World, the common purpose is: "To help make every person's experience at Disney World the happiest day of their life."[9] A compelling vision also means that people understand how their work connects to the organization as a whole. *Any employee*—the custodian, the parking gate attendant, the accounts receivable clerk, or the forklift truck driver—should be capable of taking someone on a walking tour of the business and be able to generally tell how each unit contributes to the ultimate product or service. This requires an investment in *people*. Newly hired Saturn workers go through six weeks of training so that they understand the business and the culture before they ever touch an automobile. Disney theme park summer workers, hired for just eleven weeks, go through two weeks of training, in large part to ensure they understand what Disney is all about.

There are other creative options for fostering meaning. For example, Cadillac, after its shock from the growth of luxury imports during the 1980s, took some most unusual measures to help production workers connect to their product. According to John Grettenberger, Cadillac's chief executive at that time, the Hamtramck (Detroit) plant provided phone lines for production workers to call new owners and ask how they were enjoying their new Cadillac. Engineers were encouraged to take time to regularly talk to service writers (the people who write up the repair-work covered by warranty or other work) at the Cadillac dealerships. Nearly every organization we have encountered that has made a successful transition away from appraisal has worked at and invested in these kinds of strategies, enabling people to connect their work and an overriding purpose and vision.

Promote and Provide Interesting Work

People will be energized and motivated if they are doing work that feels worthwhile and is interesting to them. As Herzberg has said, "If you want people to do a good job, give them a good job to do."[10] Everyone's interests are different. Two strategies are powerful forces in helping people find interesting work:

- *Give people freedom and choices in their work.* All managers need to understand the power of giving people *trust* and *freedom* in doing their work. This means finding ways to be more fluid and less structured, allowing people, as much as possible, to choose work that aligns with their individual interests and strengths. Part of this shift is establishing practices and writing policies that give the employee the right to independently exercise discretion and judgment. For example, FedEx Corporation has a written policy that gives authority to every employee to do whatever is necessary to handle a customer service problem. The trends toward flex-time and self-managed teams, as at Saturn, Johnsonville Sausage, and G.E., further illustrate ways of giving people choices and space in their work.

- *Offer people challenges.* Many people yearn for and thrive on having *challenge* in their work. Dr. Mihaly Csikszentmihalyi's research finds that most of us seek *challenge* and an opportunity to use our skills.[11] Challenge can be provided by offering people more responsibility and the opportunity to learn new skills and grow in other ways. This does not necessarily come from career advancement opportunities—the greatest opportunities are in the day-to-day work—again, fluid approaches to jobs will enable this to happen. Providing new challenges is not a quick fix for everyone, however. Some people are content to do a good job without novel challenges, just knowing they contribute to a worthwhile service or product. Others may be at a particular point in their career or personal life where new challenges are not desired, even though they are happy to give you good performance every day. These differences in individual outlook obviously point to the need for employees to be self-reflective and choose what works best for them.

Involving people more in decisions also provides interesting work and motivation. A Gallup poll commissioned by the American Society of Quality a few years ago asked a large sample of American workers to name the best way to motivate people to increase quality and productivity. The results:

- 33% *"Let me do more to put my ideas into action."*
- 17% *"Listen to my ideas for improvement."*
- 27% *"Pay me more."*
- 19% *"Give me more recognition."*
- 4% *Did not respond.*

Despite the continued hype our culture puts on money and recognition, more people said they would be motivated *if their ideas were heard* and they had *opportunities to apply them.*[12]

Create a Climate of People Working Together

In so many ways, conventional organizations emphasize *the individual*—individual goals and appraisals are examples of this. Instead, foster ways for people to work *together,* to *share meaning,* and *connect* with one another. If you are moving away from appraisal, there's no better time to promote collaboration and working in teams. This "connected" environment is not achieved through team-building alone but requires a fundamental shift in management, the way assignments are made, and how accountability is emphasized.

To some, these initiatives toward meaning, interesting work, and collaborative teams may feel like lofty and unrealistic ideals. But, at an increasing rate, these kinds of initiatives are taking hold and radically transforming work, with great business results to boot. Pick up any issue of *Fast Company* magazine, and you will find wonderful, detailed examples of this revolution. Go to the management section of your local bookstore or to any progressive management conference and you will find innumerable, firsthand accounts. The world is fundamentally re-inventing the work, finding new patterns and ways to enable people to connect meaning and spirit in their work. As this connection is strengthened, people find *joy* in their work. And motivation abounds.

Conclusion

As we said at the start, the dynamics of people, money, and motivation are too complex to fully understand. However, if your organization takes time to clarify what it is trying to achieve *and* builds from healthy underlying assumptions, it can create more effective compensation practices and a positive work environment. In the next chapter, we look at issues closely tied to pay—promotions and career advancement.

Review of Chapter Assumptions

Conventional Assumption

> **People will withhold their best efforts if they are not extrinsically rewarded, i.e., money motivates better performance.**

Alternative Assumptions

- Healthy people are intrinsically motivated to perform well when the work is meaningful.

- Pay is not a motivator but can be a powerful de-motivator when it is inequitable.

- Intrinsic motivation may be diminished or impaired by a number of factors including fear, excessive control, distrust, and encouraging focus on extrinsic motivators.

Conventional Assumptions

Pay is not fair unless it is linked to performance level (i.e., better performers of a job expect to be paid better than poorer performers in the same job).

People want to be paid based on their individual contribution.

Alternative Assumptions

- The vast majority of people see themselves as superior performers.

- Most people are not superior performers, but this is very difficult for them to see.

- People who contribute more expect to be paid more.

- Without education, people do not understand or appreciate the problems associated with measuring individual performance, people's tendency to inflate the value of their own performance, and other dynamics impacting attempts to connect pay to individual contribution.

7

Staffing, Promotions, and Development

There is no need to institutionalize the process of helping people with their future. The way to decrease someone's dependency on us is to keep clear that their future is in their hands.

Peter Block, *Stewardship*

Employees need to take personal responsibility for their own career development.

Paul Squires and Seymour Adler, *Performance Appraisal*

Like compensation, career advancement is a sensitive issue. Depending on the individual and how things turn out, it may be a motivating factor or a de-motivating factor. When people talk about a *good* employer, one of the first things they often mention is opportunities for promotion—they say the selection process is open and fair, or proudly exclaim, "Our company promotes from within." On the other hand, perceived unfairness in advancement drastically impairs loyalty, commitment, and motivation. To keep employees happy, and to comply with civil rights laws, employers increasingly are relying on "objective" processes and tools for promotion and career advancement. A good many organizations, in varying degrees, rely on appraisals to screen and select applicants because of its objective appearance.

In this chapter, we examine the role of appraisal in

187

decisions of promotion and career advancement. Does appraisal contribute to objective and fair promotion processes? Is it even possible to have an *objective* promotion process? In answering these questions, we focus on the great disparity between the officially recognized promotion process and what really happens. We also separately discuss employee development and career track advancements as well as the application of appraisals in *deselection,* i.e., in layoff, RIF, and job abolishment. Using new assumptions, examples, and case studies, we illuminate alternative ways to deal with promotions and career advancement *without* appraisal.

■ Creating a Common Language

The terminology for internal promotions, career advancement, and staffing issues can be confusing. To be sure we are on a common wavelength, let us designate and clarify our terms.

Promotion or Selection Process. We use these terms to refer to *competitive* promotions in which the person seeking the promotion ordinarily competes against one or more persons, whether all internal or involving external candidates.

Career Track Advancement. By *career track advancement,* we mean employees moving to a higher level job on a predetermined pattern or schedule to the next pay grade level. Normally, movement is contingent upon the attainment of specified proficiencies, competencies, experience, maturity, skills, knowledge, or abilities. These requirements for advancing are evidenced in a variety of ways including one or more of the following: time in job, experience, documented learning, additional education, completion of training, assessment tools and processes, and/or attainment of license or professional certification. Typically, these promotions are noncompetitive. With the possible exception of budget constraints, people are allowed to advance to the next job or pay level as soon as they meet the specified criteria. Sometimes these advancements are referred to by other names, such as career ladder, career path, or job progression. For example, career track advancement for engineers in a company might have four levels: Engineer Trainee, Engineer I, Engineer II, and finally Senior Engineer.

Career Planning and Career Management. These terms are often confused or used interchangeably. To be technically correct, the former applies to individuals, the latter the organization. Hence, *career planning* is "the process through which individual employees identify and implement steps to attain career goals" while *career management* is "the process through which organizations select, assess, assign, and develop employees to provide a pool of qualified people to meet future needs."[1] Yet another term, *career development*, applies to both.

Layoff, RIF, and Job Abolishment. These terms also are confused and erroneously used interchangeably. A *layoff* is an intended temporary suspension of employment based on economic constraints (or other causes unrelated to individual performance, such as reconstruction of a factory or seasonal weather patterns). In a layoff, it is expected, but not assured, that the laid-off person will be called back upon improvement of financial conditions or other change. *RIF* is an acronym for *reduction in force*, a downsizing, or "right" sizing methodology. In a RIF, the organization terminates people in designated positions, with relatively permanent intention, in order to reduce its total level of employment to meet financial or efficiency objectives. *Job abolishments* may be triggered by financial, strategic, technological, or restructuring objectives, but they are not necessarily linked to a reduction in total employee numbers. For example, a job may become obsolete and be replaced by a different kind of job. For instance, a bank may abolish teller jobs but at the same time create jobs to maintain ATMs.

■ The Myth of the OBJECTIVE Selection

Assumption

Promotions should be based on an objective, not subjective, decision process.

Employers have come to realize that the perception of unfair promotion decisions can drive people away and, in a single flash, decimate commitment and motivation. Along with increasing realization of this phenomenon, the expansion of equal opportunity (EEO) laws has accelerated the trend toward ostensibly objective promotion processes. Although employers rely on various selection structures and processes to promote *objectivity*, there is a chasm between the stated selection process and the reality of what happens. Our discussion does not necessarily insinuate bad faith—the departure from the prescribed processes can be done purely in the interest of choosing the best-qualified candidate. What we are saying is that, with rare exceptions, the formally decreed selection process is not totally objective nor does it depict what really happens.

Increasingly, formal selection processes go to great lengths to ensure that *objective* criteria are followed. Selection criteria, minimal and desired qualifications, requisite experience, and the like are often stated with detailed precision. To safeguard equal treatment of all candidates, the entire process is highly structured, with defined activities and a set sequence for each screening and selection step. The process sometimes defines the "objective" evidence upon which the selection will be based. Taken together, these elaborate processes create the guise of an entirely *objective* process. For whatever reasons, we pretend that the process is structured so that subjective judgments will not be necessary—officially we say the facts are facts, and we merely objectively apply criteria to select the best candidate. We do not know the origin of this pretense, but it seems to run deeper than a defensive reaction to EEO laws.

Part of the perception issue arises from confusion over the word *objective*. As many people assume, *objective* is not interchangeable with *fair*. In relevant part, the dictionary says *objective* means:

> (N)ot influenced by personal feelings, interpretations, and prejudice; based on the facts, unbiased; . . . dealing with things external to the mind rather than with thoughts or feelings.[2]

Conversely, *subjective* is the opposite of objective, referring to what exists in one's mind rather than the external. In light of these definitions, it's inconceivable that selection decisions could be made without some subjective influence and interpretation. For every job, legitimate intangibles need to be considered in making a good selection decision. Sometimes we call this "fit." Sometimes it's a characteristic that cannot be easily described in a posting or qualifications statement, but it nonetheless exists. A receptionist job posting requires excellent oral communication skills. Yet it says nothing about an upbeat personality that makes people feel welcome when they arrive at the company. Defining a desired personality might be difficult or perhaps such a criterion would run afoul of EEO guidelines, but we have little doubt that verification of this quality would be a primary objective in interviewing receptionist candidates, consciously or unconsciously. *Fit* also may be about the needs of a work unit. A work unit may be fractured by chemistry rifts, so a manager may make it a priority to hire someone for "the team" who is strong in interpersonal skills and connects with people in a way that brings out the best in them. In determining *fit* or special characteristics, there is no escape from making *interpretations* or relying on *personal thoughts* and *feelings*, i.e., subjective judgment. In this computer age, if we could rely solely on objective criteria, we could feed in the data and let the computer choose the next senior vice president! But this isn't the case. All critical business decisions, including selection, are about judgment and intuition as much as they are about objective facts.

In light of these realities, selection and promotion decisions are neither objective or subjective—they are *both*. A claims manager hiring an insurance adjuster knows that a qualified applicant must have excellent verbal and written skills, computational skills, knowledge of tort law, the legal system, and insurance practices and terminology. But a good candidate also must have the difficult-to-discern psychological propensities and abilities, such as an inclination to be resourceful, an ability to instinctively sense what is happening (when fraud may be involved), and the knack of making good judgments with little guidance and structure. If you had a pool of candidates without adjusting experience, it would require considerable art and intuition to figure out who best demonstrated these kinds of attributes.

Consider how much more difficult it gets in choosing a person for a management position. Assume you were choosing a plant manager for a location with a unique history, work environment, and an unusual set of immediate challenges. Though the company has standard qualifications for plant managers in a job description with enumerated specifications, the search can only be successful if the company finds a candidate who is *a good fit* for the required situation. It would be difficult to articulate with precision the unique qualifications for the ideal candidate—in fact, often that is unknowable. Moreover, each candidate comes with his or her own set of strengths and weaknesses. To arrive at what is believed to be the best choice, each candidate must be viewed from multiple perspectives, with reflection and thought, weighing the pluses and minuses. This is largely subjective judgment.

Consequently, the selection process for promotions, *in reality*, is almost never constricted to the structured criteria and the formal steps. The official process professes to be "objective" and neutral in the form of applications, resumes, preferred or required degrees, academic transcripts, reference letters, formal reference checks, screening committee recommendations, and, often times, the candidate's purportedly objective past appraisals. While certainly these indicators can be helpful, managers deciding promotions have limited faith in the official selection system. This causes them to go outside the system because they do not trust it to deliver reliable information about *fatal* weaknesses (not a team player, afraid to make difficult decisions) or more subjective qualities (managerial style, drive, thinking ability, people skills). Selecting managers invariably resort to informal reference checks, whether or not such is permitted by policy. They *always* know someone who has the inside scoop, additional insights, and, more importantly, information that the manager trusts. Moreover, for good or bad, decision making about promotions is also driven by emotional factors. Leadership expert Paul Wieand has observed that, "emotion—more than intellectual ability—drives our thinking, our decision making, and our interactions with others."[3] Perhaps for this reason and the desire to get the good information they need, managers making promotion decisions take it on themselves to enrich the formal "objective" process by going out and getting other information.

What is happening in this unofficial part of the selection process is no different than what we do in our personal lives. When we need a child care provider, a doctor, or a contractor to remodel our home, what do we do? We do not rely on promotion materials, a resume, or the licensing bureau report—we call trusted friends, ask for references, and try to talk to others who will give us candid, first hand information on the more subtle and important issues.

A selection process may be structured and designed to promote *fairness, consistency,* and equal access to relevant *information,* but it cannot eliminate the use of subjective criteria and judgments or reliance on informal processes and resources. Saying in our selection policy that only objective criteria are "discussable" will nurture the development of informal, under-the-table systems. Moreover, such practice could lead employees to think that being promoted is a matter of working hard and keeping their noses clean (no negative remarks in the official personnel record), and then they will be acknowledged and plucked from the system (known at GM as the "Chevy Angel Theory"). With some sense of what really happens in determining promotions, let us examine the typical role of performance appraisal in the "objective" side of the process.

■ The Drawbacks of Appraisals in Selection Decisions

In the search for objectivity in promotions and career advancement, many organizations have turned to appraisal. After all, it's a written record of performance with the definitive criteria, numeric scales, and other bells and whistles—it creates a powerful illusion of objectivity. Many organizations prohibit people with unsatisfactory ratings from even bidding on promotions. Some require a minimum appraisal score for eligibility. Others use appraisals as a formal screening tool for promotion applicants (for example, having a committee review appraisals and other credentials to select a pool of most-qualified candidates). This practice is common in government agencies under civil service rules. In other organizations, there is no *formal* practice or custom of relying on appraisals in the process, but they are nonetheless referenced by screeners and selectors. Internal applicants commonly use past appraisals as evidence of their qualifications in the same way that external candidates use letters of reference.

In sum, we can say that appraisals, formally and informally, are used to weed out the patently unqualified, to choose a pool of preliminary candidates, or to advance the final candidates. However, we have not found any organization that awards *competitive* promotions solely upon performance appraisal outcomes.

In theory, appraisals are relied upon in the selection process to illuminate weaknesses and strengths so best performers can be chosen. We learned in Chapter 3 about the inescapable bias, filters, rating errors, and flaws that engender distortions, inconsistencies, and invalid appraisal outcomes. We also learned that when appraisal is tied to personnel decisions, such as promotion, political maneuvering and distortion by managers and employees alike abound. Hence, if we want to make promotion decisions based on good information, appraisal is not a reliable tool.

Even if we assume that appraisals provide completely accurate information, they often would not be a good selection tool for competitive promotions. But we assume this is the case, making the following assumption:

Assumption

Performing well in one job predicts success in performing well in another job.

Certainly, in some situations, this assumption holds true. In other situations, success in a related job may be relevant, but by itself is not a good predictor. In other situations, it is hardly relevant at all. So often, with little thought, we promote the best performer to supervisor even though the person's people and leadership skills are untested, unknown, or sorely lacking. As organizations have come to realize in recent decades, it is not a *natural* leap to move from technical proficiency to being a good supervisor, planner, or leader. Moreover, the higher one goes up the ladder, the less important is hands-on, technical expertise.

As awareness of this disparity has increased, more organizations are adopting "dual tracks" to allow those without managerial skills to be promoted to jobs that do not require supervision and formal leadership. We are not suggesting that performance in a prior job is irrelevant—in the overwhelming majority of cases, prior performance in a different job has *some* predictive value of success in another job (for example, to ascertain reliability, social skills, analytical skills, or other general qualities), but *overall* performance in the prior job often is not a reliable predictive tool. For example, an auto mechanic gets an overall poor evaluation because he can't handle more difficult repairs. However, he has good communication and people skills and consequently is better qualified than superior mechanics for a service writer position because his mechanical expertise is less important in that job, while his people and communication skills are critical for success.

■ The Impact of EEO Laws

Assumption

Using appraisal as a screening tool makes it more difficult for EEO agencies and advocates to challenge a promotion process.

The increased emphasis on more objective selection processes no doubt stems at least in part from the proliferation of equal employment opportunity (EEO) laws in the United States, Canada, Western Europe, and elsewhere, extending protection against discrimination based on gender, race, age, disability, and other grounds. In the U.S., investigations by the Equal Employment Opportunity Commission and affiliated state agencies have resulted in class action lawsuits and multimillion dollar judgments. More than ever, employers attempt to document and validate their selection processes to reduce liability exposure. The law is particularly tough because it does not require any evidence of an *intent* to discriminate. For example, if an employer's pattern of promotions shows that women or African-Americans are significantly less likely to be promoted, the employer must prove that its selection methods are valid and reliable.

Consequently, employers are aggressively attempting to incorporate selection tools and methods that are objective, fair, and likely to be free from bias. Appraisal is alluring in this regard. For example, we may think of screening interviews as subjective and affected by the biases of the interviewers. By contrast, we somehow treat appraisal records as though they were more objective—because they are written documents and purportedly reflect work records, performance, and accomplishments. The precise ratings and supporting rationale makes them look like a truly objective resource. Because of this, for decades in the public sector and now in the private sector, appraisal is used as an official screening tool for competitive promotion, either at the eligibility stage, screening the initial pool, or choosing final candidates.

Despite good intentions by organizations using appraisal as a screening tool for promotions, it does not create any unique advantages versus other selection methods. First, notwithstanding its objective criteria and formal ratings, appraisal is subjective and reflective of bias and rating errors. In EEO litigation, these biases and rating errors are commonly uncovered (more on this in the next chapter). Second, under federal EEO laws in the U.S., an employer must demonstrate reliability and validity if it uses appraisal as a test or criterion for promotion selections and other staffing decisions.[4] The EEOC's tests for proving validity and reliability are rigorous and complicated. Because of the subjective nature of appraisal, it is often difficult for an employer to meet its burden of proving that it is a reliable and valid instrument. An inherent problem with appraisal is that it is an assessment of a promotion candidate's *current* or *prior* job performance, and as already discussed, it may have little predictive or content validity relative to qualification for the promotion position.

In addition to legal issues relating to validity, appraisals are problematic for employers because sometimes they leave evidence of taint and bias. For example, Ann Hopkins, a CPA, was denied promotion to partner with the Price Waterhouse accounting firm. From various written evaluations of her performance prepared by her colleagues, she was able to prove that her denial was based on sexual stereotyping of her performance and behaviors. By using multiple raters, the accounting firm had intended a fair decision, but ratings were nonetheless biased and, worse yet, they provided the concrete evidence Hopkins needed to get a favorable ruling from the U.S. Supreme Court.[5]

With or without appraisal, defending EEO charges and lawsuits in selection cases is an onerous burden. Any alternative means of selection, of course, would be subject to the same scrutiny and potential liability. Our point is that appraisal is not a particularly reliable tool for bolstering the objectivity of promotion screening and decision making. Despite its appearance, it is *not* objective information and it offers no particular advantage for the employer in defending EEO claims versus other alternative approaches we discuss later in this chapter.

■ Promotions Without Appraisal

Within the space of one chapter, we cannot apprise you of the unlimited options an organization has in making promotion decisions without appraisal. In parting from appraisal, begin with the confidence that the lion's share of employers, particularly in the private sector, do not formally require or rely on appraisal for screening and selection. We have encountered many employers that disconnected appraisal from the promotion process because of bad experiences or realizing its weaknesses as a predictive tool. (For example, in organizations that rely on appraisal for promotions, it is not uncommon for supervisors to avoid the hassle of a documented discharge by giving glowing appraisals to "bad apples" to enable their transfer or promotion to someone else's department!)

In designing an alternative approach, start by going back to the basic question—*What are the competencies required to do the job?* From this you can develop clearly defined job requirements and determine the most appropriate selection devices. To promote fairness and reduce legal exposure, be prepared to demonstrate that your screening and selection methods and criteria are valid and reliable. The U.S. Equal Employment Opportunity Commission has issued formal guidance on selection criteria in a publication called the *Uniform Guidelines on Employee Selection*.[6] Essentially, the guidelines draw from validity and reliability principles commonly accepted by psychologists. Employers subject to U.S. civil rights laws should validate their criteria under these guidelines, and, if over time, a particular selection method will be applied to a large number of promotions, seek assistance from an industrial psychologist and attorney familiar with EEO requirements. Any tests or criteria used in the selection, such as standardized tests, psychological profiles, and even minimum education or experience requirements, should be studied for validity, reliability, and to ensure there is no adverse impact against protected classes. A large Alaskan cannery ended up in a prolonged legal battle, with years of litigation and appeals all the way to the U.S. Supreme Court, because it utilized promotion criteria and channels that put production workers at a disadvantage (versus white-collar workers) in seeking administrative and managerial promotions.[7]

Since appraisal is most popular in managerial, administrative, and professional jobs, we can suggest a few nonappraisal, widely accepted methods of making promotion decisions in these kinds of jobs. Consider a combination of some of the following possibilities: internal reference checks, assessment centers, prequalifying training, structured interviews, behavioral description interviews.

Internal Reference Check

With respect to internal promotion candidates, information can be readily acquired from various people within the organization, including present and former supervisors, co-workers, and subordinates, through formal and informal channels. Information is sought to verify demonstrated abilities and experiences, and, perhaps more importantly, ascertain whether the candidate is a good fit and the right person for the job with its particular demands and nuances.

Some would say, isn't the gathering up of such information really an evaluation or appraisal? And, if so, wouldn't it be easier if the organization routinely compiled such performance information so it would be readily

available for promotion decisions? Not really, even though there are simi-
larities (such as how the person performed in the prior job). An internal
reference check is different from appraisal in at least three significant respects:

1. An internal reference check evaluation is expressly tailored to get relevant information about a candidate's abilities and qualifications for
   the *particular* position applied for—it is not a general finding of how
   the person was performing in the prior job. The prior example of the
   mechanic seeking to be a service writer illustrates this point.

2. A reference check is a just-in-time evaluation, not one collected on
   the employee's anniversary ten months earlier.

3. A reference check is an interactive process during which the inter-
   viewer can clarify responses and pinpoint critical aspects and concerns about the candidate's qualifications and suitability for the open
   position.

As for the imagined convenience of having ready-to-review appraisals, it makes little sense to force everyone to undergo the stressful and
sometimes demoralizing effects of appraisal every year, just in case they
apply for a promotion. The ultimate product generated by appraisal would
also be grossly inferior to reference-check inquiries fashioned around specific job selection criteria.

Some may argue that promotion systems that rely on informal information do not fairly let people know where they stand, why promotions
are denied, or what they need to do to increase their chances of being promoted. It's further argued that appraisal would fill this information void.
The truth is, even with appraisals, people don't know where they stand,
possibly excepting those at the far ends of the spectrum. The often-
encountered, sharp dichotomy between the appraisal results and what is
said to reference callers demonstrates its lack of reliability. Moreover, it's
clear that appraisals linked to promotion advancement are much more
likely to be distorted than appraisals that are detached from personnel decisions.[8] The solution is not to continually try to figure out ways to force
raters to put it accurately on paper—myriad approaches have invariably
failed. Rather, the solution is to recognize the *true* dynamics of the promotion process and educate and acclimate *all employees* on how to access
informal and honest information—about their performance, where they
stand, and the like. The promotion process is just one more compelling
justification for urging people to become more skilled and savvy in going

out and getting the feedback they want and need—if they develop the skills, they can access this information for themselves on a timely basis.

Assessment Centers

In recent decades, larger companies in the United States, United Kingdom, Israel, and elsewhere have relied upon *assessment centers* to screen and help select internal candidates, and they are mostly used for people wishing to advance to supervisory or managerial jobs. The "center" is not a physical place but a compilation of coordinated assessment endeavors, during which an individual's qualifications and traits are assessed. Typically, assessment-center participants perform various simulated tasks (such as working through an in-basket, making a presentation, or counseling a poor-performing employee), alone or with others, while being observed by a team of assessors. A team of evaluators is used because the judgments required are highly subjective in nature, and multiple perspectives provide some check against individual bias. Assessment centers attempt to measure aptitude and ability of more abstract skills, such as intelligence, cognitive skills, the capability of making business judgments, the ability to work in teams, and communication and people skills in general. In varying degrees, assessment centers have been shown to be more successful than interviews and conventional tests in assessing fit and the traits that predict success in managerial jobs.[9] There is nothing magical about this method that makes it work better than conventional selection methods, but through trial and error and measuring predictive outcomes, it may prove to be a very helpful screening tool in moving people from the ranks to managerial jobs.[10] It also can be used as an assessment tool for training and development needs of managers and others.

Prequalifying Training

Often people are hired for a job and then trained to do it. In this model, however, a person trains *first*, and through successful completion of training, demonstrates her ability or aptitude to do the job. The completion of training is a minimal requirement for application or a factor that will be given substantial weight in evaluating candidates. For example, the Madison Police Department (see upcoming case study) has developed an internal promotion process that requires prequalifying training along with just-in-time internal reference checks.

Structured Interviews with Candidates

While candidates may exaggerate their qualifications, a good interview can reveal genuine insights about a person and efficiently identify other relevant information, much of which is verifiable. A *structured* interview, using concrete objectives and a standardized pattern of questions, can significantly increase the fairness of the process and help in defending a subsequent legal challenge. Surprisingly, interview at whim, or with few remnants of consistency, still seems to be the prevailing practice—one survey revealed that only 35% of 245 firms surveyed were using structured interviews.[11] Among organizations that deploy structured approaches, some only structure the *content* of the interview itself, drawing on questions specifically related to the analysis of the job. Other organizations, however, also structure the interview *evaluation*—using detailed notes, the same group of multiple interviewers for all candidates, and rating scales to promote objectivity.[12] Are these methods any less subjective than appraisals? Not really. As discussed, there's no way to avoid subjective judgments, especially in filling managerial jobs. What is different is that the subjective judgments are specifically tailored for the job applied for, rather than for the applicant's existing job or prior job.

Behavioral Description Interview

A structured approach of increasing popularity is the *behavioral description interview* (BDI), also known by many generic and commercial names. It differs from a popular approach known as the *situation interview* in which applicants are asked, "How would you handle this?" and similar questions that hypothetically attempt to ascertain how a person *might* perform a task in the applied-for job. Conversely, BDI attempts to glean how a candidate *has actually* handled situations similar to those required in the applied-for position in their *present or a prior* job. The method is loosely structured with concrete objectives and questions such as:

- *In your current or prior job, have you ever (specify task or situation)?*
- *What were the circumstances?*
- *How did you handle it?*
- *Why did you take that approach?*

The underlying idea of this approach is that it's more helpful to know what an applicant has done in contrast to hearing him talk about what he *would do*. For example, if the position applied for requires negotiation skills, the candidate would be asked to talk about an experience in which she had conducted negotiations under certain conditions—what she did, how she handled difficulties, the outcome, and so on. Probing questions help validate and provide deeper meaning from examples given by the candidate. Obviously, this method is also subjective and could be undermined by less-than-truthful responses. We have worked with and talked to many organizations that have found this method to be a very valuable selection tool. Consulting services and off-the-shelf products that facilitate BDI, such as the *Targeted Selection*® model, offered by the DDI Company in Pittsburgh, are available to H.R. professionals.

Finally, we would be remiss in talking about nonappraisal promotion systems if we did not underscore the importance of *educating* the people in your organization. We have talked about the critical *informal* aspects of the promotion process. The solution is not to drive those aspects away but to help everyone understand informal systems and their purpose. For example, to be responsible for their own careers, people must learn that 80–90% of job offers in the external job market arise from networking rather than postings or advertisements. Networking is a fact of organizational life. By teaching the skills of networking, building relationships, getting good and timely feedback, and other skills, employees can become powerful players in the real political system (including its favorable connotations) that drives corporate decisions, including promotions. Development of political skills, though essential, is not a substitute for growth and development in improving one's qualification, our next topic.

Case Study

Madison Police Department Promotion Process

Each year, the Madison Police Department (MPD) goes through a series of steps to decide who will be promoted to sergeant, lieutenant, and captain. Figure 7.1 details the nine steps of the process.

Before anyone is truly a candidate, he or she must first complete a two-week leadership course that teaches systems thinking, improvement tools, and basic supervisory skills (step 2). Mike Masterson, Captain of the MPD Personnel and Training Team, notes that this training aims to foster "an adult, results-oriented, learning environment where we can demonstrate teamwork and the cooperation we want in the department." The class issues no grades or scores but is satisfactorily completed with the participants' presentation of an improvement project that demonstrates the use of systems theory and process improvement tools. The project may be completed alone or with a team of other leadership school candidates. To the degree that the project demonstrates the use of learning tools (refer to details in the Chapter 4 MPD case study), it is approved by a panel of reviewers, consisting of superiors and those most affected by the proposed improvement. Completion of the project provides a tangible way for officers to demonstrate their leadership skills.

The remaining steps provide a highly interactive and supportive process in which candidates get the information they need to assess what happened with their candidacy. Note that the process requires that nonadvancing candidates get feedback on the assessment at the screening level (step 3) and after the Management Team has made its final recommendations to the Chief (steps 8 and 9). Moreover, the process requires that every candidate not advanced in the final rounds be assisted with a development plan to strengthen their qualifications for the following year's promotion cycle.

Another strength of the process is that it provides just-in-time fact gathering on candidates' credentials (step 5). Each commander, usually a captain, is responsible to do fact-finding interviews with co-workers, direct reports, and superiors for any candidate under his or her direction and then must organize and present the findings to the Management Team (step 6).

At every level, the process emphasizes openness, collaboration, and the sharing of information. No promotion model is perfect. Subjective judgments are unavoidable, and certainly such is a critical aspect of the MPD model. However, the MPD model in many ways demonstrates alignment with more realistic assumptions about the dynamics of promotion and people's need to have information about where they stand and what they need to do to better their opportunities in the future.

■ Appraisal and Employee Growth and Development

Assumption

The organization and supervisors are responsible for employees' development.

Among many faulty assumptions around employee development is the idea that an organization must take the lead and push people to ensure that they will do the right things to develop. We encounter a large number of organizations that are striving to be people friendly and espouse heartfelt values about creating a supportive environment and empowering people. Sometimes, however, these passions for a positive

Madison Police Department Promotion Process

Step 1 Officers interested in becoming a promotion candidate ask their supervisor to complete a form that certifies that the officer is presently performing at no less than at a satisfactory level.

Step 2 Candidates successfully complete a two-week leadership academy, leadership improvement project, and presentation of a chosen project (successful completion of the class preserves eligibility for five years).

Step 3 A review and screening panel is formed for each level of promotion (sergeant, lieutenant, captain). The panel of five people consists of:
- 1 from rank above position applied for
- 1 from rank below position applied for
- 1 at same level of position applied for
- 1 other at the same level or a level below the position applied for
- 1 community resident familiar with qualifications and community policing

Step 4 The panel is given applications, conducts interviews, and uses consensus to choose finalists—the number of finalists equals the number of anticipated openings at each level plus five. Any candidate not advanced is given feedback from the panel regarding its assessment to allow learning to occur.

Step 5 All Captains who serve as commanders for any finalist candidate conduct interviews of people who worked with that candidate to gather information on the candidate's exhibited abilities and skills relative to the predetermined qualities and characteristics required for the promotional position.

Step 6 The Management Team, consisting of all Captains, the Assistant Chief, and the Chief (with Union President sitting out due to conflict of interest), hears oral input on each candidate from that candidate's respective commanding officer with further input from other members of the Team. The discussion for each candidate is led by each candidate's respective commander.

Step 7 The Management Team uses "dialogue" to discuss the qualifications of candidates and uses consensus to decide on recommendations and input to be offered to the Chief.

Step 8 The Management Team chooses the candidates to be promoted, subject to approval by the Chief, who follows in excess of 90% of the recommendations as given.

Step 9 The respective commander of anyone NOT chosen is required to provide feedback to any nonselected candidate under their command and to work with that candidate to develop a six-month plan to strengthen that candidate's qualifications for the next round of promotions.

Figure 7.1   Madison Police Department Promotion Process

environment go too far or fall on faulty assumptions. In trying to "take care" of their people, organizations impose elaborate systems of mandated individual development plans, in which every employee and supervisor must sit down and write out short-term and long-term growth and development goals. At the same time, they must commit to documented action steps that include plans for training, external courses and workshops, and then refocus work assignments to meet experiential needs, among many other initiatives. Many organizations back up this initiative with a generous budget allocation for each employee's development. Standing alone, there is nothing wrong with development goals, action plans, and organizational support for individual growth—they are all useful and, at times, necessary. The problem is the wholesale implementation and *means* of triggering these actions.

By compelling development planning, the organization, and sometimes the supervisor, is taking responsibility for the employee's development. The strategy emerges from an unsurfaced assumption that *the organization* is responsible for people's growth and development. Though unintended, at some level the strategy is akin to a parent overseeing the best interests of the child. It denies people the power of choice and, at some psychological level, is disempowering.

H.R. professionals, however, earnestly tell us that they provide career planning and development programs to *empower* people, to help them, to enable them to make the career choices right for them. Though plainly this is the intent, designing *a compulsory* program to accomplish these goals rests on a number of attendant assumptions that are not contemplated or made explicit. An organization-wide mandatory career planning and development sends the following unintended messages:

- Employees are resistant to or derelict in managing their development and careers (*that's why it's compulsory*).

- Employees want someone else to manage or lead their development and careers for them (*this is why the supervisor is charged as a gatekeeper and initiator or co-initiator*).

- Employees do not know how to optimally manage their own development and careers (*this is why the organization defines the process for the employee*).

Under enlightened management, the first two assumptions are neither accurate nor healthy.

The third may be correct relative to the employee's *knowledge* of the development avenues and strategies, but is incorrect to the extent that it discounts every employee's inherent wisdom to choose his or her own right path. Only the employee can answer the question, "Who am I, and what is my life's work?"[13] By coercing employee development, we strip away employees' intrinsic motivation to care for themselves, to be a force in their own lives, and to take responsibility for their own well-being. Some employees readily exhibit this motivation—others must be given the space for this to emerge and grow. When organizations attempt to benevolently program employee development through forced growth initiatives and paper processing, it inevitably triggers apathy and resistance. Chris Turner's personal story provides a good perspective of how development programs sometimes are viewed outside the well-meaning H.R. department.

A key defect in most appraisal designs that call for employee development is that it automatically makes the supervisor into a mentor and career counselor. The supervisor often is not the right person to be a particular individual's mentor (and many advocates of mentoring suggest

---

Personal Story at Xerox

*Chris Turner, formerly of Xerox, shared this account of a mandated personal development process at Xerox in **Fast Company**.*

Xerox had a horrible process for promotion. Each year, everyone in the organization had to fill out reams of paperwork about what they wanted to be when they grew up. You had to list your one-year, three-year, and five-year goals. And you had to name specific positions that you were shooting for. Well, whose life ever unfolds according to a five-year plan—or even a one-year plan? That practice was absurd—but one that we all completed like mules.

Finally, I said, "I'm not going to do this any more. This process perpetuates the type of organization that I don't want to work for." So, for a few years, my boss, a good corporate soldier, filled out the paperwork for me. Other people soon caught on to the absurdity, and eventually everyone on my team quit doing it. Then I got a call from someone in HR who admitted that only 35% of all employees complied with the process. When that HR person asked me to start filling out the paperwork again, I told him that everyone knew that being promoted at Xerox had nothing to do with all that paper. To make a long story short, Xerox bagged the process.[14]

that people find mentors who are not in the role of supervisor). Effective career counseling also requires certain knowledge and skills, which often supervisors do not possess. Moreover, the supervisor has a conflict of interest in acting in the role of career counselor. Sometimes what is best for an outstanding employee is to get experience in another department or put in for a promotion. A supervisor acting as a counselor may, consciously or subconsciously, discourage this path because it will mean the loss of a high-contributing performer.

■ Alternative Approaches to Development and Growth

In advocating elimination of appraisal processes that impose one-size-fits-all development initiatives, we are not advocating the abandonment of organizational initiatives to support development. In fact, we *encourage* such initiatives for several reasons.

- Most people, at various levels of maturity and stages in their career, need access to analytical resources, vocational and career guidance, mentoring, feedback, financial backing, and other assistance in career planning and development to effectively grow to their potential or do what they really want to do.

- To remain competitive, retain good people, and for other reasons, large employers must maintain a career management plan, engage in succession planning and similar initiatives, with stated goals and well-planned strategies. These plans are particularly necessary in industries and occupational groups that are highly competitive, such as engineers, information systems professionals, and nurses. Organizations also need to ensure that people are being nurtured for leadership positions as they become available, which means helping individuals with career planning and providing the right mixes of experience and training.

- To appropriately budget and effectively plan for training and educational endeavors, an organization needs information about an individual's projected training and development activities and estimated costs in advance of the budget year.

To accomplish these tasks, systems and processes are necessary. However, these measures can be better accomplished outside of the multifunctional, do-everything appraisal. Career management and organizational initiatives will also work better if career planning is imposed involuntarily *only for compelling business reasons*. Every career development design should also, as much as possible, rely on personal choices—choices within the system if mandated, and if not, the choice to participate at all.

A 34-year-old employee may be happily situated and performing well, and, with two school-age children active in sports, may be more preoccupied with home life. Consequently, at this point in time, there is little interest in career planning or any sort of job change. Unless someone is holding a job facing technological threats or other risk of being eliminated, no one should be forced to sit down and write out career plans. (If that person has skill deficiencies and fails to seek feedback or recognize them, then co-workers and supervisors should take the initiative of providing feedback that pinpoints the problem.)

Conversely, a 20-year employee, who is facing burnout and is hungry for something new, should have support and structure available for development and transition. An employee should not have to wait until an anniversary date to initiate the first steps of making a change. The most ideal type of assistance would not be of the canned development variety offered in appraisal, but a trained career counselor, special assessment or developmental tools, or off-the-shelf programs tailored for someone looking to make a total career redirection. Better yet, an entire system or module of services could be designed and made available (to see an example, refer to the GM–Powertrain case study in Chapter 5).

In some professions, continuous skill development and verification is critical. A hospital, for example, must ensure that employees in medical professions are current and continuing to grow in emerging skills. Continuing education is necessary even for the certified nursing assistant, perhaps the lowest rung of medical positons. Dropping appraisal does not mean that skill inventories, verified in some way or another cannot continue, as the Memorial Hospital case study illustrates.

Case Study

Memorial Hospital—Fremont, Ohio

In 1995, Memorial Hospital abolished its performance appraisal and moved to a new model. As a healthcare provider, it needed to maintain a certain degree of evaluation mandated by federal rules and accreditation guidelines. One aspect of the new model requires each employee, on or about their birthday (and at additional times as *the employee* chooses), to hold a conversation with *any* department manager of the employee's choice (from the same department or any part of the hospital) about progress, achievement, communication, and education (P.A.C.E).

The goal of the meeting is not to give feedback or evaluate performance—it is *a conversation.* The goal is to have an open conversation without documentation other than the fact that the conversation has taken place. The conversation is unstructured, though a number of optional interview questions are provided for employees or managers who wish to use them. The conversation may be around improvement ideas, barriers to pride in workmanship, growth and development needs, or the employee's aspirations for his or her work unit. In preparing for the meeting, the employee also has the option of sending out customer feedback forms to internal and external customers, including co-workers and supervisors.

In another aspect of Memorial's alternative model, the *supervising* manager for each employee completes a form called *annual piece of paper,* also known as A.P.O.P. (see next page). (The name may have originated with Parkview Medical Center in Colorado which had abolished appraisal in 1993, though its replacement system was

---

Memorial Hospital
Fremont, Ohio
P.A.C.E.
(Progress, Achievement, Communication, Education)

Purpose: Improvement of the relationship between employee and the systems within which he/she works.

Instructions:

1. At a minimum employee must complete the P.A.C.E. meeting annually on his/her birthday. Employees may opt to schedule more frequent P.A.C.E. meetings during the year.

2. Employee and manager **can** utilize forms as a guideline for discussion at annual P.A.C.E. meeting. **If completed,** the Employee Recommendation page of the Employee form can be attached to the **A.P.O.P** (Annual Piece of Paper) and sent to Human Resources and then placed in the employee's file.

3. The following sections are **optional** and the employee may choose whether or not these sections would be valuable and whether it becomes a permanent part of his/her record: Patient/Family Feedback, Internal Customer Feedback, External Customer Feedback.

4. The employee has the option to solicit feedback from Customers, or the employee may ask the manager to either get feedback from specific individuals or have a manager choose.

5. Employees may choose the manager with whom to have a feedback session.

Memorial Hospital
Fremont, Ohio
A.P.O.P.
(Annual Piece of Paper)

Name _____   Birthdate _____
Hospital ID# _____   (month/day)
Position _____
Department _____
Date P.A.C.E. completed _____

1. Completed Annual P.A.C.E. discussion?   YES   NO
   Comments _____
   _____

2. Review departmental copy of job description for content, accuracy. YES NO
   Comments _____
   _____

3. Mechanism that competency is established   _____
   _____

4. Completed proficiencies. Please list or attach.
   Name_____   Date _____
   Name_____   Date _____
   Name_____   Date _____
5. Certifications/licensure registration. Please list or attach.
   Name_____   Exp. Date _____
   Name_____   Exp. Date _____
   Name_____   Exp. Date _____
6. Hospital Education Day completed. Date last attended _____

Comments   _____
                 _____
                 _____

Next scheduled meeting _____

_____   _____
Employee   Manager

---

a little different).[15] A.P.O.P. verifies that the employee had a P.A.C.E. interview by showing the date. A.P.O.P. also requires the supervisor to attach an "employee skills checklist" designed for that job. It is not evaluation of the work but verification that an employee has attained the requisite skills, completed required training, or has knowledge of hospital policy. It includes everything from knowledge of the emergency codes and absenteeism policies to the skills of changing a bandage or operating a piece of equipment. The checklist does not call for any grading of skills, but allows the supervisor to verify that the employee: (1) can perform the skill;

(2) needs review of the skill (doesn't know); or (3) indicates the employee has never done the skill (employee needs to learn or demonstrate). The form then requires the manager to indicate the method of verification by one of three means: (1) a peer worker demonstrated or instructed the employee; (2) the manager has seen the person satisfactorily perform the skill; or (3) verification through a verbal communication. In addition to the skill checklist, the supervisor must, as applicable, submit written verification of the employee's knowledge of safety, restraint/seclusion practices, infection control, and specific job proficiencies. If a requisite skill or proficiency cannot be verified, the supervising manager must work with the employee to determine a plan to accomplish it.

A.P.O.P. provides a space for the supervisor to briefly summarize skill development goals and related educational needs. In addition to the A.P.O.P. formatted information, the employee has the option of attaching the customer feedback forms she has received, as well as any recommendations she may have for her unit or otherwise. Although the process does not evaluate performance, the verification and documentation of skill attainment is sufficient to pass muster with the medical industry regulatory agencies, as discussed in Chapter 8.

■ Career Management and Mandated Development

Career management by the organization is also critical in professions where, for various reasons, it's important to the organization to have people progressing to higher levels. In the military, for example, it's up or out—a way of ensuring, at least in theory, that the careerists and higher-ranking officers are only the best. Similarly, an organization may invest many dollars in recruiting, training, and developing a good design engineer. Such an engineer may actually contribute little during the early years while she is maturing into a competent professional. For the organization to gain a full return on investment, a staff management plan and mandated development structures may be prudent and necessary courses of action. For example, a staff management plan may operate with the goal of getting every engineer hired as a trainee to the level of senior engineer in 7 to 10 years from the date of hire. Assuming a clear and logical need, structured mechanisms can be implemented in ways that are consistent with the progressive assumptions advocated throughout this book.

If structured planning and development are necessary, it is extremely important to help people understand *why* the planning is necessary, the immediate goals, and the underlying objectives. Structures will be needed to trigger and track development progress, but the ideal mechanism to deliver these needs is not the all-purpose appraisal. However, you may have to resort to forms, periodic gate checks, and written verification of development in terms of growth experiences, training, and the like. Whatever processes or systems are designed, it is important to design from healthy *underlying assumptions*—Does the system treat people as adult professionals, placing primary responsibility with the employee? Does it function to primarily *help* without excessive reliance on *control?* Does it recognize the variability of people as learners (different learning curves, different ways of learning) or assume everyone is the same? Does it allow choices?

In designing organizational career planning strategies, other pitfalls are associated with underlying assumptions. In appraisal models, we have often seen two implicit assumptions that impede truly helpful growth and development systems. The first assumption is the belief that development is about *vertical movement* of the employee. Most organizations now are beginning to realize that this does not optimize people's talents (see M.J. story). In this era of very flat organizations, it also strategically makes less and less sense. Rather than an organizational goal of getting the right people to move up the ladder, we need a commitment to try to get people to jobs where they are a good fit, knowing this will drive productivity. We are delighted to see the growing interest in off-the-shelf developmental tools and organizational programs that use broader-based approaches such as psychological profiles, occupational inventories, and instruments that reveal people's deeper interests. Where in the past organizations were barriers to midlife career changes, organizations today are increasingly finding that being catalysts for these changes is to their advantage—to retain talent and a workforce where people are happy in their work.

The second faulty assumption common in mandated development systems is that they focus on helping people *overcome weaknesses*. As discussed in the coaching chapter, more leverage and benefit may be gained by focusing on people's strengths and talents rather than their weaknesses and faults. In recent years, this assumption has gained greater acceptance.

The book, *First, Break All the Rules,* describes the results of a Gallup poll in which 80,000 managers were asked what great managers do differently. On points pertinent to employee development, the poll says great managers:

• Guide employees to the right fit, not the next rung up the ladder.

Unintended Consequence of Mandated Career Counseling

Early in my career as an H.R. professional staff member at General Motors, I (M.J.) was required to fill out short-term and long-term career planning forms. As a young, relatively inexperienced person, I honestly described career aspirations, but my manager at the time told me that they were not far-reaching enough. He suggested that any career goal less than Director of Personnel (the top job in a unit) would be potentially career limiting. He went on to explain that it could be interpreted by those who reviewed my appraisal that I was not "career-minded." I agreed to make the change, but something inside of me felt I was being dishonest.

Reflecting back, it would have been a good time for me to have creatively thought about my *real interests* in H.R., rather than just aiming at becoming the top banana. My boss had not been trained to offer that kind of insight, and he really had conflicts of interests in counseling me. What I needed was someone to help me introspectively and ask—*Who am I, and what is my life's work?*

I ultimately found that I was drawn to the organizational development aspect of H.R. and eventually my work did end up there. Though Monday morning quarterbacking is easy, I believe, with the right space, diagnostic tools, and vocational counseling, I could have discovered my destiny earlier. Had that happened, I would have been better prepared for the organizational development role that GM later assigned to me, a role that truly connected to my life passion—helping organizations transform themselves.

- Don't try to perfect each person.
- Motivate by focusing on strengths and managing around employees' weaknesses.
- Select employees based on talent, not just experience, intelligence, and determination.

These views sharply depart from conventional development approaches. Looking for talent is quite different than looking at performance. Looking for fit is different than trying to help people climb vertically. The Gallup research further found that a one-size-fits-all approach doesn't work. Great managers realize that each employee breathes his or her own "psychological oxygen" and good managers figure out what that is.[16] When employers get beyond the constraints and blinders of a focused development appraisal, they and their employees may think more creatively about career paths and development (see *Gallery Furniture* case study).

It's most encouraging to see the evidence of broader thinking about career development during the past two decades. For example, at McDonnell Douglas Space Systems, they work vigorously at career rotations for managers and potential managers, rotating them through various jobs across units and across functions. This ultimately promotes good fits and enables McDonnell Douglas to have a qualified pool of people for future needs.[17] Realizing that every engineer is not good material for formal leadership, a number of companies, including GM, IBM, AT&T, and Mobil, have created "dual ladders" to keep good engineers and other high-demand talent.[18] Those suited for management go up the management ladder, but the technical or professional ladder allows the more gifted engineers to attain more prestigious positions with greater technical challenge, more independence, and sometimes greater resources. Law firms have jumped on this bandwagon with a slightly different twist. Historically, law firms have been up-or-out like the military—people who don't make partner are asked to leave. Some larger firms have recognized that the partner track is very demanding of time and requires business-getting skills (e.g., doing the "power" lunches and hobnobbing that lands the big clients). This profile does not fit many lawyers who nonetheless are excellent attorneys. Rather than parting company with talented attorneys, some firms have created "staff attorney" positions—regular, permanent positions that are offered to experienced and talented lawyers who don't want 60-hour weeks or responsibility for marketing and maintaining accounts. Yes, the pay is less than for partners, but there are fewer hours and headaches—it seems to be a really good fit for some attorneys. As more and more organizations think about career development in broader terms, it will make less and less sense to rely on the one-size-fits-all, orchestrated approaches for employee development that commonly accompany appraisal.

Case Study Addendum

Career Development at Gallery Furniture

Although Gallery Furniture parted with appraisal several years ago (as discussed in the last chapter), the company continually tries to help people get the right fit, says President, Jim McIngvale. One way they help people who are interested in management is to give them a taste of the job. For example, sales people interested in sales management go through a 12-week management apprenticeship program. Completion of the apprenticeship only assures eligibility, not a promotion. McIngvale further explained, "Some are ready then and some are not—we are looking for people who can do leadership building, not merely people who are good in sales."

In addition to continually talking to people about their interests and career goals, Gallery Furniture offers employees personality profiles to help them find and move to the best fit. For example, a couple of years ago, the company hired as a custodian a Hispanic with limited fluency in English and no particular job skills. Over time, it became increasingly evident from his day-to-day interactions that he had an outgoing personality and was a great people person. "So last year we made him a salesman," McIngvale proudly recounted, "and he does unbelievable work. Our customers love him. He is one of our highest producing sales people."

McIngvale conceded that despite best efforts, not everyone finds the best fit. "If they don't work out in their current job, we try to find a place for them where they can be happy and do a good job." Even that sometimes doesn't pan out. "Some people don't work out because they don't like retail. Retail is a tough business, the hours are hard, and some people just don't like that," McIngvale explained. If they don't work out, "we try different ways to help them. If we can't find a good fit for them, then we part company. Some people just aren't cut out for this kind of business."

■ Appraisal and Career Track Advancement

For many professions and occupations, organizations must provide fair and reliable ways for employees to advance in noncompetitive career tracks. In a good many organizations, career track advancement is determined by appraisal ratings. We've already discussed the poor reliability and problems of appraisal in deciding pay and competitive promotions. Appraisals are equally unreliable in the context of career track advancement. Hence, the big question is: *Without appraisal, how do we determine whether people are qualified to advance to the next level?*

Official answer: It depends. In some cases, it's merely a matter of passing a test or seeing if someone can do the required task. The mechanic trainee either can or cannot correctly do a tune-up. The home-mortgage loan closer either can or cannot independently do the closing correctly. In many jobs, however, especially in the managerial and professional arenas, there will always be the need for subjective judgments about qualifications. Do the projects done by Mildred or Hank as Engineer I's demonstrate that they can assume the responsibilities of an Engineer II? Do they have the requisite analytical skills? Is their skill and experience deep enough for complex projects? Do they have what it takes to be the "lead engineer" on moderately challenging assignments? There may be objective evidence in answer to these questions, but there's no avoiding subjective interpretation and judgment. A call must be made. As in the case of promotions, we have no elixir to help you avoid subjective judgments and the problems they inevitably bring. In making these determinations without appraisal, however, consider the following suggestions.

Use Only Single Purpose Assessment and Evaluative Processes

By establishing a single-purpose assessment or evaluation, decoupling from other appraisal functions (pay, coaching, feedback, development), you will eliminate some of the causes of distortion and manipulation and get more accurate evaluations.

Use Objective Indicators

Some or all of the advancement criteria should be based on presumptions or objective indicators, e.g., a requisite number of years of experience or passing an exam (from the profession, a licensing or certification agency, or organization-designed). To avoid subjective bias and instill confidence in the system, use objective indicators to the extent that they are reliable, in part or all of the process. See "Examples of Objective Criteria for Career Advancement."

Write Clear Indicators

When subjective judgments are necessary in determining how people advance, write indicators or criteria for advancement in language that is as clear and concrete as possible. Use tangible examples if the criteria are difficult to describe in words. If multiple factors are weighed, say so. Conversely, if all criteria must be met, make that clear.

The University of Wisconsin Credit Union (case study in Chapter 4) in some areas uses career ladders in lieu of the merit pay system it extinguished with appraisal. For example, for the teller ladder, specific skills are required to perform jobs at each level above teller (see Figure 7.2). People move up to higher pay grades as they move up the ladder. The supervisor makes the assessments by simply ascertaining that the employee has

---

Examples of Objective Criteria Career Advancement

Hospital Setting. A Michigan hospital uses a career ladder for regis-tered nurses, moving from RN Nurse I to RN Nurse IV. The hospital uti-lizes a combination of specified criteria and a point system in allowing nurses to advance from one level to another. A nurse can go from I to II with two years of experience and by gaining a certain number of points based on completion of in-service training, external workshops and courses, and even for reading and writing summaries of professional journal articles. All of these measures are seen as tangible evidence of professional development and growth. Among other criteria, nurses going to level III typically need to complete their baccalaureate degree. A nurse cannot go to level IV unless she meets all the rigors of being board-certified as a specialist. As nurses climb the ladder, they move into a higher pay range with wages 8–10% higher than the prior level. The vice president of nursing and nursing directors, as well as the nurses' union, have found the system well received by the nurses and that it effectively advances the nurses who are growing and developing in their profession.

Manufacturing Setting. A General Electric plant in Durham, N.C., with 170 employees assembles jet engines with 10,000 parts that as a finished product weigh 300,000 pounds each. The pressure of building of high-quality engines with a tiny workforce requires that people rapidly advance their proficiencies and skills. The plant operates with nine self-managed teams; it does not grant any individual merit raises nor are there any opportunities for competitive promotions (there's only one supervisor in the entire plant). The plant has established three grades of jet-assembly technicians with a single wage rate for each grade. The high-est grade is capable of performing all tasks required to successfully build the GE90 jet engine. All technicians are required to be FAA-certified mechanics. Technicians advance to the higher-paid tech-2 and tech-3 lev-els by studying, training, and passing an exam. This open, objective system for career advancement has resulted in a highly energized workforce that continually improves quality and lowers costs by 10% each year.[19]

---

completed the training or otherwise has demonstrated the specific skills for the next level. Employees decide whether or not they want to try to qualify for next higher job in the ladder. Each supervisor is responsible for providing assistance and helping the employee develop training plans to attain the required skills.

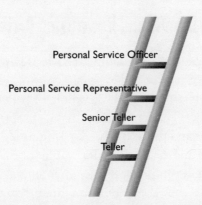

Personal Service Officer

Personal Service Representative

Senior Teller

Teller

Figure 7.2   University of Wisconsin Credit Union Career Ladder from the Position of Teller

Use a Panel of Objective Evaluators

With the popularization of 360-degree appraisals, we have learned from social scientists that multiple raters are more reliable (meaning more consistent but not necessarily more valid) than a single rater.[20] Using a panel of qualified people either to determine or to review and question findings should help to create a fairer system *and* the appearance of an equitable system. Also, it may be helpful to utilize evaluators from outside the day-to-day work area of the candidate. For example, a software engineer seeking to go from Systems Engineer II to III may need to demonstrate the successful handling of certain kinds of projects. The candidate seeking advancement could report to a panel on projects completed. The supervisor might be a witness to what projects have been done. A panel consisting of two or three qualified people, ideally from *outside the work unit*, may add some objectivity in examining and weighing what the candidate has done. In some industries, outsiders are used, e.g., the Michigan State Police has a university professor on its promotion panels.

Openly Share the Results

An honest system should also be designed to inform anyone denied advancement the nature of the deficiencies. Most of all, it should promote *learning*. A supportive organization should also ensure that denied candidates are offered assistance in addressing those deficiencies (see *Madison Police Department* process).

■ Appraisal in Making Layoffs and Downsizing Decisions

The least pleasant and most difficult staffing decisions pertain to layoffs and downsizing. Though not a prevalent practice, a surprisingly large number of corporations rely on appraisals, in whole or part, to determine who will receive pink slips. The idea behind this is, if some people must go, let's keep the good ones and throw out weak performers. It's a nice theory, but it does not work and rests on faulty assumptions. The reasons have been recounted over several chapters, e.g., appraisals cannot separate people's contributions from the system in which they work; incomplete information, biases, filters, politics, and other factors fatally impair ratings. When appraisal is used to lay off, everyone knows that it's brutally unfair. Even those who survive have bitter feelings about their co-workers losing their jobs based on the caprice of appraisal.

For example, a large telephone company announced that it was going to downsize and would use appraisal outcomes to decide who would go. An uproar followed, with people alleging that the managerial assessments were subjective and unfair. In response to this outcry, the company decided to conduct another appraisal, using a 360-degree process to increase objectivity. Peers and supervisors ranked each other from high to low. Based on the results of this exercise, the bottom 20% were notified that they were being let go. Naturally, they were upset, but what about the 80% who did not get pink-slipped? As you might expect, they railed against the decision, and the resulting anger and distraction were so severe that the company had to bring in an organizational consulting firm to help them heal the wounds.

Abolishing appraisal cannot take the emotional sting out of a downsizing initiative. Losing a job is one of the most stressful experiences in life. Losing a co-worker, valued as a person and as a colleague, likewise is a visceral experience. Using appraisal in any form, however, puts fuel on the fire. From past experience, people *know* appraisal ratings are unreliable and political. Moreover, once an organization has based RIF decisions on appraisal, you can be sure of a new electric charge in the next round of appraisal. Every criticism will be contested. Even though the organization just released the bottom 20%, all of the survivors will fear they will be marked as the "new bottom 20%" (no matter how many times you lay off the bottom 20%, you still end up with a bottom 20%). If you had any hope that appraisal might be a time for hearing feedback, learning, and improvement, the chilling and numbing effect of an appraisal-driven RIF surely will freeze that hope for years to follow.

Abolishing appraisal, or at least disconnecting it from layoff and RIF decisions, does not make the difficult decisions any easier. But at least you don't have appraisal inflaming the process. If you have determined that there is no way to avoid a downsizing (though, too often, organizations leap to that assumption when there are other options[21]), we can make a few suggestions. If positions must be abolished, an organization can explore a number of creative options including voluntary separations and extended leaves, retirement incentives, and buyouts (as did GM–Powertrain—see case study). If creative options cannot help, then the organization must do everything it can to render fair decisions *and* help people understand its efforts toward that aim. Using seniority, for whatever reason, seems to take an emotional edge off the process—the downsizing is still bitter, but seniority may be accepted better because it has an objective and determinable value and a certain element of societal acceptance. If more subjective factors are required, then, for reasons discussed with regard to career track advancement, use a committee of people. A committee that takes time to develop clear criteria, discuss, and reflect on the best choices will be somewhat more objective, at least to the extent of dampening individual bias and getting clear about thinking. Moreover, in the event of a legal challenge, juries are far more receptive to a group decision than one attributable to a single manager, whom the laid-off employee's attorney will make into Satan incarnate.

Subjective factors based on *operational needs*, though subject to arbitrary abuse, seem to be less controversial than using *individual performance* as a determinant. Operational needs assessment might include determining what positions will be essential in the streamlined organization or possibly what person has the requisite qualifications for a newly created job that combines two abolished jobs. Using seniority as a tie-breaking factor in operational-based decisions may somewhat reduce hostility toward the final decisions (nothing makes people more crazy than seeing solid performers with 20 or 25 years being let go when less-than-outstanding younger people somehow keep their jobs!).

If *performance* rather than operational considerations must be used as a factor, examine your assumptions and recall the validity and reliability problems of performance ratings. At best, a system of review and evaluation can successfully identify only the employees on the outer fringes, i.e., those who are truly outstanding or patently poor performers. If the management decision is to go deeper than that, forcing you to rank everyone, all we can say is, good luck! (You'll need it!) You may have individual sales or output records, but in a world where performance is largely driven by situational factors and the system, these data will not enable you to accurately rank people.

Case Study Addendum

GM–Powertrain—A Different Approach to Downsizing

As recounted in the Chapter 5 case study, GM–Powertrain abolished performance appraisals in 1987 as part of a transition toward a culture that focused on systems and process improvement. Notable improvement in morale and productivity followed, but in 1991, along came a bump in the road. GM Headquarters ordered staffing cuts across the corporation to reduce costs. In other GM divisions, downsizing initiatives were underway, using performance appraisal rankings to purportedly choose the worst workers. Having abolished appraisals, GM–Powertrain could not follow suit, short of reverting back to some sort of rating or ranking of employees.

In response to the edict, GM–Powertrain formed a collaborative team, consisting of line and staff employees from all disciplines including manufacturing, engineering, finance, and internal H.R. consultants. The objective of the team was to comply with the mandate to reduce labor costs while concurrently preserving the newfound culture of openness and trust. After discussion and deliberation, the team concluded that it did not want to return to any form of ranking and rating. The underlying assumptions of such a practice would send the wrong messages and take them back to what they had deliberately abolished. Instead, the team wanted to preserve and build on the emerging positive culture. Using the format of questions for predictive management and by examining underlying assumptions, the team developed an alternative way to achieve downsizing. A number of alternative approaches were adopted including: (1) elective personal leave; (2) elective retirements; (3) voluntary transfers; and (4) voluntary incentive buyouts. As a result of these measures, GM–Powertrain met the corporate mandate without exercising any involuntary layoffs or retirements.

The approach to the reduction-in-force preserved and strengthened GM–Powertrain's employee culture because the actions taken were aligned with its espoused, healthier assumptions about people. Although GM–Powertrain and all other GM divisions achieved the mandated reduction goal, there was a steep difference in impact at the human level. The other GM divisions' layoffs were *involuntary* and largely decided by performance appraisals. Following the decision process, external consultants Drake Beam & Morin conducted workshops at all GM divisions to provide assistance on career options for people leaving the company. In visiting the work sites of the various divisions, the consulting firm reportedly found a significant difference in the atmosphere of GM–Powertrain versus other GM divisions. In other divisions, there seemed to be a residue of anger, depression, and cynicism, whereas at GM–Powertrain, there was more acceptance of the changes and a positive focus on moving forward.[22]

Conclusion

Promotions, career advancement, employee development, and downsizing decisions can be better made if they are decoupled from one another and the other functions of appraisal. Subjective decisions are an inevitable part of organizational life, but orchestrated appraisals, conducted annually or otherwise, are not reliable or helpful in making these decisions. Alternative structures that are well thought out and that work from new assumptions can enable organizations to make important staffing decisions in an effective and fair manner.

In the next chapter, we deal with employees at the other end of the spectrum. We offer insights and practical advice about dealing with those who are performing poorly.

Review of Chapter Assumptions

Conventional Assumption

Promotions should be based on an objective, not subjective, decision process.

Alternative Assumptions

- Promotions should be conducted in a fair and equitable manner and be based on relevant qualifications, including good fit.
- While objectivity should be encouraged in promotion decisions, subjective judgments are necessary and helpful with regard to some aspects of such decisions.

Conventional Assumption

Performing well in one job predicts success in performing well in another job.

Alternative Assumption

- Past performance of a specific competency required in a new position is relevant information about a person's qualifications for another job.

Conventional Assumption

Using appraisal as a screening tool makes it more difficult for EEO agencies and advocates to challenge a promotion process.

Alternative Assumptions

- All screening and selection tools must be demonstrably valid and reliable to withstand EEO challenges.

- Success in a prior job does not demonstrate selection validity for a different job without evidence of content or criterion-related validity.

Conventional Assumption

The organization and supervisors are responsible for employees' development.

Alternative Assumption

- At some level, all employees want to be responsible for their development, but to enable this to happen, organizations must provide education, offer assistance, and provide a supportive environment.

8

Dispelling the Legal Myths and Dealing with Poor Performers

If you really want to help people change, empathize with them.

Carl Rogers

I don't have an attitude problem. You have a perception problem.

Dilbert (Scott Adams)

When we talk to audiences about tossing performance appraisal, invariably we see someone's eyebrows furrow, and a hand goes up. "Well, what about legal documentation," the voice of concern asks, "In these days, don't you need appraisals to protect the company from employee lawsuits?" Our answer surprises audiences: There is far more fable in that belief than truth.

In this chapter, we sift the truth from commonly held beliefs. We identify the few instances when appraisal or formal evaluation is legally mandated. We also dispel the widely held notion that appraisal provides a reliable shield against employee lawsuits, delineating the kind of documentation that *is* prudently necessary. Lastly, we shed light on the value of appraisal as a counseling tool for errant employees. In all of these discussions, we once again focus on underlying assumptions to help us better understand why we have relied upon appraisal. We pose alternative assumptions from which we can craft new practices to encourage effective counseling of sub-par employees and the prudent collection of legal documentation.

As we would hope you understand, nothing in this chapter or elsewhere in this book is intended to serve as legal advice. We touch on legal issues only with the goal of education and enlightenment. We assume that you will not act on information or advice provided without first checking with a competent attorney who is familiar with all the particular circumstances.

■ Are Appraisals Legally Required?

Assumption

Appraisal documentation is required by law.

People often hear their labor attorney addressing the need for preparing appraisals correctly. Because appraisal so often is damaging to employers' defenses, it's not surprising that attorneys would harp on this issue. Attorneys logically assume, based on their experience, that most firms are going to give people evaluations, and their assumption is valid. One comprehensive study of appraisal practice in the United States found that 87% of managers receive appraisals as do 90% of professionals at non-union firms.[1] Attorneys most commonly encounter discharge lawsuits filed by managers and professionals because they are more highly paid and consequently more likely to contest their discharge in the courtroom. Appraisals usually are preserved and consequently become "hard" evidence in these legal challenges. For these reasons, it is quite understandable that labor attorneys place great emphasis on preparing appraisals and doing so with due care.

Though labor attorneys place emphasis on appraisal, does this mean that appraisals are required by the law? In most instances, no, with notable exceptions. Appraisal spuriously poses as a fair and objective instrument in evaluating someone's performance. Consequently, a number of governmental bodies and industry regulators (who perhaps have not looked at the research) see appraisal as a way to contain favoritism and political spoils and maneuvering. They further see appraisal as a concrete way to ensure that employees are performing competently. With these noble objectives in mind, many public sector and regulatory bodies in the United States and elsewhere prescribe appraisal or some type of formal evaluation through laws, ordinances, regulations, civil service rules, and the like. We are not aware of studies or data that pin down the extent of legally mandated appraisals, but they are certainly not uncommon in the public sector. For example, we sometimes find state or local requirements for school teachers to be given formal appraisals. Civil service regulations for municipal, state, and federal employees often prescribe appraisals, either on an annual basis or in special instances. Appraisals are routinely required in the military. In the health care industry, the Health Care Finance Administration (HCFA) and Joint Commission of Accreditation of Healthcare Organizations (JCAHO), an industry regulatory agency, both require an annual evaluation of employees.

We have found that many of the legal and regulatory requirements to conduct appraisals do not prescribe a specific method or form of appraisal or evaluation, only that they be conducted or, in vague terms, that they measure competency, skills, or level of job performance. More often than blanket mandates, we find appraisal required for probationary employees moving to regular status or tenure. Employers who are legally required to conduct appraisal often are at liberty to alter their appraisal system and can do so, drawing from some of the ideas and alternative assumptions discussed in this book. In any case, every public sector employer or employer in a heavily regulated industry, as well as those with publicly licensed professionals, should specifically make an inquiry and review regulations to determine whether appraisal or formal evaluation is required. As you may understand, such mandate could severely constrict the "instead" options for employers wishing to move away from appraisal (see "Creatively Meeting a Legal Mandate").

If you are not subject to a legal or industry requirement, are there other circumstances where appraisals are legally mandated? Yes, if you have a labor union agreement or an employment contract with an individual that says appraisals will be given, then you must comply with that agreement. If you fail to follow the agreement, you may be subject to a breach-of-contract action or a grievance, in the case of a union. If you fail to do a contractually required appraisal and then discharge someone, there is a good chance that a performance-based discharge would be overturned by an arbitrator or judge. Similarly, if you state, within your

---

Creatively Meeting a Legal Mandate for Appraisal

Though appraisal or formal evaluation is sometimes mandated by law or regulations, a number of organizations have aggressively skated on thin ice to rid their organization of conventional appraisal. Although hospitals are required to conduct appraisal by law (HCFA) and their primary accreditation source (JCAHO), at least a dozen hospitals have creatively found ways to discard appraisal, or at least its most damaging aspects. The regulations do not spell out a requirement for ratings, nor do they specify who must do the appraisal. Consequently, some hospitals merely have a checklist verifying a conversation or identifying that an employee has demonstrated the skills and licensures required for their job. If your organization is subject to a legal mandate, you may find that the expectation is perhaps merely a skill check or assurance that feedback was given by someone to the employee, but there is no requirement, per se, for conventional appraisal.

In the Leander School District, in a suburb of Austin, Texas, the movement away from appraisal required some attention to the grounds for discharging tenured teachers under Texas state law. According to Deputy Superintendent Monta Akin, the district has preserved an element of annual evaluation in which the formal supervisor affirms (by completing a check list) that the teacher has minimally met requirements related to the statutory grounds. No written comments are required unless the teacher is deficient. Developmental needs of teachers are now addressed with self-assessments on a matrix of proficiencies and skills. This open developmental tool provides a basis for periodic conversations with the formal leader and has shifted "staff members' focus to *learning* that has really made a difference," Ms. Akin gleefully reports.

---

employee handbook, employment manual, or otherwise, that appraisals or evaluations will be conducted, this may constitute a legally binding promise. Absent a contractual obligation, appraisals are not expressly required by laws pertaining to discharge and discrimination.

■ Must You Do Appraisals for Legal Protection?

Assumption

Appraisals provide reliably helpful legal evidence.

Certainly appraisals *can* provide legal protection in various forms. Appraisals may serve as evidence that an employee has performed poorly, that the employee was given formal notice of the deficiencies, and that the employer took remedial measures to help the employee. Arbitrators, judges, and juries routinely give weight to appraisal evidence. A database search on U.S. court decisions found more than 528 employment and labor law cases in which one or more parties used performance appraisal as evidence.[2] Appraisal may also be useful as evidence when employers are sued for personal injury to prove that employees were properly directed, counseled, and trained.

In unionized workplaces, the employer has an onerous burden of proving it has just cause to discharge an employee for poor performance. In most industrialized countries around the globe (other than the United States), by law, employers must have "good cause" or defensible reasons to discharge an employee, for poor performance or otherwise (at least, with respect to regular, postprobationary or longer-term employees). In the United States, outside of Montana, there is no statutory or common law that generally extends rights against arbitrary discharge in non-union workplaces. Because of other legal developments in the United States, however, the employer's benefit from the doctrine of "at will" employment (a legal presumption that employers have an unfettered right to discharge) is severely limited. With the proliferation of discrimination laws (race, color, religion, national origin, gender, age, disability, veteran status, citizenship, union activity, and more) along with a spate of public policy rights (whistleblower and other antiretaliation provisions in everything from the trade security laws to the Pure Water Drinking Act), any discharged employee potentially has scores of bases upon which to sue the employer.

To defend against these suits, the employer typically has the burden of proving, in varying degrees, that it had legitimate justifications for discharge. For example, the Age Discrimination in Employment Act expressly provides a statutory defense requiring the employer to show "good cause" for a discharge.[3] Moreover, an increasing number of states have carved huge holes in the "at will" presumption, based on contracts implied by employer's policies and practices, concepts of good faith and fair dealing, and public policy grounds. Between 1970 and 1989 in the United States, employee lawsuits rose at an astounding rate of 2166% (versus only 125% in the general federal civil caseload for the same period).[4] And in the past decade, with passage of the Americans with Disabilities Act and other laws, the pace has continued to increase—job bias lawsuits filed in federal court rose from 6,936 in 1990 to 21,540 in 1998.[5] Hence, in the United States and most economically advanced nations around the world, grounds and documentation are needed to justify and defend the discharge of an employee.

Does this mean we *must* have appraisal evidence? Absent a law or legal requirement to conduct appraisals, the answer is *no*. In interpreting contracts calling for "just cause" and statutes prohibiting discriminatory discharge, arbitrators and courts by logic and common sense essentially apply very similar standards. In defending a wrongful discharge claim, through testimony, records, documentation, and other evidence, an employer ordinarily must be able to prove all of the following:

1. **Notice of Expectation.** The employee was given adequate notice of the performance expectation, work standard, rule, or requirement and the consequences of not meeting that expectation;

2. **Reasonableness.** The expectation, standard, or rule was reasonably necessary in light of efficiency, safety, or other legitimate needs;

3. **Evidence.** There is substantial evidence that the employee failed to meet the expectation or standard or comply with the rule;

4. **Fair Investigation.** Before making any decision to discharge, a fair and objective investigation was conducted;

5. **Consistently Applied Standards.** The expectation, standard, or rule that was the basis for discharge has been applied to similarly situated employees in a consistent manner; and

6. **Discharge Is a Fair Penalty.** The penalty of discharge was fair and reasonable in light of all the circumstances and consistent with the way other employees have been treated for similar infractions.[6]

Although the precise standards of proof will vary depending on the forum and case, these six elements reflect the commonly recognized requirements in defending a wrongful termination claim.

Can appraisal help an employer document the six elements? Yes. Depending on the form of appraisal, it can provide evidence that an employee had notice of performance expectations and deficiencies that occurred. Since appraisals *can* serve as helpful evidence, does this mean that employers *should* do appraisals? Out of sheer prudence, in these litigious times, every employer must have sufficient documentation. Granting this, it does not hold true that appraisals must be conducted as a matter of prudent practice. All six elements of proof can be proficiently documented and demonstrated without appraisal. Later on, we explain how this is done.

Some make the plausible argument that a mandatory appraisal process can be a way to ensure that documentation is systematically collected. They contend that supervisors tend to be lax and remiss about confronting employees with negative feedback, documenting deficiencies, and making and preserving a record that ultimately will serve the organization's best interests. The underlying premise of this argument is certainly true. We would further concede that systematic appraisals often produce beneficial documentation. They also can be exploited to accomplish that purpose (see "Building a File"). But, overall the drawbacks of

---

Building a File with Appraisal

With the drastic rise in employee lawsuits and million-dollar awards, employers have greatly heightened their focus on ensuring that they have the necessary documentation before discharge or separation. One legal researcher, John Edward Davidson, looked at the use of appraisals in employee lawsuits. He notes an increasing concern that appraisal has become more a tool to document separations than to help employees increase productivity. The courts and others have taken note of the common practice of using appraisals in "building a file" against targeted employees, he observes. "Despite the inaccuracies that plague even the most ideal appraisals," Davidson says, "most employers apparently conclude they are worthy of continued use." For what purpose? Davidson explains, "Employers are quite willing to *intentionally* abuse the appraisal process in order to insulate themselves from employment litigation." This perhaps emerging pattern is damaging to the judicial system because, he notes, "appraisals are routinely admitted into evidence." Unfortunately, juries accept them as "gospel truth," and the courts seem to give appraisals far more credibility than is warranted by their track record.

If, as Davidson reports, employers are perceiving and using appraisal as a way to create legal evidence, how will this trend impact H.R. intentions that appraisal is a tool for helping people, communication, counseling, and learning?

using systematic appraisal as a documentation tool outweigh its potential benefit. We reach this conclusion based on several points.

The Leniency Tendency

As we discussed in Chapter 3, supervisors have a strong tendency to act leniently. Forcing systematic documentation, by itself, does little to alter the causes of leniency. Data on the prevalence of leniency in appraisal underscores this. By imposing appraisal, an organization may successfully prod the supervisor into a needed conversation, but the tool does little or nothing to help supervisors overcome their reluctance, intuitive reservations, and fears about giving negative feedback and redirection.

The Two-Edged Sword

Yes, the employer can defend against wrongful discharge cases with appraisal evidence, but *employees* can also use appraisals to their advantage. Employee plaintiffs and union advocates routinely deploy appraisals to demonstrate that an employee fired for incompetence or poor performance was, in fact, a good employee. Quite often in these instances, the appraisal backfires and causes the employer to lose the case, sometimes in cases that should be a lay-down win. Let us illustrate this through a fictional story that represents hundreds of cases we have seen over the years:

> Winifred, a 20-year employee, has worked for Myron for seven years. Though Winifred is increasingly unproductive over the years and has had diminishing skills, she's a very nice person who bakes cakes on people's birthdays and readily jumps in to help in a pinch. Myron has made suggestions to her, but she is so likeable that he has not been confrontational or documented her deficiencies. Consequently, over the past seven years, at appraisal time he has given her "meets expectations" (3s) and "exceeds expectations" (4s), but no "outstandings" (5s). One day Myron gets his gold watch and heads for Florida. Then *you* get hired as Winifred's new boss. You ask her to be productive. You clearly lay out what she needs to do and offer to help. Nonetheless, she persists in her old patterns. Appraisal time comes, and, as an earnest and sincere person, you tell it like it is. Soon to follow will be charges that you are discriminating against her because of her age, Norwegian ancestry, and disability arising from her long struggle with the gout in her big toe. The problem must be YOU. After all, she has a seven-year official record that unequivocally states that she has met and *exceeded* expectations. The resulting implication is that you discriminate or you don't know how to work with people.

With stories like this happening every day, there's little wonder that most managers in these litigious times are shy about taking on poor performers. In the event of litigating the above situation, the company's attorney would try to argue that Myron rated Winifred's co-workers higher and this contrast indicates evidence of poor performance. In all likelihood, however, outsiders, such as a hearing officer or jury, would still believe that *exceeds* means *exceeds* and *meets* means *meets*. This type of unfavorable and yet convincing evidence may intimidate your company into paying a large settlement or, if the case gets to a jury, saddle it with an unfair verdict. Misuse of appraisals as evidence has been so commonplace that, the Practicing Law Institute has warned defense lawyers that "Every good word in a (discharged employee's) performance evaluation will be claimed to be universal truth in subsequent suits."[7]

While appraisals may backfire in litigation, don't they mostly help the employer? One of us (T.C.), in handling age discrimination cases for the federal government for ten years and practicing labor law for another fifteen years, has found that appraisals hurt or raise doubts about the employer's case more often than they help. Wondering if this experience held true for other labor and employment attorneys, we took a survey of attorneys belonging to the Michigan State Bar Association Labor and Employment Law Section. We collected 62 responses from attorneys who specialize in employment law matters, including discharge and discrimination cases, asking them what their experience has been in cases where appraisal was a significant issue.

Figure 8.1[8] displays their responses. Notice that only 3% of responding attorneys had found that appraisal evidence "usually" favors the employer and 31% found an overall effect favoring the employer. Though appraisal is touted as *the employer's* legal weapon, 44% of responding attorneys found that appraisal evidence favored *the employee* more than the employer. Another 25% reporting found that, on an average, the evidence equally impacted employee and employer. In other words, seven out of ten attorneys (69%) surveyed reported that appraisal evidence did not give employers a general advantage in litigating employment claims.

Despite appraisal's ability to damage an employer's defense, most labor attorneys (55% in our survey), in greater and lesser degrees, encourage the use of appraisal.[9] This happens for two reasons: (1) A good many attorneys are not fully aware of the research demonstrating the unreliability of appraisal and its unintended consequences; and (2) they encounter

ATTORNEYS' CASE EXPERIENCE WHEN APPRAISAL EVIDENCE IS AT ISSUE	PERCENT	EVIDENCE FAVORS
Usually Favors the EMPLOYEE	16%	FAVORS EMPLOYEE 44%
Favors EMPLOYEE More Often than Not	28%	
Impacts Employee and Employer about EQUALLY Overall	25%	NEUTRAL EFFECT OVERALL 25%
Favors EMPLOYER More Often than Not	28%	FAVORS EMPLOYER 31%
Usually Favors the EMPLOYER	3%	

Figure 8.1   Labor and Employment Law Attorneys' Experience with Appraisal Evidence

an epidemic degree of neglect by supervisors in documenting problem employees (with and without appraisal practices) and believe that systematic documentation, as appraisal provides, is perhaps the most effective way to make supervisors do required documentation. Like H.R. managers, many attorneys representing employers think that, with better training, administration, monitoring, and enforcement, appraisal will provide supportive evidence. The flaw in this thinking is that it assumes the administrative features of appraisal cause the rating defects, when, in fact, it's more about underlying assumptions, relationships, fear, and other psychological issues. If an organization uses appraisal solely with the goal of getting hard documentation on errant employees, then we concede that it will probably get better documentation through forced appraisal than through none at all. At the same time, however, it will also get documentation that will backfire, as well as the costly, adverse effects of appraisal that we have discussed throughout this entire book.

Undermining Employer Credibility

Aside from providing favorable evidence for the employee, appraisals can backfire another way in employee lawsuits. As a labor and employment law attorney, I (T.C.) often find that appraisals indirectly undermine the employer's credibility. Performance-based discharges frequently rely on *valid* subjective judgments about performance deficiencies that cannot be documented with hard evidence. Over the years, I have seen many cases in which the separated employee has been marked down in several performance areas in the last appraisal that precipitated the termination. In testing the accuracy of the appraisal, typically the sub-par ratings can be corroborated by the testimony of the supervisor and co-workers. In many cases, however, one or more of the appraisal criteria reflect on something that can be contradicted by objective record evidence. If the employee's attorney can plainly demonstrate this contradiction, it has a powerful effect in undermining the employer's credibility in other subjective areas, where the veracity of the supervisor is critical. (See "Discrediting Appraisals".) This erosion of credibility routinely happens in cases where the employer, overall, has good justification for the dismissal.

The specific criteria of appraisal, the filled-in boxes, and numerical ratings may give the appearance of objectivity, but the black-and-white specificity can backlash against the employer. Because appraisals are frequently painstakingly specific, the exact results of one employee can be compared against another. This comparison opens the door to transforming honest mistakes into an attack on the employer's credibility. Appraisals, because of their broad coverage of the job, perhaps tempt supervisors into downgrading in categories where the evidence is unclear (the "horn" effect of being poor in one area influencing the rating in other areas). Without appraisal, documentation of performance deficiency can be more appropriately focused on only the most critical aspects.

Creating Grounds for Lawsuits

Appraisal, by its nature or within the context of a situation, may establish or bolster grounds for many types of lawsuits. We can give several examples:

- Appraisals that allegedly contain inaccurate or false information may give rise to a claim for defamation (such as libel) against the employer and the rater.

- Raters may be sued for negligence in which it is alleged that careless preparation of the appraisal has resulted in gross inaccuracies that triggered discharge or other economic loss.[10]

Discrediting Appraisals Without Expert Testimony

To illustrate more tangibly how a rating in one performance area undermines the credibility of other ratings, T.C. offers two personal experiences:

- A hospital clerk in a large Chicago hospital was discharged after being evaluated poorly for quality of work, quantity of work, and excessive tardiness. It was true that she was tardy often. The EEOC verified this and closed the case. The Labor Department, pursuing the same case under a different statute, took time to pull the time cards for every employee who worked in that department. It turned out that the discharged employee had the *best* on-time rate in the department. Apparently, closing and relocating parking lots had caused tardiness for everyone over the prior year. The remaining appraisal outcomes, though perhaps valid, were put in doubt by this verifiable error in judgment (perhaps made in good faith as a result of the "horn" effect—see Chapter 3). The case ended with the employee being reinstated with 100% back pay and benefits.

- A case manager with an insurance company was discharged after she received poor ratings in several performance areas. A wrongful discharge suit was filed. A token settlement was offered and refused, and depositions followed. For two days the employee's supervisor was questioned about the accuracy of the employee's and others' ratings in the same job. In one performance area, and to a lesser degree in another, hard data clearly revealed that the plaintiff had been unfairly and inconsistently rated. Consequently, the ratings in other areas, based on subjective evidence, were cast in a dark shadow of doubt. A few days later, the employee was offered a full year's salary in settlement, which was satisfactory because she had already found a better paying job.

- Appraisal has been held to be a tangible job benefit under Title VII, giving rise to claims of discrimination or even sexual harassment under Title VII.[11] An adverse appraisal may constitute sufficient evidence to establish the preliminary proof of discrimination (known as the *prima facie* case).[12] Even *positive* appraisals have been used to bolster claims that an employee was discriminatorily denied information needed to improve (yes, they get you coming and going!).[13]

- A practice of appraisal may be used to support a claim of an implied contract for continued employment (i.e., that the employee has a *de facto* agreement that he could not be fired without good cause).[14]

- Appraisal evidence may be used to challenge layoff and RIF decisions to refute the employer's claim that the eliminated employee performed less favorably (relying on claims of age discrimination, wrongful discharge, breach of layoff policy, and other claims). A shining example is a 1996 court case in which Texas Instruments was sued by the EEOC for allegedly engaging in age bias because they disproportionately had retained younger persons during a reduction in force. Laid-off older workers had received favorable performance reviews prior to the layoff. To defend against the lawsuit, Texas Instruments ironically was forced to argue that its own appraisal system did not provide "worthwhile" or "useful" information in deciding who would be terminated on a merit basis. Of course, proving that appraisal is an unreliable measuring stick was hardly a challenge, and Texas Instruments won the lawsuit.[15]

- Grossly unfair or unduly offensive appraisals may also significantly increase awards for emotional pain and punitive damages. In extreme cases, when combined with other evidence of harsh mistreatment, they may give an employee good cause to quit, opening the door for a "constructive discharge" claim (a legal theory in which the litigant says he was in effect fired because the conditions were so adverse they forced resignation).

Actually, this list could continue, but the gist is that, while appraisals can provide a form of legal protection, they open the door to a variety of potential liabilities, some of which would not be present in an alternative documentation system.

Impeding Feedback and Remedial Measures

If you are conducting appraisal with the aim of gathering evidence against employees, it is indirectly or directly linked to a discipline and discharge process. Over time, other employees may detect or learn about this linkage, and fear will be associated with the process. The resulting fear not only impedes listening and reception of feedback as a "noise" factor but causes undue stress that undermines productivity.

Unintended Consequences

As discussed throughout this book, appraisal triggers demoralizing effects, game-playing, and other toxins unintended by its designers. Even if appraisal can be demonstrated to instigate better documentation efforts by supervisors or provide advantageous evidence, does the overall gain to the organization offset all of the counterproductive effects? We think not. In a modest-sized company of 500, the cost of losing one or two employee lawsuits may be a half-million or million dollars every few years, an amount large enough to cause concern. But on the other hand, what is the cost of demoralizing half the workforce through the annual ritual of appraisal? How would you calculate the cost of disheartened and angry employees, deflated confidence, diminished motivation, wasted time at the drinking fountain, and the erosion of employee commitment? If the employer has alternative means of prudently getting the documentation needed to defend lawsuits without the pernicious effects of appraisal, it makes sense to turn to those alternative avenues.

■ Getting the Documentation You Need Without Appraisal

If appraisal is not a good way to gather employee documentation, what is? Before answering this question, we urge you to look at your primary goals. What is the mission of your organization? Are you in business to defend lawsuits or to provide high-quality services and products to your customers? Do your employee policies aim *primarily* at limiting exposure to employee lawsuits? Or do they aim at creating a milieu that fosters commitment and high performance by an energized workforce? "Both," may be goals, but sometimes you must choose. Even without appraisal, you could orchestrate reams of checklists for supervisors to fill out every week about each employee's productivity, errors, and deficiencies. Very likely this would give you plenty of evidence to defend a lawsuit. At the same time, the impact of such monitoring would send messages of distrust, engender fear, and undermine commitment.

What we are advocating is a properly balanced approach. Working from different assumptions, your policies and practices foremost should express confidence in people and convey trust. At the same time, it's realistic to expect the need for some involuntary separations. When these instances arise, the likelihood of having appropriate documentation may be enhanced by having prudent documentation practices and policies in place. Virtually every organization we encountered that has abolished appraisal has in place a corrective action policy or prescribed progressive discipline steps that ensure that necessary documentation—the required written records and notices of counseling, assistance plans, the consequences of not improving, and the like. We found this to be true at both "at will" and "just cause" organizations, whether union or non-union.

In addition to well-written policies and disciplinary procedures, every supervisor should understand the basics of good documentation. Without appraisal as a driver of documentation for errant employees, what kind of documentation is useful to make and preserve? Essentially, you want to make and preserve any evidence that substantiates the six elements of proof covered earlier. Figure 8.2 identifies some of the tangible ways of documenting without appraisal.

With or without appraisal, supervisors should continually try to keep some informal documentation of noted significant deficiencies, critical incidents, or other notes on what is going well or not (pretty much what is encouraged in traditional appraisal training for supervisors). This does not mean a change in coaching style, or walking up to people and saying "bad" every time a deficiency is observed. The purpose is to have information that, in cumulative form, indicates either a continuing problem or random and isolated instances that don't amount to much. If kept conscientiously, the informal documentation will tell the supervisor who needs special help. When the employee appears to be in deep trouble, such notations can provide a foundation for accurate information in the counseling memos and for legal documentation, should the situation deteriorate.

For example, I (T.C.) had a truck-stop client who discharged a waitperson for tardiness, improper guest checks, abuse of breaks, and other offenses. The employee filed a charge with the National Labor Relations Board, alleging that she was fired because she had talked with co-workers about bringing in a union. The Board Examiner came to the truck stop, reviewed the copious detailed documentation, but was still not satisfied. He wanted to see whether or not the documentation was merely a ploy of building a file against a targeted employee. To the Examiner's surprise, the manager pulled out a drawer of files, one for every waitperson, cook, or dishwasher who had worked there for five years prior. In every file, without exception, there was a simple sheet of deficiencies, showing the date

Lawsuit Defense Requirement	Means of Meeting Documentation Requirements Without Appraisal
1. Notice of Expectation, Standard, or Rule	Employee policies and handbooks, orientation checklists, training documentation, job descriptions, meeting agendas and minutes, e-mail, and memoranda to employees.
2. Necessity of Expectation, Standard, or Rule	The rule either speaks for itself (sleeping on the job) or is demonstrated through industry standards, safety laws, organizational objectives and goals, financial and efficiency data, and notices and memoranda to employees, among other evidence.
3. Employee Failed to Meet Expectation, Standard, or Rule	Memoranda, counseling documentation, and formal notice of warnings, reprimands, discipline, and discharge may describe deficiency, along with corroborating evidence from innumerable sources, such as production and efficiency data, the employee's work products, records of critical incidents, customer and co-worker complaints, signed statements and witness notes, and time and attendance records.
4. Fair and Objective Investigation Was Conducted	Investigation diaries, meeting notes, notes of interviews with the affected employee and witnesses, and the like are preserved and dated. In notice of discharge to the employee/file, determining factors are recounted.
5. Expectation, Standard, or Rule Is Consistently Enforced	Records of all similarly situated employees with the same degree of performance deficiencies or who committed similar infractions are preserved for a reasonable period of time (several years).
6. Recourse of Discharge Is Fair and Consistent with Treatment of Others	Seriousness of deficiency can be demonstrated by actual or possible impact on the organization (losses, exposure to liability, etc.) Discipline and discharge records document how the employer treated others with similar deficiencies or infractions.

Figure 8.2   Documentation Without Appraisal

and nature of the offense. The very best employees had notations, just like the bad ones, but fewer in number (e.g., tardy on this date, incorrect guest check on this date, and so on). She explained how she made it a habit to make a notation each time she experienced any problem. The case was dismissed by the NLRB the next day. The truck-stop manager was a very positive person who got along well with her workers. She explained that she did not take up the issues of the notations unless the issue was an emerging pattern or serious (e.g., shortages). Though few managers would be as meticulous as this truck-stop manager, regular documentation can be encouraged in the absence of appraisal—it can be done discreetly and with an attitude of having good information and learning, rather than "catching" people.

In a performance-related discharge, with or without appraisal, you need to be sure that the paper trail of the performance problems and your remedial efforts to counsel and assist the employee before discharging is continuous. Too often, managers think of compiling a paper trail only at the point they want separation, then they rush the "improvement program" and try to fire a 17-year employee with a three-month paper trail. The four and a half years they earnestly tried to help the employee are not documented. The deficient paper trail leaves the impression of a very unfair or biased discharge and is the basic ingredient of a lawsuit.

Whenever serious performance problems arise, hold formal meetings with the employee, provide the necessary guidance and counseling, and document, document, document. In lieu of appraisal documentation, you can send the employees memoranda, e-mails, and formal notices of deficiency at any appropriate time. If the remedial measures fail to correct performance-related problems and, in the end, involuntary separation is necessary, you will need to have written memoranda or documentation that minimally demonstrate all of the following elements:

- **The employee clearly knew what was expected of him or her.**

- **The employee was given all necessary information, training, and resources needed to perform adequately.**

- **The particulars relating to the performance deficiencies triggering the involuntary separation.** For example, if the employee repeatedly failed to complete major projects on time—what projects were not done or late, how did the employee know they were a priority, the consequences of the employee's failure to timely complete the projects, and the like.

- **The details of how and when the employee was advised of the deficiencies.** For example, documentation of the content and times of counseling and meetings with the employee, forewarning the employee that termination would be the result of continued poor performance.

- **The particulars on any special help, counseling, assistance, retraining, and other measures offered to help the employee correct the deficiencies.**

Obviously, this is a bare bones simplification of what and how to document performance deficiencies of a serious nature. An outstanding source that has been updated through the years is a very small book called *Supervisor's Guide to Documenting Employee Discipline* by Lee T. Patterson and Michael R. Deblieux. Flowcharts lay out the process with easy-to-follow guidelines, and, best of all, the *Guide* provides examples of counseling and disciplinary memoranda (see "Legal Documentation" in *Further Reading and Resources*).

In dropping appraisal as a part of the documentation strategy, organizations are often concerned that supervisors will fail to get the necessary documentation without some reminder or triggering mechanism. Among organizations practicing appraisal, the appraisal in theory is supposed to accomplish this. Without appraisal, how would this be encouraged? One answer is training supervisors and raising awareness that, in an appraisal-free organization, documenting performance issues any time they get serious is particularly important. As discussed, providing some structured steps and easy-to-use forms or templates may get greater cooperation in getting timely documentation. Some organizations that have abolished appraisal, such as GM–Powertrain and Michigan State University, have systems that, on an annual basis, require supervisors to write an appraisal for any employee who is not minimally meeting expectations.

Case Study

Michigan State University

Serving more than 44,000 students, Michigan State University (MSU) employs more than 5,700 clerical, technical, and service employees and over 1,200 employees in managerial, administrative, and nonfaculty professional positions. Virtually all non-exempt employees belong to a labor union. Like most universities, MSU had required appraisal for its exempt and non-exempt staff positions for several decades. Revision and revampment occurred periodically, with a new version put in place in 1991. Though geared toward employee excellence, with the latest bells and whistles, the tool was complicated and confusing, with numerous categories, all rated on a 5-point scale with narrative comments. For many, the appraisal process determined the "merit" pay adjustment for employees moving upward on an established pay range.

MSU's retreat from the practice of appraisal began with the personal experience of one employee. In 1993, H.R. professional Lauren Marinez was promoted to Assistant Director of Human Resources, a position that oversees the compensation function for all nonfaculty personnel. Not long after her promotion, Marinez was expected to write appraisals for her direct reports in the H.R. office. One of her reports was a valued colleague and friend who was her peer for many years. The idea of sitting down with him and rating him on scales made her extremely uncomfortable. After struggling with this for several days, her consternation culminated in an idea. She approached her boss, Denise Anderton, the H.R. Director, and asked if she could be excused from doing a formal appraisal. Marinez told her boss that she just didn't feel comfortable doing his appraisal. Then she asked, "Could I just talk to Jeff? I don't want to assign him a number, but I'd just like to have a conversation with him instead of doing the appraisal." Somewhat to her surprise, Anderton said yes with little hesitation. Marinez then met with Jeff, offering no report card, but just having a conversation around performance-related issues. Marinez recalled how well it turned out. "We had a dialogue about our work and didn't waste energy and time talking about ratings. We just talked. We understood one another. That is what it's all about." Jeff also found the conversation to be positive and helpful.

The conversation worked out so well that it gave Marinez an idea. She realized that most people on campus did not like giving and receiving ratings and this resulted in low utilization of the system. Marinez told her boss how well the conversation had gone, "If it worked well for us—why couldn't we just ask people to have a conversation instead of going through the paperwork?" They talked about the poor utilization rate with the current system and concluded the idea was worth exploring. Together they began the search for alternatives.

A few weeks later, the H.R. department received a formal charge from MSU President Peter McPherson to begin exploring ways to depart from a conventional appraisal system. In the months that followed, Marinez and her colleagues looked at the whole question of appraisal and the possibility of a simple alternative. They took time to study the issue of motivation, referring to Herzberg and McGregor. They attended workshops on the issue by Alfie Kohn, Peter Scholtes, Mary Jenkins, and Joel-Cutcher Gershenfeld. They looked at the correlation between merit pay and what people got out of it. They concluded the university got very little from the system then in place. They found that the numbers got in the way of meaningful conversation and enabling people to grow and develop. They learned that ratings were not accurate and didn't provide helpful information. In the end, the important questions were—Did they need any kind of rating and how could they eliminate the barriers presented by conventional appraisal? They looked at initiatives of other organizations, including DuPont, GM–Powertrain, Eastern Realty Management Investment Company, and others. They were most enamored, however, with the A.P.O.P. process adopted by Parkview Medical Center in Colorado (see *Memorial Hospital* case study in Chapter 7). A.P.O.P. stands for "annual piece of paper" and is a nonappraisal approach to an annual conversation that includes no performance review, no ratings, and virtually no documentation. Parkview's approach seemed to be what MSU was looking for.

The primary replacement to appraisal was called the Performance Development Program (PDP). The goal is not to rate performance or measure performance but to promote alignment of expectations and goals. Its explanatory form states that the substance of the program is derived from "trust in employees" and "communication between employees and supervisors, not in program paperwork."

The resulting form (see opposite page) is one page on which the supervisor checks eight boxes (with no rating) verifying that a discussion occurred, close in proximity to the employee's anniversary. The topics for discussion include performance; strengths and opportunities for growth; barriers to effective work performance; process improvement possibilities; future growth needs; the employee's feedback to the supervisor; and anything else either one wanted to talk about. The supervisor is given three lines for comments, if any. As a check relative to legal documentation, the form at the bottom contains one set of yes/no boxes, affirming or negating that the employee's performance meets minimum expectations. If the box indicating "no" is checked, then the supervisor must in effect provide comprehensive performance feedback in writing and work with the employee in developing a corrective action plan. This box is checked for between 2 and 3% of the employees annually. For the remaining 98%, no evaluation or written documentation is required beyond the verification of the conversation and the "yes" box being checked.

The process discards the majority of problems associated with conventional appraisal while ensuring that, if an employee is not performing at an acceptable level, the supervisor will take the additional step of documenting the problems, giving notice to the employee of the deficiencies, and beginning appropriate corrective action. That documentation process, called "Performance Improvement Plan," requires more elaborate documentation of both the deficiencies and planning of corrective measures. The plan requires a formal follow-up 90 days later. If, at that juncture, the problems are not resolved, and there is no indication of substantial improvement, the situation goes into the formal progressive discipline process, which ultimately may lead to involuntary separation.

In the five years since implementation, the PDP conversation and documentation process has proved to be very successful. The supervisors enjoy the flexibility, conversation, and communication occurring in the place of embittered discussion. The grievances and complaints previously associated with appraisal have all but disappeared. The university has worked hard at training all supervisors on an array of coaching concepts and tools, including human motivation, feedback, ways of identifying and helping people develop competencies, process improvement, and effective coaching, counseling, and communication tools. Compliance increased from 50% with the former appraisal system to between 85 and 88% each year since the adoption of PDP.

MICHIGAN STATE
U N I V E R S I T Y
Performance Development Program

Employee: _____   SS# _____

Job Title: _____

MAU/Department: _____   Date Due: _____

This form is to annually document that the following topics have been discussed. Supporting documentation should be retained by the department.

AGENDA	Check Off When Done
■ Discuss employee's performance on primary responsibilities/priorities in the past year. *(A written summary of responsibilities/priorities should have been previously provided to the employee, if requested.)* - Revise written responsibilities/priorities for the coming year, as needed. *(If revised, provide updated copy to the employee upon request.)* - Discuss how they relate to overall unit objectives.	☐
■ Discuss employee's strengths/areas for growth in critical performance factors (see back).	☐
■ Discuss barriers to effective work performance and job satisfaction.	☐
■ Discuss possible work process improvements.	☐
■ Discuss employee's development (over past year; future needs for current job; long-term career goals and development needs to achieve them).	☐
■ Discuss whether employee continues to grow to meet future needs and demands of the changing environment.	☐
■ Discuss employee's feedback/constructive suggestions for supervisor.	☐
■ Discuss anything else the employee or supervisor would like to address.	☐

Supervisor/Employee Comments: _____
_____
_____

Employee meets or exceeds current expectations: Yes ☐   No ☐ *

These topics have been discussed by:

Employee Signature _____ Date _____

Supervisor Signature _____ Date _____

*If no, Performance Improvement Plan needs to be completed (form available from Human Resources at 3-4330).

When Performance Development Program discussion is completed, provide a copy to employee, retain a copy for department file, and send original to Human Resources, 120 Nisbet Building.

Critical Performance Factors

The following are examples of general performance factors that may be considered during performance review discussions. Other performance factors that are specific to your unit's strategic plan or the employee's development plan may also be used.

Organizational Success

- Teamwork/Cooperation (within and across units)
- Customer Orientation
- Commitment to Continuous Quality/ Process Improvement
- Creativity/Innovation

- Flexibility/Adaptability to Change
- Continuous Learning/Development
- Displays Vision
- Leadership/Initiative

Making People Matter

- Respect for Others
- Interpersonal Skills
- Supports Diversity and Understands Related Issues
- Honesty/Fairness
- Builds Trust

- Recognizes Others' Achievements
- Understands Others' Perspectives
- Resolves Conflicts Constructively
- Positive Attitude

Job Effectiveness

- Planning/Organization
- Problem Solving/Judgment
- Makes Effective Decisions
- Takes Responsibility
- Achieves Results

- Communicates Effectively
- Dependability/Attendance
- Job/Organizational Knowledge
- Productivity

Additional Factors for Supervisors

- Coaches/Counsels/Evaluates Staff
- Identifies Areas for and Supports Employee Development Opportunities
- Encourages Teamwork and Group Achievement
- Leads Change/Achieves Support of Objectives
- Enables and Empowers Staff
- Strives to Achieve Diverse Staff at all Levels
- Understands Diversity Issues and Creates Supportive Environment for Diverse Employees

> ### *Education* for People Managers
>
> Mostly we hear about supervisors getting *trained* on the skills and techniques for effectively working with people. Psychologist and management consultant Richard Farson, however, suggests that you cannot improve people management through training. "*Training*," he says, "leads to the development of skills and techniques," but "techniques don't work well in human relations." What is required, says Dr. Farson, is *education.* Education, he explains, does not lead to a technique but to *information,* which can lead to *knowledge,* which may lead to *understanding* and *wisdom.* Wisdom may lead to "humility, compassion, and respect—qualities that are fundamental to effective leadership." While *training* makes people more alike (with everyone learning the same skills), *education* helps people examine their own personal experiences, a foundation for meaningful change. Dr. Farson observes that, with the right *education,* "managers can gain self-understanding, learn about their own interpersonal styles, their reactions to and the impact on others, prejudices and blind spots, strengths and weaknesses.[16]

A final caution in promoting good documentation is warranted. While there may be some need to encourage and train supervisors on effective documentation without appraisal, do not lose sight of your ultimate goal—building a healthy work climate and culture where people every day are energized and committed to do a good job. Excessive emphasis on documentation can chill relationships, generate fear, and convey distrust. Training and information about the legal points on documentation are helpful, but they must be given in the context of *education* and helping supervisors artfully balance effective leadership with the more mundane chores of providing paper trails to protect the organization in litigious times. See "*Education* for People Managers."

■ Appraisal as a Counseling Tool for Poor Performers

Assumption

Appraisal is an effective analytical and counseling tool for dealing with employees who are performing poorly.

While appraisal is dispensable for legal documentation, is it a helpful counseling tool for an employee with performance problems? At this point in the book, you already know our answer: *No*, for several reasons. First, as discussed in earlier chapters, scales and ratings conjure up needless negativity, barring openness to change and receiving feedback. Second, in the early stage of dealing with deficiencies, formally documenting negative feedback in writing (through appraisal or otherwise) may tend to make people more defensive. If it's going in the personnel file, one's reputation is at stake—rather than a meaningful exchange, tension or an argument is more likely to ensue. Without appraisal, the supervisor has the option of pursuing informal, less threatening methods before resorting to a documented approach. If appraisals are mandated, however, the supervisor is forced to document the deficiency whether the timing is right or not. Failure to do so would undermine the supervisor's and organization's credibility in the event that the employee's performance problem continues or worsens. Systematic appraisal denies the option of what is right for the given situation.

Yes, counseling within the format of appraisal may be appropriate or helpful in some situations. As discussed in Chapter 4, formal evaluation may be advantageous for probationary employees as a gate check or for counseling a poor performing employee who is lost in the job and struggling in a number of performance areas. On the other hand, if you have an accounting clerk who cannot get the numbers right, then counsel and document on that issue—the message will be clear and unambiguous. By contrast, using an appraisal in that situation may cloud the message. Rather than hearing that getting the numbers right is a dire problem needing immediate attention, the employee hears praise for her oral communication skills, well-organized files, and prompt turn-around of work. The person walks out thinking, "I'm doing pretty good. I am above average in six out of seven areas." Encouragement and positive feedback should be a daily habit of supervisors, but a counseling session documenting serious deficiencies is not the time or place to sing someone's praises.

Finally, the format of appraisal may unintentionally encourage supervisors to think about performance problems in constrictive ways. For example, appraisal criteria may draw the supervisor's focus to a list of job duties, predetermined performance goals, or competencies to be measured. These approaches are about looking at the pieces rather than the whole. A performance problem requires thinking about a wide range of causes and potential remedies. Between the lines of the deficient ratings, what is really going on? Is there a system cause? Is there a relationship issue with the supervisor or co-workers? Is something going on in the employee's personal life? Is the person a good fit for the nature of the work? Is the overall job excessively burdened? Focusing on established criteria or measurements, as appraisal encourages, tends to take the conversation away from the broader, deeper issues that so often are the cause of performance deficiencies. Accordingly, reliance on appraisal as the primary counseling and discipline-related tool may discourage more open conversations, meaningful reflection, and deep probing of underlying issues and causes.

■ Dealing with Problem Employees

Assumption

Poor performance arises from laziness, dereliction, and irresponsibility.

Short of providing a compendium on how to deal with problem employees, we think any organization moving away from appraisal must take time to reorient managers and supervisors toward looking at performance problems in new ways. Again, we are talking about a shift in assumptions. If supervisors approach every performance problem with the assumption that the employee has chosen to be derelict in performing his job duties, they approach the problem too narrowly, perhaps with the wrong focus. Applying new assumptions is not a Pollyannish approach that ignores the possibility of bad apples—sometimes employees *are* lazy or suffer emotional maladies that put them beyond help. While a shift toward healthier assumptions does not deny this possibility, it brings a more expansive view that takes into account a broader base of possibilities, including saying goodbye to the employees. As discussed earlier in the book, more often than not, performance problems are *not* attributable to the individual for lack of trying. Figure 8.3 attempts to give some visual perspective to the various causes of performance deficiencies. Note that the causes of poor performance may arise from the system or from causes beyond the individual's control. Harvard Business Professor and author Dr. Michael Beer shared a similar view regarding poor performers (see "Some Observations").

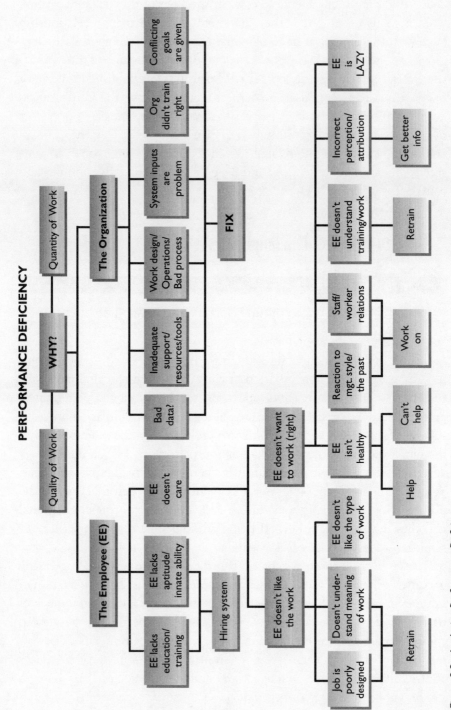

Figure 8.3   *Analyzing Performance Deficiency*

Some Observations on Appraisals and Performance

Dr. Michael Beer kindly took time to share his thoughts with us on appraisal and related management issues, and here is a summary of his comments:

CEOs and H.R. executives resist dropping appraisals because they want linear ways to control performance, and they believe appraisal is a tool that will help. They don't trust people down below, so they need something objective to ensure the work is being done. They persist in appraisal because of implicit notions that we must try to fit people into the system, the department, the company. This is a legitimate concern, and it is a good idea and worthwhile to try to find ways to get consistent modes of management, but appraisals and elaborate administrative processes do not accomplish this. Large companies cannot create a form to cover every situation within the entire organization.

Appraisals continue because everyone else does it—it is part of the landscape of management. And it fits our linear way of thinking. In Western society, we have difficulty in looking at the circularity of things, indirect causes, and unintended consequences—we look for the direct line. If there is a problem, we tell the person he screwed up, instead of thinking of the circular and contextual causes and the design of the system. Poor performance issues often are about fit. Most performance problems are not about people who are duds, but about people who are in the wrong job or with the wrong company.

While performance discussions are important, and learning must occur, appraisals do not contribute much to improvement of systems and making performance more effective. Appraisal systems are deeply flawed, make people unhappy, and cause defensiveness. They are not necessary to improve performance. Instead, we must look for ways to help the work unit in what is important, asking how do we change structure and culture to get better performance.

To break away from appraisal, first, companies must have the guts to break away from what everyone else is doing. Second, they must create alternative ways to deal with performance and understand performance. Foremost, they must focus on high-performance *systems,* i.e., the organizational culture, what the customer wants, goals, people having a voice, units having information and autonomy, and feedback from actions and the results of work units and the company. These actions will help people be more performance-oriented and help them care about performance and high standards. These strategies will make appraisals unnecessary.

Instead of appraising people, Dr. Beer calls for organizational assessment using the Organizational Fitness Profiling method. This proven approach, used by Merck, Honeywell, Hewlett-Packard, and others, involves a series of open and fact-based dialogues looking at values, alignment of strategies, barriers and opportunities. The goal of Fitness Profiling is strategic organization learning, enabling management to "assess the 'fit' between competitive realities and the organization's capabilities to succeed in meeting those realities."[17]

Assume you have ruled out the various system causes, and you have an individual who is not performing. At this point, the options fall into three categories:

1. **Help the individual improve to an acceptable level.**

2. **Alter the job or find a position that is better aligned with the individual's skills and potential.**

3. **Take measures to remove the employee from the organization in a manner that is respectful and caring.**

Choosing the correct course depends on the facts and good judgment. Option 1 should always be the beginning point unless it's crystal clear that any such efforts would be futile. Option 2 affirms a belief in people and is supportive. Many successful organizations work hard at trying to avoid involuntary separations—they try to get people into the right job. Exercising option 2 is not done in the spirit of laxity or in condoning less than optimal performance, but is based on a belief that people will perform best when the fit is right. Organizations that readily dismiss poor performers create a cloud of fear for the remaining employees and rupture morale. (While it is demoralizing to keep a nonproductive person in a job, we have found over the years that such person's co-workers still expect that person to be treated fairly—they get quite upset about unfair treatment even when the nonperformance was plainly evident.) In the event that finding a better fit is not wise, justifiable, or possible, then option 3, saying good-bye, must be pursued.

The box, "Questions to Ask," provides a list of questions for the organization to help choose the most appropriate among options 1, 2, and 3.

When these questions do not lead to other solutions, and option 3, involuntary separation, appears to be the only logical course, there is another option. Sometimes open and honest dialogue about the issues with the individual will lead to voluntary departure. For legal reasons, certain safeguards must be taken before pressing involuntary separation. Except for probationary or temporary employees, or, in the case of willful misconduct as opposed to failure to perform, involuntary separation should not occur unless remedial measures (assistance, training, etc.) have been provided and documented. There should be verifiable evidence and written documentation as discussed earlier in the chapter. Consultation with labor counsel may also be wise, particularly when terminating managerial and professional employees in the higher earning brackets.

Questions to Ask When Facing a Serious Performance Problem

Though no list will have all the right questions, this list is intended to encourage more expansive thinking when an organization must deal with an individual whose performance level is seriously in question.

- Is the substandard performance a pattern or recent development?

- Is this the first incident of this type, or have variations happened in the past?

- Can the observations of the supervisor be confirmed by others?

- Is there a personal, chemistry, or political issue that may have triggered the problem?

- Does the person have the necessary skills, knowledge, abilities, temperament to do the job?

- Has the person received adequate training, guidance, and feedback?

- Does the person like the work? (This is different from whether or not they like the company.)

- Has the performance deficiency/problem been observed with other people in the same or other jobs?

- How long has the person been in the job? Could sub-par performance be explained by insufficient time on the learning curve, not progressing with the learning curve, stagnation, or burnout?

- Has the job undergone significant change recently or over the past few years?

- Has there been a change in the workload volume, increase in stressors, staffing shortages, or other changes that may be triggering the performance issue?

- Have management and performance expectations changed? Does the individual understand these changes?

- Are system barriers causing performance problems that are not the individual's fault?

- Does the employee have the proper tools, equipment, personnel support, work environment?

Conclusion

People problems and poor performance issues are tough with or without appraisal. Dropping appraisal, we think, provides more options and greater freedom in choosing the best recourse. In protecting the employer's legal interests, deploying appraisal seems to have more disadvantages than advantages, especially if nonappraisal is accompanied by prudent documentation practices. Dropping appraisal places a greater burden on the organization to ensure that it has enlightened leaders, which requires nothing less than a relentless effort of "educating" the formal leadership and nurturing a culture that takes a healthier view of people. That culture cannot emerge or thrive unless organizational structures undergo radical change. In the next chapter, we help you roll up your sleeves so you can begin the process of designing alternative practices and systems in place of appraisal.

Review of Chapter Assumptions

Conventional Assumption

Appraisal documentation is required by law.

Alternative Assumptions

- Appraisals generally are not required by law.
- Some public sector and regulatory agencies mandate formal evaluation of performance.

Conventional Assumption

Appraisals provide reliably helpful legal evidence.

Alternative Assumptions

- Appraisal evidence may benefit either the employer or the employee.
- Employers can defend against employee lawsuits by properly documenting performance deficiencies.
- Performance deficiencies may be documented and evidenced by innumerable sources.

Conventional Assumption

Appraisal is an effective analytical and counseling tool for dealing with employees who are performing poorly.

Alternative Assumptions

- Employees viewed as performing poorly expect to get prompt notice, good information about the nature of the deficiency, and assistance as appropriate.

- The best counseling tool for an employee performing poorly depends on the individual, the situation, and the style of the supervisor.

Conventional Assumption

Poor performance arises from laziness, dereliction, and irresponsibility.

Alternative Assumptions

- Determining the nature and causes of performance deficiencies involves assessment of many complex and interrelated factors.

- Performance deficiencies sometimes arise because the individual is at fault, but more often deficiencies arise from other causes, including the system, fitness for the job, and relationship issues.

Part Three

How to Get There: The Transition to Alternatives

To be fully free to create,
we must first find
the courage and
the willingness to let go:
Let go of the strategies
that have worked
for us in the past . . .
Let go of our bias,
the foundation
of our illusions.
—Gordon MacKenzie

9

Disconnecting Appraisal and Designing Alternatives

The realization of ignorance is the beginning of wisdom. You will find that the more you realize you don't know, the more you will understand.

G. I. Gurdjieff, *Teachings of Gurdjieff*

If everyone desired to do his or her job correctly and on time, and could be trusted to act with integrity and in support of the firm's aims and goals, what would your organization's processes and procedures look like?

Dr. John Whitney

When we talk to audiences about abolishing performance appraisals, in greater and greater numbers we see nodding heads and ready acceptance of this idea. This reaction is not surprising considering the high rate of dissatisfaction with the process. Invariably we also find audiences very anxious to get to the next step—*What do you do instead?* It seems our audiences expect us to hand out a list of steps along with forms that they can copy and go back and implement the following Monday. If you're of the same mindset, we're sorry to break your bubble—there are no best practices or processes that you can just copy and implement. If you want genuine, lasting success in transforming to a workplace culture without appraisal, you must roll up your sleeves, gather a team of passionate people, and do the hard work of designing with a clean sheet of paper. Anything less is a waste of your energy and a surefire recipe for failure.

Though we offer no packaged formula for designing alternatives to performance appraisal, we do lay out some step-by-step guidance on how to get there. If the prior chapters have motivated you to rid your organization of appraisals, it's crucial that you refrain from leaping into changes without an understanding of design and the process of change, our focus here and in the next chapter.

■ Overview of the Design Process

Successful design of appraisal alternatives requires nothing less than engaging key stakeholders in an iterative process of deep questioning and thinking. This is hard work and it takes time—possibly a year or two in a smaller organization of a few hundred or less, and maybe several years in organizations with several thousand employees or complex matrixes of corporate structure. The process takes time because the task is much more than merely creating a design. You may start out thinking you are designing a *single* practice to replace appraisal. As you go down the path, however, you'll quickly discover that you are really designing *several* systems to replace all the things you had loaded onto appraisal.

Before you brainstorm new possibilities and strategies, you will need to do some assessment and deep probing of your existing practices. Somewhere early on, you will also need to gain a clear sense of the overall mission. The ultimate aim is not about designing alternatives—it's about transforming your work culture and people systems to garner greater commitment and alignment with your organizational vision, values, and goals. Beyond design, it will take time to communicate your ideas to those affected, listen to them, and redesign based on their input. In most situations, you will be running trial clinics and pilots and implementing changes in phases. And these too will trigger further redesign.

Though the actual work of designing is complex and challenging, it can be interesting and fun. Foremost, it should be a *learning* experience in which you and the organization as a whole learn together and discover new paths that can move your organizational culture forward (see systems thinker Jamshid Gharajedaghi's comments). It may bolster your confidence to see a concrete list of the first seven steps we recommend for cre-

> ### Jamshid Gharajedaghi on the Goals of Process Design
>
> Designers seek to choose rather than predict the future. They try to understand rational, emotional, and cultural dimensions of choice and to produce a design that satisfies a multitude of functions. The design methodology requires that designers learn how to use what they already know, learn how to realize what they do not know, and learn how to learn what they need to know. Finally, producing a design requires an awareness of how activities of one part of a system affect and are affected by other parts. This awareness requires understanding the nature of interactions among the parts.[1]

ating alternatives to performance appraisal, followed by discussion. The remaining steps are covered in the next chapter.

■ Quick Overview of Initial Steps

Step 1: Conduct a preliminary assessment of the need for change. Take time to investigate, study, and give some forethought—look from afar at what is not working, get some sense of your overall mission, and then choose the one particular function of appraisal that you initially want to tackle.

Step 2: Approach top management to get a charter that reflects your particular focus and any boundaries of your design process. You let top management know what needs to be fixed and get their blessing and formal support, defining the objectives, givens, and parameters of the project.

Step 3: Form a small design team of passionate stakeholders. You can't do it alone—form the initial design team by gathering a small group of carefully chosen people who are excited about the possibility of creating a better workplace.

Step 4: Methodically examine the appraisal process you are replacing. Look at the old system and carefully identify its aims, outcomes, structure, and underlying assumptions.

Step 5: Clarify the overall objective for your alternative systems. Based on your learning, restate the overriding purpose and detail specific objectives of the alternative system you intend to design.

Step 6: Develop an alternative set of underlying assumptions. Using various creative tools, ascertain the new set of assumptions upon which you will build the alternative system.

Step 7: Develop a new design. Relative to your focal function, define the aim, determine indicators of success, explore models, and create the key concepts and skeletal framework for a proposed model.

■ Step 1: Assess the Need for Change

No doubt you are dissatisfied with your appraisal system. Probably without any insights from this book, you already had some thoughts on how and why it failed. You also have spoken to colleagues and others in the organization and have a good sense that people would support a real alternative. We caution you, however, not to be overconfident. Recall from way back in Chapter 1 not to expect the people in your organization to give you a standing ovation when you announce your idea about throwing out appraisals. Many people cling to the illusion that they need appraisal to tell them where they stand. Others who have not gone through the thinking in this book may misunderstand any talk about *abolishing appraisal* because, effective or not, they associate appraisal with goals of fostering feedback, helping people, and making fair decisions about pay and career advancement. Because they have not examined the underlying assumptions of appraisal, they see its perennial problems only as something that needs to be fixed in the process. They probably haven't looked at the unintended effects of appraisal. Few people in your organization have ever pondered the possibility that appraisal is hopelessly flawed or even that something else was possible. So if you send out a corporate-wide e-mail asking who would like to help the organization end appraisal, you will probably get a very mixed reaction, at best.

Rather than asking others to support abolishment, begin the process with your own education. Take some time to investigate and assess the appraisal practice in your organization. It will be easier and more effective if you can get two or three people of like mind to help you make this preliminary assessment. With your start-up colleagues, take a long look at the appraisal practice in your organization and ponder questions such as these:

- Do the people in our organization seem satisfied with our current appraisal process?

- Is there a particular aspect that causes the most dissatisfaction or renders our appraisal process ineffective? Or are people just indifferent and underwhelmed?

- Has our organization gone through umpteen revisions of the appraisal process and forms?

- Do people in our organization gladly participate in the process? Or do we see procrastination and prolific prodding to get supervisors and employees to participate?

- Are there indicators of dissatisfaction from data our organization has collected from sources such as employee attitude surveys, exit interviews, feedback gathered on our appraisal system, grievances or complaints filed with H.R. or EEO offices?

- When appraisals are spoken about at lunch, in the break room, or by the water cooler, do people indicate respect, enthusiasm, and appreciation for the process? Or do we hear sarcasm, fear, indifference, or putting down the process?

- In the day-to-day work environment throughout the year, do the people in our organization pay attention to the goals, personal development, and other links to our appraisal process? Or do people seem connected to these links only during the few weeks before and after the appraisal process?

- Do we find that some of the functions of the appraisal process, such as coaching, feedback, and employee development, are undermined because of conflicting functions (determining pay, focus on ratings, etc.)?

The answers may not always be evident. In some instances, you may need to look at data or historical information. Short of conducting a scientific study, on a low-key level, you could conduct some interviews or question selected individuals by e-mail.

Once you have completed your preliminary investigation and assessment, use your intuition and give some thought to where the greatest dissatisfaction and dysfunction lie. This critical step may seem premature, but, as a monster of many functions, appraisal cannot be taken on whole for reasons explained in Chapter 1. An effective plan of attack is to break off pieces and take on one piece at a time. Breaking apart the functions of appraisal to examine each piece separately is called *decoupling* or sometimes *debundling* (see "Debundling").

To do a good job and get energy behind the project, you will need to have a focal point or perhaps a couple of closely related focal points. The stated mission should not be—*to abolish performance appraisals and create alternatives*. This would engender little enthusiasm. It makes no substantive statement about *what you want to do*.

Narrow your focus to the function of appraisal that will be your initial focus, for example, *to create a system for effective feedback*. The findings of your preliminary investigation and assessment should point to one or two areas of particular concern in your current appraisal system. If your organization has never had appraisal, the initial focus would be around the function of greatest interest. Choosing an initial area of focus does not mean that the other functions will be dropped. They will be dealt with later. If there's a keen interest in several appraisal functions, for reasons that should be clear from the discussion and research presented in the function chapters (Chapters 4–8), we strongly encourage your team to choose feedback or development as an initial focus rather than the more sensitive issue of pay or promotion—the sorting out and design steps will flow much better if stickier issues are done after completing building blocks in other functional areas. Moreover, at that point, you'll be working from experience. Once you discover the focal point of your mission, you're ready for the next step—talking to top leadership.

■ Step 2: Get a Charter from Top Management

Nearly everyone who has earned his or her stripes in organizational life has suffered the bitter disappointment of having a promising, ongoing project undermined by upper management. Such an experience is painful and crushes the spirit. To avoid such a fate in designing alternatives to appraisal, at the beginning, middle, and ending stages, check in with top management to get their blessing. This is particularly important in the

---

Debundling

Peter Scholtes, author of *The Leader's Handbook,* defines *debundling* as taking apart "all of the various separate service providers or perceived benefits" that appraisal offers to the organization. He recommends four sequential steps for debundling:

1. Make a list of the functions, benefits, and services you had hoped to achieve under your appraisal system.

2. For *each* benefit or service on your list, ask whether it is important enough that the organization wants to find a way to accomplish it.

3. If yes, take the benefit or service and treat it as a separate function, disconnecting it from other functions.

4. For each separated function, ask what is the best way to deliver the intended benefit or service (examining the purpose, values, premises, etc. and determining the best action to achieve the desired function).[2]

---

case of appraisal. For whatever reason, CEOs seem to have a reflexive penchant for insisting on appraisal, perhaps emanating from their subscription to perceived conventional wisdom, rather than from deep thought or validated experience. We have encountered several CEOs who normally cut slack to the H.R. department but interceded and imposed edicts with regard to the sacred cows of appraisal and pay for performance.

To avoid such a fate, get an audience with top management and speak with conviction about your mission. Share with them your overriding concerns and your preliminary assessment. Be clear and specific about your focus—again, not talking about a goal to abolish or change appraisals, but to find a better way to deal with the function or concern of X (e.g., a system to foster better coaching and growth of employees, or a pay system that will not cause annual widespread grief and dissension because it's seen as political and arbitrarily unfair). Listen to their responses and gain a realistic sense of what they can support and keep an open mind about what they are not ready for.

Once you have reconciled your mission with their input, you're ready for the benediction. Ask them to "charter" a design team to work on the issue. A *charter* is a somewhat formal charge or statement, in which the organization officially embraces an endeavor, such as exploration of new ways to achieve employee development. In painstakingly clear form, you'll need to discuss with them the following:

- The purpose and main objectives of the design team—the focal area of what needs to be fixed and what your team will work on

- The anticipated composite of the design team participants (probably not the particular people, but a general description of the selection criteria)

- The design process, including anticipated means of getting input and support from the organization's various sectors

- Any anticipated need for internal and external resources, including any foreseeable financial resources required

- Any other boundaries or givens that may significantly impact the design process or end product.

In asking top management to charter your team, you are asking the leadership to make an earnest commitment to your mission and anoint the team to take on the task. At this stage you are not asking for a carte blanche sign-off—you can even tell them when you plan to revisit. Instead, you are seeking their pledge to not interfere with the design team

---

What If You're the Top Banana?

If you are the CEO, COO, or business owner, Step 2, of course, would be different but nonetheless essential. Though you are the top banana, you know that a transition away from appraisal, like any other significant organizational change, cannot be accomplished by a directive. If you are passionate about exploring alternatives, you must deploy all of your intuitive, persuasive, listening, and leadership skills to foster openness and enthusiastic support from a critical mass within the organization. Even though *you* fully support this initiative, you still need a small team of advocates to make an initial presentation to the key players in H.R., finance, product areas, etc. Likewise, a design team should be formed, and, as indicated in the remaining steps, continue to meet with top management as a group, even if you are personally involved with the design team's efforts.

and keep an open mind on the issues, except for any limitations or conditions stated up-front. While top management is present, record on a flipchart the key points of the charter. Promptly follow-up with a written charter, memo, or protocol suitable for your organization.

■ Step 3: Form a Design Team

Pulling together an ideal design team is not easy—it requires some forethought and judgment. The ideal design team represents the entire organization, which will provide a broad perspective and create a beginning base of support. In a perfect world of democratic ideals, you would want to bring together a vertical and horizontal slice of the organization. The idea is to put together a team that integrates the perspectives of all the various stakeholders. A broad-based team of this nature, however, would not work well in all organizations but may be worth seriously considering if you can say yes to *all* of the following questions about your organization:

- Do we have a nonpatriarchal, high-trust organization where everyone feels comfortable to speak freely? (For a good litmus test, ask: When your organization holds meetings, is the conversation in the restroom after the meeting different than the one that took place in the meeting room? If yes, your organization fails this test!)

- Do we have a relatively open, seamless organization without a caste system and with subtle boundaries between the job classes, such as executive, managerial, professional, clerical, technical, skilled, and unskilled?

- Does our organization have a *proven* track record of successfully using diverse teams, consisting of both managers and nonmanagerial employees, and in dealing with sensitive, challenging, and emotional issues, such as pay or handling a downsizing?

Organizations with more than 500 employees that could say yes to all three of these questions are a rarity. In any case, if your organization passes the test, you may be successful in working with a widely diverse, democratic team with representation from every level and all functional areas. (If you intend to include nonmanagerial employees in your team, in the United States, you will need to seek legal counsel regarding labor law implications.)[3]

If you're not blessed with an unusually open, high-trust organization as we've described, we advise you not to use the design of appraisal alternatives as your first try at democracy. Appraisal is a highly charged issue, and its obscure nature makes it extremely challenging. Accordingly, start with a design team that is narrow in scope, which does not preclude anyone's participation but is simply a productive way to design a plan through logical steps of education and involvement. As much as possible, you want to get the natural, normal politics and dynamics of the organization out of the way. It's also very important to meet people "where they're at" and bring them along in a way that is helpful and comfortable. In later steps of the design process, we prescribe methods to ensure involvement and input *from everyone* in the organization prior to the final design.

This "narrow" version design team still brings together divergent perspectives and a healthy mix of people. We recommend that you try to convene the major stakeholders, drawing relatively equally from people who give appraisals and people who receive appraisals. Rather than trying to bring the whole vertical ladder into the room, compose the team of people who are within two or three levels of each other in the hierarchy. For example, do not bring a high-level vice president or director onto a team if you plan to include employees from line-level or unskilled job areas. Our experience, with the exception of highly open organizations, is that the presence of high-level people produces a significant chilling effect on the participation and forthrightness of people from the lower rungs of the organizational ladder. In selecting design team members, you can draw from lower or higher levels, as long as the span of levels is not great. We find that working from somewhere in the middle of the organization works particularly well. For example, you could have middle managers and supervisors and a similar-sized component of professional and administrative employees who don't supervise but are recipients of appraisal. In addition to these guidelines, be sure that the team otherwise reflects the diverse nature of organization. We use the term *diverse* to include traditional diversity (gender, race, ethnicity, age, disability) as well as diversity in representing the various functions, departments, and work locations.

Diversity in perspectives and outlook is invaluable. You are not looking to fill a team with people who are predisposed to abolish performance appraisal—this would deprive the team of credibility and severely limit its creative potential. What you do need are participants who: (1) have a sincere and preferably passionate interest in the "people" issues and the overall good of your organization; (2) are open to new thinking, exploration, and learning; and (3) are *opinion leaders* in your organization. By opinion leaders, we don't mean *opinionated* people. Opinion leaders are people who are respected and valued for their ideas. Their strength is not derived from title or position, but from their commitment, caring qualities, common sense, intelligence, charisma, superior performance, long experience, or some combination of these qualities. An ideal design team size is ten to twelve people. While diverse representation, as delineated above, is necessary, this goal should not balloon the size of the team. It will be difficult to get more than a dozen people to create a cohesive plan or even meet regularly (this is a long-term project). Hence, you may need to strike some creative compromises to balance size and the need for diverse representation.

Beyond getting a diverse group of opinion leaders, think also about the personalities, dynamics, and interplay of the people you are bringing together. Designing appraisal alternatives is a long-term project, necessitating many hours of discussion, reflection, and inquiry. Use your intuition and artful skills to assemble an enthusiastic group that can work well together.

If your organization has one or more labor unions that represent a significant portion of the people affected by your appraisal practice, it may be helpful to include them on the design team. If the relationship is relatively congenial and cooperative, we strongly encourage inclusion because many decisions related to changing or abolishing appraisal will constitute a "mandatory bargaining subject," which means you are legally required to negotiate any changes that impact wages or the terms and conditions of employment. If you are blessed with a reasonably cooperative relationship, it will be much easier to negotiate these terms if union representatives are seated on the design team from the beginning. We generally have found labor organizations to be positive and supportive of the organization's open examination of appraisal—they hear the same gripes you do! In larger organizations, we have observed that broad-based "democratic" design teams are particularly effective when a cooperative but strong labor union actively participates in the design process. In any case, partnering with the union from the beginning will make it easier to build trust and create acceptance of contemplated changes.

■ Step 4: Look at the Past–A Critical Step

Once you have the design team in place, bring them together for an overview of the mission and charter. You may want to share your preliminary thoughts and how your initial assessment led you to choose your focal points. Review with the team the input from top management, including the givens and parameters of your charter. Allow team members time to respond, ask questions, and express their thoughts about the process and where you are headed.

Then the real work begins, with a process of reflection and education. In this step, the team examines the former appraisal system and carefully identifies its aims, outcomes, and underlying assumptions. This step is much more than a warm-up exercise. To move on to alternatives that will really make a difference, it is absolutely critical that the team takes the necessary time to explore and reflect on the organization's past practice of appraisal, work culture, and belief systems about people, work, improvement, motivation, and appraisal itself. This education process is best accomplished by allowing unrushed time to ponder five questions about your present (or most recent) appraisal process:

1. What are its purposes, goals, and objectives?

2. What results and outcomes have we seen and experienced?

3. What are its features and characteristics?

4. What are its underlying assumptions relative to our particular area of focus?

5. What links or connections can we make between the results we get and the underlying assumptions?

Answering these questions requires probing, thinking, reflection, dialogue, and discussion, along with charting the responses. Consequently, plan a minimum of four hours, and, in larger complex organizations, a full day. We will discuss the process of this inquiry for each question separately.

Question 1: What are the purposes, goals, and objectives of our appraisal process? With this question, you are seeking the team's perception of why appraisals are conducted. Rephrase the question to get them thinking: *What is the purpose of performance appraisal? Why do we have ap-*

> ## What if your organization is new or never had appraisals?
>
> If you work in an organization that is new, never had appraisals, or let them lapse long ago, it's important to work through the five questions from a slightly different angle. With no organizational memory of appraisals, the team can answer the questions in the context of their experiences with appraisals in other workplaces. With estimates as high as 89% of organizations in the United States using appraisal, most of your team will likely have had some experience in giving or receiving appraisals. If not, they can draw on their experience with "appraisals" in school or college—a grade is really an appraisal of sorts. In addition to the five questions, ask the group whether the underlying assumptions of conventional appraisal can be identified in the management style and human resources practices of your organization.

praisals? Be sure that answers are about what appraisals are *intended* to do and not a critique or description of personal experiences. Even though, in accordance with your charter, you are focusing on a particular function, such as feedback or pay, in this question and in the next two questions, allow the team to broadly define the purposes, outcomes, and characteristics of performance appraisal. At this early education stage, it will be difficult for people to sort out the various functions. Letting them see the *decoupling* of appraisal is an underlying goal of the education process.

As we discussed in Chapter 1, the purposes behind appraisal are useful and positive, and you can expect their responses to likewise be positive. If someone identifies a negative purpose, in all likelihood it's not an intended function of appraisal, but a criticism of what they've experienced. If it's the latter, don't list it as a purpose or function, but save it as a reply for the next question. The list you end up with may look something like our list of sample responses in Chapter 1 (Figure 1.1). Once you have exhaustively recorded the various purposes of your present appraisal system, tape them up on the wall so they can be referenced during subsequent questions.

Question 2: What results and outcomes have we seen or experienced?
Like the last question, this question is intended to provoke free-flowing answers. Ask the question in different ways to help the team recall their experiences:

- What have we personally experienced in connection with our appraisal process? What behaviors in ourselves and others have we seen?

- What are the results, effects, and outcomes we have seen—good, bad, or indifferent?

- How is the process viewed by the people here? What associations do we have with the process?

We find that everyone contributes answers to these questions, relaying personal stories and perceptions of the process. Most of the responses will be critical, negative, and even sarcastic. Some responses may be matter-of-fact neutral. You will likely hear one or two sincere accounts of favorable experiences with the process. Record all of their answers in a nonjudgmental way, asking questions only to clarify their statements. Many of their responses will seem disconnected from the purpose and design of appraisal—you must still write down those answers. Most of the responses, it will turn out, are actually unintended consequences and effects. For example, someone may say the process has been a de-motivating experience or that people changed their behaviors in the weeks immediately prior to the review. These and other unintended consequences of appraisal are a part of the experience. We have provided a list of examples of responses to question 2 to give you some sense of what you may hear. Of course, your team's list will look quite different, though we invariably find the same pattern of issues. You likely will fill up two or three sheets on a flipchart with this question.

Question 3: What are the characteristics and features of our appraisal process? The last question focused on people's *experiences* with appraisal. In this question, we're asking the team to describe the *characteristics* and visible design *features* of your organization's appraisal process. This question always requires prompting because many participants will not readily recognize what is meant by *characteristic*. Start the team off with some examples, such as:

- It's a once-a-year event

- Everyone must do it—it's mandated

- Feedback is documented

- It's retained in the employee's personnel file.

Then allow the team to add to the list other characteristics and fea-

Examples of Responses to Question 2

What are the results and outcomes of appraisal?

- Focuses on weaknesses and deficiencies
- Standards are inconsistently applied from one supervisor to another
- People are not listening; preoccupied with the bottom line—money or overall rating!
- Tied to documenting bad performers for termination
- Causes fear and apprehension
- Ratings seem arbitrary—supervisors don't really know who did what
- Demoralizes those who do worse than expected
- Conversations are guarded and superficial
- Many people (including supervisors) are just going through the motions
- Unfairly blames people or credits people
- Ratings don't always mean what they say
- Lets people know where they stand with the boss
- Conversation often is forced —"whatever" attitude
- Goals are reviewed and fixed
- People get help on training needs
- Not always done as scheduled—people procrastinate, we're too busy
- Short-lived effects
- Lots of surprises
- Arguments and heated conversations

tures of your organization's appraisal process. Some individuals may be stuck in the *experiences* or *functions* thinking mode, so be sure each response qualifies as a *characteristic* before writing it down. The items they will add vary depending on the kind of appraisal process, but in typical systems, we see answers such as:

- Personnel provides forms
- The meeting is scheduled by the supervisor
- There are ratings and scales

- The employee must sign the document
- Feedback is given, some good and some areas needing improvement
- The form contains a training and development planning section
- The supervisor's boss must sign off before it is official
- If an employee has unsatisfactory ratings, an improvement plan must be attached.

Allow the team to continue until all of the important features of your process have been listed. The answers to this question will be very helpful in answering the next.

Question 4: What are the underlying assumptions of our appraisal process relating to our particular area of focus? This question is particularly challenging for design teams. The reason is that few of us have had practice or experience in thinking about underlying assumptions. Before posing the question, you must clearly define what is meant by *underlying assumption* and give some easy-to-understand examples. Additional background is in Chapter 1, and other resources on assumptions are identified under *Designing New H.R. Systems, Further Reading and Resources.* After getting the group comfortable with the concept of underlying assumptions, turn the focus to the particular function you have chosen to work on (feedback, coaching, development, promotion, pay, or whatever it is). For example, if your initial goal is to design a better feedback system, you would ask—*What are our beliefs and assumptions in our existing system as to how and when feedback occurs? What do we assume or accept as "given" in expecting our existing feedback system to work?*

A good way to get the team started is have everyone take a look at the *characteristic* list (question 3). Identify the characteristics related to the function you are working on. Ask them *why* a particular feature is in your appraisal process. You may need to repeat *why* several times to get at the deeply rooted reason. Sometimes the repetition of *why* is known as the "Five-Whys" method or perspective to encourage people to go at least five levels deep in looking for root causes. For example, if your focus is feedback, you might look at the characteristic—*feedback is documented.* If you ask *why,* they may say—*to create a record of performance.* Asking *why* again might get—*to protect the organization in the event of litigation.* At this deeper level, you usually will be looking at an assumption, i.e., "we assume appraisals protect the organization in the event of litigation." You should ask these *why* questions with each characteristic or feature that broadly or specifically relates to your chosen area of function. Other assumptions relating to current practice may not necessarily be derived from the *characteristic* list.

Let the team work through its own answers. If they have difficulty warming up, give them some examples from assumptions in the chapter that corresponds to the function you are working on. If people suggest any broad-based assumptions, such as improving individuals improves organizational performance, include those on your list. If they suggest underlying assumptions unrelated to your chosen function area, list them elsewhere in a "parking lot," so you can draw from them at a later time.

We find that people who are inexperienced in unearthing assumptions frequently suggest concepts that are not assumptions. Rather than identifying premises or beliefs we hold as true in the design or conception of appraisal (e.g., *rating is a helpful form of feedback* or *raters can be fair and objective*), participants may cross over to describing the *experience* of appraisal (*ratings are de-motivating* or *raters are biased*). The *experience* with appraisals was covered in question 2. Accordingly, in this question, keep the responses to what we *ideally* hold to be true if the appraisal process were to function effectively. The idea with this question is to surface as many assumptions, beliefs, and premises as possible so their validity can be examined in question 5. When you can see that the team has adequately covered the key assumptions of your chosen function area, you're ready for the creative challenge of the next step.

Question 5: What links or connections can we make between the results we get and the underlying assumptions? In this step, have the team look at the *assumptions* list and the *experience* list already completed. To get the creative juices flowing, put both lists side by side. Ask the team to look at both and try to see any logical connections between the validity of the assumptions and the outcomes received. For example, a person may see that the assumption—*a one-size-fits-all method of coaching is effective*—is inconsistent with the outcome chart that shows that people's reaction to appraisal is quite variable. Many other examples of inconsistencies have been discussed in the first eight chapters. In comparing assumptions and outcomes, there's no need to go through either chart point by point, but give your team the opportunity to think about the connections and identify the more obvious linkages.

An important learning in this step is the connection between appraisals and *unintended* outcomes or consequences. As your team attempts to find links between underlying assumptions and appraisal outcomes, help them understand the concept of *unintended consequences* (see box). Encourage them to identify appraisal outcomes that fit in that category. There's no need to exhaust the discussion of assumptions and outcomes, but allow the team enough time to elicit some of the more obvious connections. During the next steps of the design process, you will continue to examine the connection between assumptions and the results appraisal delivers.

▪ Step 5: Revisit and Clarify the Overall Objective

After spending several hours working through the five questions in Step 4, the team is ready to take the first concrete step toward the design of a new process. Though you are focused on a specific mission around a single function of appraisal, some of the work thus far has taken broader perspectives. Hopefully that work has given the team a deeper understanding of the complexity of appraisal in terms of purpose, assumptions, outcomes, and effects. With this stronger base of knowledge, revisit your mission, and assess its accuracy and clarity.

Designing an alternative system to appraisal is a form of improvement. An effective strategy for improving or creating any process or practice begins by getting clear answers to three questions:

- **What are we trying to accomplish?**
- **How will we know a change will result in an improvement?**
- **What changes can we make that will result in an improvement?**[5]

As the first question suggests, in this step the team is trying to make a more definitive statement about what it's trying to create. For example, a clarified mission might look like:

> Our goal is to design one or more practices that will foster a work environment in which: (1) feedback and information are valued as a means to improvement; and (2) the employee, rather than the supervisor, is primarily responsible for deciding the method and timing of obtaining feedback for the purpose of improvement.

Take time to think about what you have learned, and create your own

---

Unintended Consequences

The phenomenon of *unintended consequences* is not a characteristic unique to appraisal. Any policy or practice, no matter how good the design, yields unintended consequences. And often the unintended consequences are precisely the opposite of what was intended. Psychologist Richard Farson recognizes this as a universal paradox of human intentions.[4] For example, washing machines were invented to reduce the time people had to spend washing clothes. The outcome: Time spent washing *increased* because the machine made it easier to wash, raising the expectation for people to wear cleaner clothes.

In implementing appraisals, organizations expect to increase feedback given to employees. An unintended effect of formalizing a process, however, is that some supervisors will give *less* feedback and delay feedback because the appraisal process conditions them to see feedback as a once-a-year process. Even well-designed, *healthy* alternatives to appraisal will have unintended consequences. For example, a company abolishing appraisals shifts the responsibility for getting feedback to the employee. A number of employees, however, may view this new approach as supervisors shirking their responsibility. Consequently, employees become *less* willing to seek feedback. This consequence could, of course, be a viewed as a design, training, or implementation flaw, but, perhaps not.

Unexpected consequences are to human resources practices as flies are to kitchens. You can put screens on your windows and doors, but somehow flies always end up in your kitchen. In designing policies, you can follow every known effective strategy and precaution, but you will always get unintended consequences. This is one reason why policy and design work is iterative and a never-ending cycle.

---

statement of the objective, definitively stating in your own words the overriding purpose and intended direction of your design effort. Remember, replacing appraisal is *not* a worthy or helpful statement of objective—be sure you have debundled, and clearly focus on the one function of the former appraisal system that seems most important to your organization.

Briefly take up the next question for an improvement effort—*How will we know a change will result in an improvement?* Try to define the outcome and effects of a successful change. Again, using the feedback function as an example, you may talk about a possible shift in the culture, where people would take a greater interest in seeking feedback, sharing information, and using it to make improvements. There would be multiple avenues of feedback that people could access based on their own preference, need, and timing. There would be evidence that people are using those avenues and benefiting from them. At this point, there's no need to develop any specific yardsticks to validate success—that can wait until later in the design process.

The last question—*What changes can we make that will result in an improvement?*—is part of the design step that should not begin until you have completed Step 6, identifying the assumptions around which you will design.

■ Step 6: Build from a New Set of Assumptions

Creating and choosing a new set of assumptions is the most critical and challenging aspect of the design process. Underlying assumptions are the foundation upon which your new design will rest. In this step, you are trying to weed out the undesirable assumptions of your former appraisal system. If you fail to adequately root out the undesired assumptions of the former practice, the new system will duplicate its unintended effects. In addition to rooting out the old, the team must devote time to the task of developing a new set of underlying assumptions.

Your team has already prepared for this step by making the assumptions of your former appraisal system explicit. Some of those assumptions are useful as written, some will need to be modified, and many will need to be tossed. In their place, challenge your team to create new assumptions, consistent with what reasonably can be accepted as true and the desired organizational culture.

As we discussed in the functional chapters, alternative assumptions often are idealistic, e.g., people are intrinsically motivated to do a good job, but idealism is not grounds for rejection. Remember, as emphasized throughout this book, your overriding goal is not merely to design an alternative system but to create a new work environment in which *commitment* can emerge. When employees are committed, they take personal responsibility to learn, grow, and improve their individual performance. Espousing healthier goals about people is not a flight from reality but an effective way to encourage employees to behave in new ways. People appear and act for you in the way you frame them—this is called *the*

Douglas McGregor on Changing Our Assumptions

So long as the manager fails to question the validity of his personal assumptions, he is unlikely to avail himself of what is available in science. And much is there. The knowledge of the social sciences is not sparse, but it frequently contradicts personal experiences and threatens some cherished illusions. The easy way out is rejection, since one can always find imperfections and inadequacies in scientific knowledge.[6]

Pygmalion effect. Though silent and unseen, the underlying assumptions of your human resources practices plainly tell your employees how you see them. Seeing employees in a new light, without other measures, will not precipitate a profound cultural shift, but it can fertilize the soil from which real change can grow.

Building human resources upon healthier perceptions of people requires great courage. We attend business conferences and read the latest progressive books on managing people—they pretty much tell us to expect the best in people, that is, that people are intrinsically motivated to do a good job and can be trusted to act in the best interest of the organization. Hearing this, we nod our heads, and a voice inside us says, "Yes, people have these qualities." But when it comes to actually *changing* our human resources policies and practices, we retreat from these notions in a cowardly fashion. Then we rationalize, "They're nice ideas, but have little to do with the *real* world we live in." In the box, Douglas McGregor offers some insights that partly explain this retreat from what he called Theory Y assumptions, i.e., a healthier view of people. His contemporary, Abraham Maslow, also recognized managers' stubborn adherence to the more negative or Theory X perception of people. Maslow said this obstinate persistence "rests entirely on habit and tradition" and becomes "a kind of self-fulfilling prophecy."[7] Maslow acknowledged that our skepticism regarding healthier views is justifiable but also said our resolute and dogged faith in Theory X expectations is unsound, noting:

> . . . I would say that there is insufficient grounding for a firm and final trust in Theory Y management philosophy; but then I would hastily add that there is even less firm evidence for Theory X. If one adds up all the researches that have actually been done under scientific auspices and in the industrial situation itself, practically all of them come out on the side of one

or another version of Theory Y; practically none of them come out in favor of Theory X philosophy except in small and detailed and specific special circumstances.[8]

Though Maslow wrote these words nearly four decades ago, the research would not stack up much differently today, as you may have noted in Chapters 4 and 6. While much is yet to be learned from designing human resources systems around healthier assumptions, our experience resoundingly indicates they bring very positive effects.

If you can muster the courage to design around healthier assumptions, start the process of creating new assumptions by looking at the old ones. Go through each assumption and ask whether it holds true based on your organization's experience or available research. More important, ask whether the assumption supports and is consistent with the work environment and culture you are trying to create. For example, if your organization professes to empower employees, are your assumptions consistent with this belief? If your former system saddled supervisors with the role of initiating feedback and appraisals, it may have stemmed from the underlying assumption—*It's the supervisor's responsibility to give people feedback to improve job performance*. Such assumption runs counter to the notion of empowered employees. Your team may reject or modify this assumption, replacing it with one or more new assumptions, such as—*When the receiver seeks and gathers feedback, it's more likely to be heard, thereby improving performance*. Reflecting on the earlier work around the characteristics of appraisals and the five whys, continue the process of reviewing, keeping, modifying, or rejecting assumptions of the former system.

Replacing unwanted assumptions and creating new ones requires both patience and artful tools. For example, one creative tool is called *assumption reversal*, i.e., looking at an assumption and seeing whether an opposite statement creates a helpful new assumption. Another creative tool is called *parallel thinking*, i.e., taking a concept from a totally different context and seeing if it provides insight into creating a new assumption. For example, auto dealers are wooing customers by placing sticker prices on cars telling the customer the exact, no-haggle price. The underlying assumption is: *Openness and straightforward information is more important in building customer loyalty than creating the image that customers are getting a special treatment*. Borrowing from this assumption for organizational people systems, we might create a promotion process around a similar assumption: *People want access to open and straightforward information about what will enable them to advance their career.* Often, to get the right assumption, there is no creative tool—just raw creative juices. You simply need to take time to ponder the kind of system you are building and ask: What are the underlying premises and beliefs required to make it work?

The design process is iterative. In subsequent design, as you clarify your intended purpose, it's vitally important to take time to recheck your assumptions against your specific design features. Your preliminary creation of an alternative set of assumptions will be sufficient to take you into the next step—the design itself. The working product you take with you might look something like the GM–Powertrain example in Figure 9.1.[9] That list represents assumptions extracted and replaced by a design team at GM–Powertrain as it created new feedback and development systems to replace a pay-for-performance appraisal system.

■ Step 7: Begin the Process of Design

In this step the real fun begins. Your team likely has found little excitement in wordsmithing a charter, examining the old system, or rebuilding assumptions. Early on, few participants fully appreciate the value of these preliminary steps. With a clear vision of what you are trying to achieve and a new set of underlying assumptions, you are ready to design a new practice or strategy to partly replace your former appraisal system.

Hopefully, the preceding chapters on the various functional areas have provided some initial insights on possible ideas for design. Looking for *ideas* from other models is valuable and encouraged, but resist the temptation to copy some other organization's purported success. Each organization is unique, and genuine success can emerge only if you take time to craft an alternative that is accurately attuned to your organization's culture and systems. Any idea you wish to borrow in whole or part must be tested against your new set of underlying assumptions, as well as for its consistency with your current and desired workplace culture.

The nature of "design work" may be a new experience for some of you, and having a good mental model will make all the difference. In designing a practice or policy, we naturally tend to focus on and design around a particular *solution* or *answer.* This perspective hinders successful design. Design is the process of *making a prediction.* If we do X, we predict the result will be Y. Implementing the design tells us if our prediction is

Prior Assumptions	New Assumptions
Money motivates people to work.	• Money motivates people to get money (not necessarily to generate improvement). • Money's motivational power is short-term—there is little sustaining power. • The size of pay increases needs to continually increase to have the same impact. • It can be very de-motivating to receive less pay than you think you deserve.
An individual's performance can be objectively evaluated.	• Assessment of an individual's performance is fraught with subjectivity. • An individual's performance level cannot be measured apart from the system in which the individual works. • Subjectivity and bias in judgment cannot be overcome by good intentions. • The Company cannot identify with reliable accuracy the best and poorest performers within a given group of workers.
Improving the performance of individuals improves the performance of the organization.	• Improving the performance of systems and processes improves the performance of the organization.
Internal competition improves performance.	• Internal collaboration improves performance.
People are inherently lazy and cannot be trusted.	• People want to do their best and are trustworthy.
People take what leaders say at face value.	• People interpret what leaders say through observing their behavior.

Figure 9.1   Underlying Assumptions at GM–Powertrain

right or wrong—it asks and answers a question. Implementation enables learning to occur and may lead us to a new design which, in turn, is yet another prediction. Designing alternatives to performance appraisal is also prediction. For example, if we design a career ladder to replace performance ratings as a means of promoting people, we are predicting that our design will result in qualified people being promoted to more responsible positions. Another design team predicts that, if appraisals are discontinued, with proper training supervisors will reliably provide assistance, counseling, and legal documentation for employees who are performing poorly. These predictions may prove to be accurate, inaccurate, or a shade in between.

Designing with prediction in mind enhances clarity and the opportunity for learning. Without a clearly stated prediction, little learning can result. Predictions are closely linked to the design's underlying assumptions, which, more or less, are also tested in a new design. Explicitly stated predictions will make it easier to plan measuring sticks, determine whether an alternative is working, and ascertain the occurrence of unintended consequences. Design may be viewed as a *test* or *experiment* that leads to learning. An experimental perspective will energize the members of your design team, enabling them to relax and let go of any notion that they must craft a perfect solution. They will come to understand that the challenge is mostly about organizational learning.

Though the team may begin to take on an experimental perspective, at this stage your team is *not* yet ready to mold anything close to a detailed design. The finished product will come later. Rather, the immediate objective is to construct a skeletal framework or model that minimally includes the following elements:

1. A clear statement of aim or purpose;

2. The underlying assumptions of the intended design;

3. The key features and components of the recommended model; and

4. An indication of any significant resources that may be required.

Once you have developed your proposed model to sufficiently cover the above points, you're ready to take your model back to upper management and then out into the organization to get feedback and guidance before putting on the final touches. These and related points are covered in the final chapter.

10

Creating Consensus and Confidence for Change

The last thing we ought to do is replace existing ideas about organizations with yet another idea and go on as we have before believing we have the solution.
Dick Richards, *Artful Work*

People may genuinely become excited by a beautiful idea and even support it wholeheartedly. But as the idea moves closer to implementation, insecurity and self-doubt set in. The supporters of the idea may then subconsciously sabotage their own efforts to prevent the change.
Jamshid Gharajedaghi, *Systems Thinking*

In organizational life, a good idea on paper hardly bodes success. Too often, good ideas bite the dust long before they are tried or brought to fruition. To succeed, a good idea must run an obstacle course, jumping hurdles and climbing over formidable barriers. The bigger the organization, the bigger the obstacles. Organizations are structured for stability and homeostasis, not change. Organizations are ingrained to play it safe. Change is risk. And we who work in organizations, as human beings, are also resistant to change. It's both a natural and learned response. Change brings the unforeseen, and this engenders fear. Things could get worse. So, we have a predilection to stay with the devil we know. We also resist change because breaking patterns requires a great deal of mental effort and emotional energy—it seems easier to endure the present mediocrity and misery.

Appraisal has been an artifact of organizational life for decades. Accordingly, expect formidable resistance if you seek to abolish appraisal, notwithstanding its widespread unpopularity. After all, most people have experienced some form of appraisal throughout their worklife. And before work they got appraisals in the form of report cards for many years in school. Old habits die hard.

The challenge in dropping appraisal is more than breaking a habit. And it's more than designing a slick, state-of-the-art alternative. The *real* challenge is to create a *radically different culture*—a culture spawned from healthier assumptions and the convergent thinking that is reshaping organization life today. As discussed in Chapter 2, this new thinking alters our long-established perspective of people—shifting from the view that people are inherently lazy, irresponsible, and self-centered to a heartfelt belief that people are responsible adults who, under the right conditions, will commit and give their best efforts to worthy organizational goals. While discarding appraisal is a good start in shedding the "old" thinking, successful transition requires an atmosphere of openness, trust, and a zealous commitment to cultural transformation. This transition requires nothing less than education for everyone, structures for learning, experimentation, patience, and a long-term commitment to persevere in the face of obstacles. We cannot instruct you on how to gather these ingredients, but want to be sure, as you bog down in the design process, that you don't lose sight of the true objective.

With this thought, we continue with the remaining design and implementation steps for crafting alternatives to appraisal. Continuing from the last chapter, we complete the series of steps that allow for new designs to be refined and garner grassroots support.

■ Overview of Remaining Steps

The remaining nine steps for transition from appraisal to alternative strategies are listed in short form below, followed by some additional suggestions and discussion of common pitfalls. The steps are not intended to be dogmatic. In some instances, it will make sense to combine steps, to circle back, or deploy other variations. Follow your gut. Here are the next nine steps:

Step 8: Plan an organizational communication and educational strat-

egy. Drawing from the foundation of knowledge about organizational and individual *change* and *transition*, develop a strategy for helping all stakeholders understand the need for and aims of intended alternative systems.

Step 9: Gather feedback on the new designs from stakeholders. In the form of an unfinished product, present your model framework and concepts, including the aim and underlying assumptions, to employees and managers to gather feedback.

Step 10: Analyze feedback results and refine the design. Keep track of and learn from the stakeholders' feedback any implications for implementation and whether any changes in the preliminary model are necessary.

Step 11: Go back to the top leadership. To avoid an untimely veto later, revisit top executives and review the scope of your intended design to get their blessing on the final course corrections.

Step 12: Complete the design and devise an implementation strategy. Make your design model specific and create the necessary tools, processes, and procedures needed for implementation. Clearly define the roles for employees, managers, and the H.R. department. Decide on a time line and determine the necessary financial, staffing, and expert resources.

Step 13: Plan a pilot run. Ascertain the benefits of a trial run on a small scale, analyze results, and make needed adjustments to your design and implementation strategy.

Step 14: Present the final design and secure approval from top leadership. Advise and get the organization's top leadership team's okay on the final design.

Step 15: Educate and train on the alternative system. Develop and implement a plan to help all affected stakeholders understand the purpose and processes of the newly designed system.

Step 16: Implement, monitor results, and continuously improve. With information and data gathering tools in place, implement the new design. Look at data and outcomes, including unintended consequences, gather feedback, and redesign as needed.

Figure 10.1 provides an overview of all sixteen steps, including the seven from Chapter 9.

16. Implement, Monitor & Improve
15. Educate & Train
14. Secure Final Approval
13. Plan a Pilot Run
12. Complete Design/Strategy
11. Review with Top Leadership
10. Analyze Feedback/Refine Design
9. Gather Feedback from Stakeholders
8. Plan Communication/Education
7. Create New Design
6. Develop New Underlying Assumptions
5. Clarify Objectives in Redesign
4. Examine Existing Appraisal & Related Practices
3. Form Design Team Comprised of Stakeholders
2. Charter with Top Management
1. Make Preliminary Assessment

Figure 10.1   Sixteen-Step Program to Recovery from Appraisal

Step 8: Devise a Communication and Educational Strategy

In Step 7 from Chapter 9, you developed a tentative design for a *single* function, decoupling that function, such as feedback, compensation, or professional development, from the other functions of your former appraisal process. Though the design team may represent a broad spectrum of the organization, it's not wise to rely entirely on their informal communication about the process. If your former appraisal process was connected to pay, career advancement, discipline, and other significant issues, and word is out that some type of new design is underway, it's a sure bet that people will speculate and circulate rumors. Sometimes the rumors feed fear.

An effective communication plan can curtail the pernicious effects of water-cooler paranoia. Devising a good communication plan is no great mystery. The objective is simply to provide all affected stakeholders of the former appraisal process and of the new design with clear communication on the aim and intended steps of the process. Most important, the communication must help stakeholders understand the need for alternative systems, i.e., why the prior system did not deliver, the strategic advantage of decoupling, and precisely what the new design is expected to achieve. At the same time, they should be given assurance that these steps will be taken only with cautious and deliberate speed, allowing appropriate feedback at various stages.

The design committee should receive some basic training on *change theory*, i.e., the widely accepted explanation of the dynamics and underpinnings of organizational change used by organizational development specialists in strategizing the implementation of organizational change. This understanding will help the design team better anticipate the typical reactions of people dealing with change. With this knowledge, they can give attention to those needs in the implementation plan. Because of the potent effects of change dynamics, active and passive resistance may be expected, even if the proposed design is a good one. The team and other supporters of the change need to understand that commonly encountered resistance is not necessarily an attack on the merit of their intended plan or efforts.

Effective strategies for working through change dynamics is more than we can present here. Someone from within or without the organization should have a good understanding of change theory and related strategies for your organization. Critical components of effective change strategy in this type of situation will be able to:

- Help people understand the failings of the former appraisal process and the need for an improvement.

- Allow, at various stages, avenues for people to express their ideas and feelings about the changes being considered and proposed.

- Prepare communications to affected employees and stakeholders in the organization, letting them know in plain language how the proposed alternative would work and possibly impact them.

At this point in the design process, the design team is *not* attempting to persuade stakeholders to accept any particular design. The goal is to establish a foundation of trust that will be helpful later when the dynamics of change come into play. Accordingly, the team should plan the measures needed to provide general information and educate people about the goals and expectations of the intended design. At the same time, everyone should realize that the design team will be making alterations and that periodic updates will be provided along the way.

Each culture has its own customs for communication, but here are some informational tools we've seen:

- Circulating flyers, organization-wide e-mails, or placing items in employee newsletters or on electronic bulletin boards

- Holding informal "coffee and donut" or "brown bag" sessions for people who are curious or interested

- Scheduling formal informational meetings

- Using the labor-management committee (where unionized employees are involved)

- Setting up an internal web page, where people can access meeting minutes, proposed ideas, and otherwise follow the progress of the initiative.

Although some discretion must be exercised about sending out half-baked information (which, in effect, is misleading), having a bias toward open and honest information about the activities of the design team is helpful. Timely and reliable information builds trust, leaving the door open for acceptance and support.

■ Step 9: Gather Feedback from Stakeholders

At this stage, you want to gather feedback from stakeholders on the initial, tentative design you crafted back at Step 7. You are not presenting a final product to a group of prospective customers but making a gate check to ensure that the ideas and thinking are on track. There is no finished product—you're merely sharing the *concept* underlying the design, not the details. This involves describing and illustrating the proposed model and explaining how it would work.

The best process we know of to get this kind of feedback is to conduct *clinics*, bringing together a diverse group of stakeholders in one room at the same time. To ensure the free flow of information, schedule *separate* sessions for nonmanagerial employees and another for supervisors and managers. Separate sessions ensure that the needs of both constituencies are addressed since they are quite different and often contradictory. In a larger organization, you likely will need to conduct several clinics to get a broad spectrum of input.

At each session, present your model in the form of an unfinished product, including its characteristics, the "givens," and framework. Make the aim and objectives clear, and explicitly identify the underlying assumptions (explaining how they were derived). The right questions, of course, must be tailored to the objectives, the design features, and expected and expressed concerns. This process is not particularly easy because it requires a great deal of forethought about what questions you really want answered and thinking of ways to ask the questions that will get you the most helpful information. The design team's objective in conducting the clinic is to get answers to the following questions:

- *Does the proposed design have the right objectives?*

- *Is the design consistent with the stated objectives?*

- *Will the design be effective in meeting its objectives?*

- *Will the implementation plan render the design to be effective?*

- *What have we missed or overlooked?*

Use these questions as a guide in constructing the clinic questions. Begin the session by presenting the key information—the objectives, design, assumptions, and implementation plan—in a helpful way. You will need to employ a well-thought-out, interactive technique. Then ask the participants to give you feedback with questions that will draw out good information. In Figure 10.2, we provide a sample of list of questions that might be used for a clinic on a proposed professional development system. Ask the questions in a way that will enable you to confirm what you think you are hearing. One way to do this is to synthesize and record key points on a flipchart, and each time you write something down, confirm with the group that it reflects what they are saying.

A neutral facilitator may be more successful in gathering honest feedback in a way that does not evoke defensive listening. By the end of the session, you should have some sense of the comfort level of your audience. Typically, a single clinic session will run 1 to 2 hours. The stakeholder participants will tell you things they don't understand, raise new concerns, and make helpful suggestions. They may affirm your theory as valid

Assume that you are implementing a new system to facilitate career counseling and advancement within determined professional ladders. You may have questions along the following lines:

Question	Target Audience	
	Professionals	Managers
Will this system help you understand the process of career advancement?	X	
Does the system help you understand what you need to do to progress to higher levels?	X	
Will this system make it easier for you and your supervisor to communicate about your career advancement?	X	
Will this system enable you or the supervisor to better plan the experiential and educational requirements in meeting your career goals?	X	X
Do you think this system will be easy to use?	X	X
On a scale of 1–10, what level of confidence do you have that this system will accomplish the stated objectives?	X	X
In the long run, do you think this system will be flexible enough to adjust as criteria for professional advancement changes?	X	X
Do you believe this system will make it easier for you to communicate to subordinates the company's career advancement opportunities and processes?		X
Do you believe this system will be valid and reliable in determining the readiness of employees to advance to the next level? Why or why not?		X
How can the implementation plan make it easier for managers to understand and work with this new system?		X
Will the proposed system impact, favorably or unfavorably, any other human resources or management practices? What? How?		X

Figure 10.2   Sample Clinic Questions

or tell you why it won't work. Carefully record or chart their responses and rationales; also watch for nonverbals and messages between the lines.

Toward the end of the clinic, an effective way to check on what you heard or might have missed is a quick survey, such as the one in Figure 10.3. These surveys are designed to give a quick sense of where people have concerns or a lack of confidence.

CRITERIA	SCALE		
	Disagree		Agree
The proposed purposes and objectives of the new design are appropriate. Is there a need for: ■ Additions? ■ Modifications? ■ Deletions?	1 2 3 4 5 6 7 8 9 10		
The underlying assumptions are accurate.	1 2 3 4 5 6 7 8 9 10		
The design accurately reflects the stated purpose and objectives.	1 2 3 4 5 6 7 8 9 10		
This design can be effectively implemented in our organization.	1 2 3 4 5 6 7 8 9 10		

Figure 10.3   Clinic Instant Survey Tool

Each question in Figure 10.3 can be posted on the wall, so that participants can cast their vote by placing a check mark over the appropriate number on the scale. Everyone gets an immediate sense of the reaction of the room. This diagnostic tool leads you to the next layer of questions. If you get high scores, you ask why. If you get medium or low marks, it's critical to understand why. For example, you may ask: "A number of you did not think that our implementation plan would work well, could you tell us more about your specific concerns?" If you are trying to implement a new feedback system driven by receivers, for instance, you may hear a prediction that supervisors with directive styles of leadership will have difficulty in getting comfortable with the new system. People may begin asking them lots of questions, and they're not used to that—the supervisors may take the questions as threatening, intrusive, annoying, too time-consuming, and so on. After getting clear about their concern, you can ask them about possible changes or additions to correct the concern. For example, relative to the concerns about supervisors adjusting to the new feedback model, you could ask whether it would be helpful to establish managerial support groups, in which managers could openly talk to one another about their experiences and how they are handling subordinates' requests for feedback.

Upon completion of the clinics and compilation of the results, you will have information to help you determine if your design is on track or if modification is required. You also will have a good sense of where the pitfalls might be in the implementation phase. The challenge for the team is to sort out which feedback points to a design flaw and which is more a reflection of barriers to be addressed in preparing the organization for transition.

■ Step 10: Refine the Design

In this step, you try to apply what you learned in the clinics. What design modifications are needed? What did you learn that is relevant to implementation planning? The objective now is to make adjustments based on the input you received. Do not overreact to one person's input or advice unless confirmed by others or it's an obvious flaw. As the saying goes, you cannot please all the people all the time. Clinic participants may be clear about the problem, but don't tell you exactly what to fix or how to fix it— you have to figure it out (as Dr. Deming would say, no heart patient ever asked for a pacemaker, no automobile owner ever asked for fuel injection). The design team shouldn't be defensive about any criticism since the task is about learning.

In refining the design, it's critical that you revisit underlying assumptions. In designing alternatives to performance appraisal, we frequently find that the design team ends up with something that takes on characteristics and assumptions associated with appraisal. (See "Common Errors"). Examples provided in the case studies throughout the book will give you ideas on creative possibilities for alternative designs.

At the end of this step, you will have a more concrete product. You will have items that explain the process, such as a written summary of objectives, underlying assumptions, givens, the processes, people affected and involved, resources required, anticipated training, communication measures, possible targets for a pilot, and likely time lines for implementation. You'll likely have flowcharts and rough drafts of key instructions or forms and anything else that helps translate the conceptual design into something more tangible. Tentatively decide on a time line, and determine the necessary financial, staffing, and expert resources, including required internal and external support. This step is not about completing the design or carrying out every detail of planning but about getting the

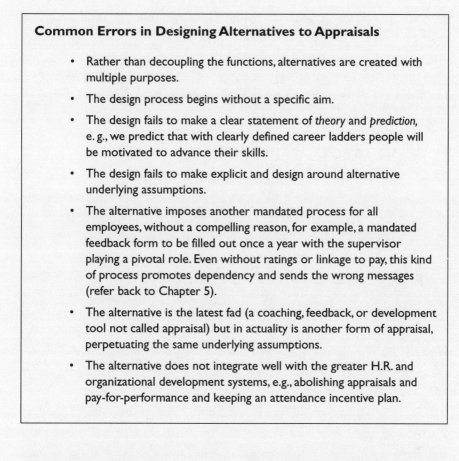

Common Errors in Designing Alternatives to Appraisals

- Rather than decoupling the functions, alternatives are created with multiple purposes.

- The design process begins without a specific aim.

- The design fails to make a clear statement of *theory* and *prediction,* e. g., we predict that with clearly defined career ladders people will be motivated to advance their skills.

- The design fails to make explicit and design around alternative underlying assumptions.

- The alternative imposes another mandated process for all employees, without a compelling reason, for example, a mandated feedback form to be filled out once a year with the supervisor playing a pivotal role. Even without ratings or linkage to pay, this kind of process promotes dependency and sends the wrong messages (refer back to Chapter 5).

- The alternative is the latest fad (a coaching, feedback, or development tool not called appraisal) but in actuality is another form of appraisal, perpetuating the same underlying assumptions.

- The alternative does not integrate well with the greater H.R. and organizational development systems, e.g., abolishing appraisals and pay-for-performance and keeping an attendance incentive plan.

design and intended plan to a more substantive level to allow further reflection and scrutiny.

■ Step 11: Get Another Blessing

Once more you need to go back to the top leadership. No, we are not assuming that your CEO is obsessively controlling. Even if top management allows autonomy in functional areas of the organization, systems that replace appraisal often go to the heart of managing people. They can have powerful impact in altering the organizational culture for the better. The alternative practice must have *solid support* from top management. The risk of making an inaccurate assumption regarding upper management support for the new initiative is too great to not do this check. We've seen many organizing teams egg-faced and heartbroken when, at the advanced stage of design or at implementation, upper management axes the project. Accordingly, revisit top executives to review the salient features and scope of your intended design and implementation, share the clinic results, and get their blessing on final course corrections.

■ Step 12: Complete the Design and Devise an Implementation Strategy

You now have talked to your customers and have a good sense that your design is on track. Upper management has made a commitment to support the project. You know with certainty that the necessary resources, including financial, will be available. Any labor union barriers have been addressed. Hence, all of the roadblocks are out of the way and you're ready to complete the design.

At the end of this step, you will have a final statement of objectives, underlying assumptions, defined indicators of success, clearly defined roles for all the players, and all of the processes, procedures, and forms needed for delivery. Finalize your strategy and plan for requisite communication, training, required resources, and implementation steps. In most instances, your implementation plan should call for starting with a pilot.

Case Study

Electronic Data Corporation (EDS)—
Working Within Corporate Mandates

Within large corporations, appraisal frequently is mandated corporate-wide. When people from these organizations are confronted with the idea of abandoning appraisal, they say something like, "Well, we couldn't think of that because corporate says we must do appraisals." Sometimes, by taking time to understand what corporate really wants, you may be surprised to learn there's some flexibility. And this is the story here.

EDS is a colossal company with 130,000 associates in 45 countries, providing information technology services generating $16 billion dollars per year. EDS requires a multisource appraisal for all associates, including six steps:

1. A manager solicits feedback sources from the associate.

2. The associate gives the manager a list of people from whom feedback will be requested.

3. A manager sends corporate's standard forms to people on the associate's list, plus any additional questions or forms the manager chooses to add.

4. The manager collects the feedback and distills answers.

5. The manager meets with the associate to review the feedback received.

6. The form is signed by the associate and manager and sent to H.R.

Of course, all this equates to a form of appraisal, even though it's progressive in the sense of letting the associate choose the raters.

A small unit of 35 associates, however, pondered the possibility of a different path. That unit is the Quality Consulting and Resource Center (QCRC), which provides information and consulting services to the company on process and system improvement. Given what the people in that department do, they were fully aware that appraisal is not effective. They further found that it was not really contributing to their personal growth. As a result of this dissatisfaction, the associates in QCRC were interested in pursuing a nonappraisal approach to feedback. According to Eric Budd, an associate there at the time of transition, the staff asked corporate H.R. if it could have "a variance" and do something other than the six-step requirement. To its credit, H.R. was open-minded, and offered some flexibility with given parameters. It agreed that the customary appraisal practice could be waived, provided that: (1) feedback is gathered annually from multiple sources; (2) the associate reviews the feedback received with another EDS associate; and (3) the manager and the associate sign the feedback form.

The positive feature of the new approach was that it allowed the associate to choose another associate to review the feedback compiled. This enabled the participant associate to do the process with someone who ideally fits his or her personal needs in terms of a feedback coach with the right expertise, personal style, trust, and other factors. Working from corporate's parameters, a team of people in the unit devised an 8-step process as illustrated in Figure 10.4. The process has been used for two years, and the associates in the unit have overwhelmingly found the process to be more helpful and enjoyable than the conventional appraisal.

Though the EDS variation is still a form of appraisal, with some of its inherent flaws, it is strikingly more progressive than most "state of the art" appraisal practices in terms of: (1) trust in the associate; (2) giving the associate great freedom in getting the right feedback sources; and (3) letting the associate play the greatest role in driving the process.

■ Step 13: Plan a Pilot

We are amazed how often we find corporations with five, ten, or twenty thousand employees that take a new idea and, cold-turkey, apply it across the entire workforce. One would think that common sense alone would

1. An annual date of feedback is scheduled, and the participant associate chooses a reviewer. Any associate (peer or leader) may be the reviewer.
2. The participant chooses trusted sources among peers, customers, suppliers, etc., who have knowledge of his or her performance.
3. The participant designs the feedback questions and distributes them to the selected sources.
4. The participant receives feedback directly from those sources.
5. The participant compiles the information received and meets with a reviewing associate.
6. The participant and reviewing associate meet to discuss the feedback and allow the reviewing associate to offer support and insight.
7. The participant creates a developmental action plan and, if desired, obtains assistance from the reviewing associate.
8. The participant arranges support and picks someone to have a weekly conversation about progress on the development plan.

Figure 10.4   EDS QCRC Business Unit Feedback Process

suffice to tell you to first give a new idea a small-scale, trial run. With rare exceptions, every new human resources initiative, practice, procedure, or policy should first be tried on a small-scale basis. Typically referred to as a *pilot*, the goal is to ascertain the benefits and weaknesses of the new system in a smaller environment. The pilot is designed to allow *learning* to occur, meaning you will have clear-cut questions and know what data you must gather to answer those questions. For example, if you design a new documentation and corrective system for "errant" employees, at the end of the pilot you may want to know:

Was the system utilized? Was it utilized correctly? Did it help employees improve or encourage supervisors to find better fits? Did it have unintended consequences? Did supervisors find it to be efficient and helpful? When legal action, grievances or charges arose, did the system provide adequate documentation? Was the documentation accepted as valid by reviewing parties, such as a civil rights agency, arbitrator, or hearing officer?

To some degree, the pilot can be designed to collect data and information, especially with the use of commonly available databases. On the other hand, some of these questions will require follow-up surveys, interviews, customer focus groups, and other assessment tools. We strongly recommend the inclusion of one or more open-ended, interactive assessment tools to ensure that you get back optimal information.

Once you have gathered the results and feedback from the pilot, determine if there were consistent messages about what needed to be strengthened, what was confusing, or other problems. If it appears that the problems can be remedied, go back to your design with an open mind. Look again and make the needed adjustments to your design, its tools, and processes. If your pilot reveals a major bounce, you may need to go back to one of the earlier steps and again redesign, conduct clinics, and talk to top management. As disappointing as this is, it's better than having a major flop (see "The Perils of Going for the Whole Enchilada").

Case Study

The Perils of Going for the Whole Enchilada

An internationally established industrial design company with over 500 employees realized that its traditional appraisal process did not meet any of its expectations. Appraisal had been a long standing practice within its culture, of which nearly 80% were from professions requiring four-year degrees. The former practice used scales, long forms, and was connected to merit pay practices that were fraught with inconsistences, political manipulation, and other problems.

Undertaking a quality management initiative, the company embraced the idea that real improvement would only occur if systems and processes were improved in alignment with customer feedback and needs. A design team worked very hard at coming up with an alternative. The aim of the alternative was *improvement*. It developed a structured process that required work units as teams to gather customer feedback. It then expected that the unit supervisor would get the unit to address these issues as a team. The alternative plan further called for the supervisor to initiate measures to get customer feedback for the unit and individuals. In addition to addressing customer issues as a team, the supervisor would, under the plan, meet with each employee to discuss the ramifications of the feedback to their individual work. Together they would look for opportunities for improvement, with emphasis on systems analysis, process improvement, and gathering data.

In implementing the new plan, appraisal was scrapped altogether. The new plan was implemented company-wide. The idea was to shift to a customer-feedback driven culture, using system and data learning tools. Employees and supervisors were trained. Flowcharts on the suggested steps were disseminated. Improvement tools were taught. The new plan, however, never took hold. Usage of the process was hit and miss at best. Some supervisors and employees carped that they were not getting feedback. There was great variability—some managers were having conversations with people; others were not. Some gathered customer data, others said it was hard to get. Over two or three years, the initiative fizzled, and eventually the CEO asked for a new initiative that involved an individual structured feedback process but stopped short of appraisal.

What can be learned here? They had dedicated designers with good ideas. In many ways, the design team was on the right track, with a good understanding of how improvement could take place. They had a clear vision of people talking to their customers, and units working as a team using customer feedback to look for opportunities for improvement. The design encouraged good improvement tools such as using theory, data, measurement, and continued experimentation.

In part, the difficulty may have stemmed from a need for more education before implementation, though considerable efforts in this direction were expended. It's more likely, however, that the problem stemmed from trying to implement company-wide, in one fell swoop, the most challenging aspects of quality management. We learned in the late 1980s and early 1990s that implementing quality management on a wide-scale basis is exceedingly difficult, probably impossible in an organization of any size. Their idea was a good one, but too tall an order to expect in a short transition. If the designers had conducted a pilot, they would have known this. The plan also seems to be multifunctional. While the major goal was improving organizational performance, the process also rolled in expectations for coaching individuals and individual feedback gleaned from customer feedback. Clearer decoupling may have been more helpful. As a culture steeped in traditional appraisal, they may have started with some half steps, such as structured individual feedback without ratings, and then, over a period of years, worked to transform the culture to a quality management mode.

■ Step 14: Unveil the Final Design

After making final adjustments based on the pilot, advise the organization's key, high-profile leaders of the details and implementation schedule of the final product, which may include yet another visit to the executive management team. The important thing is to be sure that, as much as possible, the formal and informal leaders of the organization are on board. It takes only one or two of these individuals to derail the entire project. While you cannot proselytize every leader into being an ardent supporter, you can at least try to convince those who are lukewarm to give tacit support and stay out of the way in order to give the idea a fair chance.

■ Step 15: Educate and Train on the Alternative Systems

At this juncture, everything appears to be in order and it's time to roll out the new initiative. Given the legacy of appraisals in our work culture and the resulting mindsets, education is perhaps the most critical aspect of widespread implementation. People must understand *the why* as much as *the what*. Help them understand that the design team is not claiming that the new initiative will solve all problems or that it is "the answer." Rather, the project is a grand scale experiment that hopefully will yield *learning* and the opportunity to make subsequent changes based on that learning. These educational goals will not be met without a rock-solid communication and training plan. Don't leap over this step in a rush to implement your idea.

■ Step 16: Implement and Continuously Improve

Recognize that 95% of successful new measures will do *worse* in the beginning than what they replace. You probably have seen this happen with a new software program. In the beginning, people moan and groan. They tell you that old system worked better. The speed of routine work suddenly drops. Then, over time, people get used to the new system and the improvements are evident to everyone. No one would even think about going back to that awful software system of the past. Since we know this is the behavior pattern for *successful* initiatives, it's important to give the new system time before deciding if it needs fixing.

Remember, too, that implementation is not the end. It is experimentation and learning, always. Do not *own* the process in a way that makes you defensive to feedback and criticism. "A complaint is a gift," Janelle Barlow and Claus Moller, authors of a book by the same name, tell us.[1] People who take time to give you negative feedback, in most instances, care about the organization. So often, a complaint will offer an invaluable insight.

As you receive the feedback, take the longer view. Do not overreact to one piece of feedback. Stay with the intended design. Trying to fix the practice based on every criticism will surely give you a mess. On the other hand, keep track of the feedback, complaints, and system data, and see if there are opportunities for deliberate, well-thought-out improvements. In monitoring the efficacy, don't just look to see if objectives are being met. Every organizational intervention will produce some unintended consequences. They are often hard to see, but with observation and reflection, they are discernible.

■ The Remaining Functions of Appraisal

In completing the above cycle, you probably worked on the one function of the former appraisal process that was viewed as most important and troubling. Assuming you reach some level of success, a design team should again be gathered to work on the next most important issue. For example, everyone wanted a culture where good feedback was provided in a timely manner. Your initiative has successfully addressed that problem. The next most troubling problem may be something else—How can we pay people fairly? How can we develop a promotion process that is open and understandable? How can we ensure good documentation in the event of a legal problem? How can we develop a way to ensure that people are growing and gaining skills as required? How can we get everyone involved in improving the performance of the organization? And the list goes on. Remember, take these on one at a time. Bunching them together could take you back to the problems of appraisal.

If you cannot move the leaders of your organization to fathom the possibility of abolishing appraisal, take a look at some of the half-step ideas.

One last word of encouragement. We conducted interviews with twenty organizations of varying sizes and within a broad spectrum of industries, including the public sector. We talked to another thirty organizations in lesser degrees. As a result of all these contacts, we did not encounter one organization that had suffered any significant problems as a result of abandoning appraisal. We encountered only four or five who felt some disappointment with the transition and parts of their stories are in this book. The remainder found the experience overwhelmingly positive, especially in contributing to the successful transformation of their work culture. A number of these organizations have gone 8, 10, and 12 years without appraisal.

The growing list of organizations that have dropped appraisal or

Consideration of Half-Steps

Dropping appraisal in any organization where it has had a long history calls for a major mind shift. Remember that dropping appraisal means little if the culture does not shift. If people are managing with the belief that people are inherently lazy, untrustworthy, and motivated entirely by self-interest, tossing your appraisal process will reap no benefit. The shift in thinking will be new to *everyone*. Employees at every level will need time to adjust to the new ways of viewing work.

Accordingly, for organizations with a recent history of appraisal, it's often unwise to drop appraisal cold turkey. Instead, the design team should consider partial measures or stepping stones to get to abolishment. A graduated strategy would be to dismantle the appraisal in steps, paring away some of the more damaging aspects of appraisal over a period of time. At the same time, organizational development initiatives, leadership training, and ongoing education should help people to learn to think with alternative assumptions. With success in this initiative, at some point, the complete dropping of appraisal will appear logical to all of the stakeholders. Below is an assortment of half-step measures that organizations can use in moving away from conventional appraisal:

- Eliminate ratings if you can. If not, pass-fail is the next best thing. A tri-level scale (outstanding, meeting expectations, and not meeting expectations) is less destructive than the conventional multilevel scales.

- Decouple appraisal from other processes (pay, promotions, discipline, etc.). Disconnecting appraisal from pay will reap many benefits, especially in improving the reception of feedback and development suggestions. If pay is disconnected, try to conduct appraisals at a different time of the year from when pay raises are granted. Disconnecting appraisal from discipline will reduce fear.

- Make the process a collaborative task, shifting responsibilities to the employee as much as possible. Employee selection of the feedback sources is a particularly helpful way to shift responsibility.

- Have the appraisal prepared by the employee and limit the supervisor's role to input and final approval.

- Do not require appraisals to be placed in the personnel file—perhaps the supervisor would keep it or just the employee—legally required or prudent information can be preserved as needed.

- Instead of appraisal, use a mandatory, written feedback system, with no scales or connection to pay (again, not as the ultimate goal, but as a transitional process).

- As discussed in Chapter 8, require appraisal only for employees who are not meeting expectations.

- Allow each department to decide if it will use appraisal or alternative systems, while asking each department to be accountable for the achievement of certain objectives (see *EDS* case study).

substantially eliminated the elements of conventional appraisal, either across the board or within segments of the organization, include: Alcatel Network Systems (TX), Berrett-Koehler Publishers (CA), Ceridian Corporation (MN), Eastman Chemical (TN), Entré Computer Services (MI); Gallery Furniture (TX), General Motors–Powertrain Division (MI), Glenroy, Inc. (WI), Grand Rapids Ophthalmology (MI), Kelly Allan Associates, Ltd. (OH), Leander School District (TX); City of Madison Police Department (WI), Marshall Industries (CA), Michigan State University (MI), Memorial Hospital (OH), Modineer Corporation (MI), Parkview Medical Center (CO); Peaker Services (MI), Peterbilt–Wisconsin (WI) and Peterbilt–Illinois (IL), PQ Systems (OH), SAS Institute (NC); Southwest Missouri State University (MO), Voyager Information Service (MI), Wheaton Franciscan Services (IL), Wisconsin Public Service Corporation (WI), and the University of Wisconsin Credit Union (WI). In Yorkshire, England, Marshall PLC, a building materials manufacturer with 2,800 employees, abolished appraisals in 1995.

In addition to organizations consciously moving away from appraisal, hundreds more are slicing away, one piece at a time, the most damaging aspects of appraisal—discontinuing numeric ratings and scales, separating feedback and development from pay decisions, keeping written feedback out of the official personnel file (now done with officers in the U.S. Air Force), and more. Perhaps your design team may have more confidence knowing that many organizations parted with appraisal and many more are headed that way.

Conclusion

Free
at
Last!

If you don't know where you are going, you might end up someplace else.
Lawrence Peter (Yogi) Berra

Free at last! Free at last! Thank almighty God that we are free at last!
Dr. Martin L. King, Jr.

This book is about starting over. Abolishing appraisal is *not* the goal—it's only an obstacle that stands in the way of the goal. Dropping appraisal gives us new freedom—the freedom to think in radically different ways about how to unleash the human spirit in our workplaces. The real goal is building a culture that makes this possible.

Culture is derived from an old Latin word that means "place that is tilled." In our workplaces, the soil and tilth are our beliefs, values, thinking, and customs that we manifest in our organizational structures, management styles, and day-to-day practices. If we renew and rebuild our organizations upon good soil, free of the toxins of the old thinking, we can advance in ways never imagined. To make this happen, we must nurture and till the soil by patiently allowing people to learn

---

A New World View

Joseph Jaworski, author of *Synchronicity*, reflects on the emerging world:

(I)t's important to see the world as full of possibilities—to shift our world view from one of resignation to possibility. But if we are to participate in the unfolding process of the universe, we must let life flow through us, rather than attempt to control life.

(O)ur mental model of the world must shift from images of a clockwork, machinelike universe that is fixed and determined, to the model of a universe that is open, dynamic, interconnected, and full of living qualities. . . .   Once we see this fundamentally open quality of the universe, it immediately opens up for us the potential for change; we see that the future is not fixed, and we shift from resignation to a sense of possibility.[1]

---

and transform. It will take time. It will require us to earnestly redesign our structures and practices based on a new set of assumptions that complement our new vision of people and work.

No, we have not told you, and we cannot tell you, exactly what to do instead of appraisal. Viable alternatives to appraisal can emerge only within the context of your unique organization, with its distinct history, traditions, systems, values, and vision. The transformation can never come from the best practice of another organization. There are, perhaps, better practices, as Dr. Deming used to say, but no best practice for your organization and its particular needs. The alternative to appraisal is not a new five-page form or an intricate scheme to motivate people and garner their commitment. It's a totally new view of the work world and the world in general.

The particular alternative strategies we employ in place of appraisal are not especially important—but our *mindset is everything*. We must go down the new path not only with new assumptions and beliefs but with a sense of excitement and wonderment, with a willingness to take risks and cope with the uneasy feeling of unsettlement and transition. On this journey, we must be ready to stumble, experience setbacks, and endure the caustic criticism of the naysayers who are ready the first time we falter, to say "I told you so."

Beyond our emotional readiness to be a change leader, we must be ready for hard work and a long road. As Maslow observed, "enlightened management works best for the long run; it may not work for the short run."[2] When people see that, replacing appraisal, is not creating a single process, but four, or six, or seven new systems and strategies, they say, "That's a ton of work!" The challenge is so daunting that you will be tempted to return to appraisal, saying maybe this time we can get it right. Perhaps, a new appraisal won't be perfect, the thinking goes, but no replacement system would be perfect either. This is true—replacements to appraisal will leave unsolved some of the most difficult problems. Subjective judgments, required for fair pay or equitable promotions, will always result in some dissatisfaction, intended and unintended bias, and some sense that it is not working perfectly well.

But despite the inevitable struggle in creating desirable alternatives to appraisal, continuing with appraisal is beating a dead horse. Some of you may have been disappointed that we did not take more time to write about all the latest flavors of appraisal and how they stack up. H.R. professionals are pelted every day with reams of promotional materials about the new appraisal method that really will motivate, improve performance, and build commitment. They say "don't do appraisal"—do competency modeling, performance management, team appraisals, performance scorecards, 360-degree feedback, knowledge-based assessments, and the list goes on and on. It seems that, when you get to the bottom line, however, these supposedly new methods essentially are only novel variations or mixtures of what we have seen for decades. The driving force behind all of them is still control, and worst of all, the underlying assumptions are largely unchanged. For us to spend time analyzing the trends in appraisal would be the same as if we were environmental naturalists who didn't believe in zoos. In such case, we really wouldn't be keen on evaluating the latest advancements in caging animals, which works better, and so on. As we have discussed, in a context different than appraisal, some of the newer tools may offer helpful insights. When these tools are used as systematic appraisal, however, they bring most of appraisal's unhealthy assumptions and its unintended, damaging effects.

Performance appraisal does not and cannot work. It's a new century now. It's time to start over and look for new ways to liberate the human spirit in organizational life. Let us close with thoughts from T. S. Eliot:

> And to make an end is to make a beginning.
> The end is where we start from . . .
>
> And the end of all our exploring
> Will be to arrive where we started
> And know the place for the first time. . .[3]

▪ What To Do Instead of Appraisal—A Summary

Function	What To Do Instead
Transitioning Away from Appraisal (Chapters 9–10)	✓ Use a broad-based team to design alternatives based on healthy assumptions. ✓ Separate the functions (pay, feedback, development, etc.), clarify the aim, and design to accomplish that one specific purpose. ✓ Educate everyone in the organization about the need for and direction of intended change.
Improving Organizational Performance (Chapter 2)	✓ Foster a compelling shared sense of purpose and direction for the future. ✓ Create a work climate that trusts and respects people as responsible adults. ✓ Train everyone to understand and apply system and process improvement methods.
Coaching Employees (Chapter 4)	✓ Encourage everyone to take responsibility to get the coaching assistance that will best serve their individual needs and the particular situation. ✓ Provide employees and supervisors with training and an array of elective tools that facilitate alignment, improvement, goal setting, development, and the like. ✓ Use appraisal format as a coaching tool only if it is the most appropriate counseling tool for the particular employee and situation.
Feedback (Chapter 5)	✓ Enlighten everyone on the value of feedback, information, and communication in improving the performance of individuals and the organization. ✓ Train everyone in the organization to be effective *receivers* of feedback. ✓ Foster a work culture where feedback is integrated into the day-to-day work. ✓ Make available to all supervisors and employees elective feedback tools and formats, including 360-degree feedback systems, customer feedback, and process feedback methods.

Compensation *(Chapter 6)*	✓ Study and educate everyone on the realities of human motivation and the intended and unintended effects associated with compensation systems. ✓ Adopt profit or gain-sharing practices that equitably benefit everyone when the overall organization is successful. ✓ Foster pay practices that allow increases based on market adjustment, longevity and maturity progressions, attainment of specific skills, reclassification, and cost of living. ✓ Consider systems that can provide special increases or lump sums for those very rare individuals who truly stand out as exceptional performers. ✓ Create a compensation system that is easily understood and clearly distinguishes market, longevity, cost of living, and merit factors.
Promotions and *Career* *Advancement* *(Chapter 7)*	✓ Create open promotion and career advancement systems that clearly articulate both the objective and subjective criteria. ✓ Conduct just-in-time reference checks and use state-of-the-art interview techniques to fairly and accurately assess each candidate's potential for the position sought. ✓ Use panels of people to screen promotion applicants and to evaluate eligibility for career advancement.
Development *(Chapter 7)*	✓ Encourage and train people to be responsible for their own development and professional growth. ✓ Provide access to professional development assessment and counseling tools, career counseling, and funding for training and education. ✓ Mandate career planning and development only where there is a critical need.
Legal *Documentation* *and Helping* *Poor Performers* *(Chapter 8)*	✓ Educate all supervisors on the origins of poor performance, the importance of good fit, and ways to work with people in need of special help. ✓ Conduct appraisal only where legally required or prudently necessary (e.g., employees ending probationary status). ✓ Train supervisors on the array of ways to document unacceptable performance. ✓ Establish formal counseling and corrective action systems for poor performance.

What the Sages Say On Performance Appraisal and Related Issues

Kelly Allan

Filling out a form is *inspection*, not feedback. . . .History has taught us that relying on inspection is costly, improves nothing for very long, and makes the organization less competitive. . . .Anyone who equates delivering feedback with filling out forms has lost the battle for smart appraisal before it's begun.[1]

Dr. Michael Beer

Evidence has been accumulating for years that performance appraisal systems, no matter how well designed, do not differentiate employees sufficiently to make valid and reliable compensation, promotion, and layoff decisions. They do not necessarily even lead to better coaching. Instead these systems have become bureaucratic nightmares and have put human resources professionals in the role of "cop."[2]

Philip Crosby

The performance review, no matter how well the format is designed, is a one-way street. Someone the individual didn't select gets to perform a very personal internal examination. There are no certificates on the wall stating the qualifications of the reviewer. Yet the effect on the individual's present and future is as real as if everyone knew what he or she were doing. . . .The reviews, which are supposed to give information to management about employees, do the reverse. The employees quickly realize that management has no way of knowing who is the fairest of them all, except through luck and instinct.[3]

Dr. W. Edwards Deming

(The annual review) nourishes short-term performance, annihilates long-term planning, builds fear, demolishes teamwork, nourishes rivalry and politics. . . .It leaves people bitter, crushed, bruised, battered, desolate, despondent, dejected, feeling inferior, some even depressed, unfit for work for weeks after receipt of rating, unable to comprehend why they are inferior. It is unfair, as it ascribes to the people in a group differences that may be caused totally by the system that they work in.[4]

Dr. William Glasser

"No human being should ever evaluate another human being." If we would practice this recommendation, we would get rid of one of the most destructive things we do to each other, because it is distrust, antagonism, and anger that is almost always generated by being forced to submit to evaluation of others.[5]

David H. Maister

Many firms with performance-based rewards systems are fooling themselves. They think that because they match financial rewards with performance, they are therefore good at tackling performance issues. But the opposite may be true. The more the firm relies on rewards to deal with performance problems, the less effective the performance counseling tends to be because performance issues are treated as the responsibility of the individual, not the firm. In essence, performance-based rewards systems represent, in many cases, a perfect excuse to abdicate responsibility for coaching, counseling and assisting—an excuse not to manage.[6]

Douglas McGregor

. . . (A)s far as the assumptions of conventional appraisal are concerned, we still have what is practically identical with a program for product inspection. . . .(R)esistance to conventional appraisal programs is eminently sound. It reflects an unwillingness to treat human beings like physical objects. The needs of the organization are obviously important, but when they come into conflict with our convictions about the worth and dignity of the human personality, one or the other must give.[7]

Peter Scholtes

Despite their apparent reasonableness, performance appraisals are not reasonable. They suffer from one flaw upon another. . . .When all is said and done, the conventional performance evaluation system is more like a lottery than an objective observation process.[8]

Margaret Wheatley and Myron Kellner-Rogers

We collect information from measures that tell us how we are doing—whether we're up to standard, whether we are meeting our goals. But these measures lock us into learning only about a predetermined world. They keep us distracted from questioning our experience in a way that could create greater possibilities. They don't ask us a question why we're doing what we're doing. They don't ask us to notice what learning is available from all those things we decided not to measure."[9]

■ Further Reading and Resources

On Alternative Approaches Generally

Imperato, Gina. 1998 (September)."Tales of Tomorrow." *Fast Company*, pp. 145–56.

Scholtes, Peter R. 1998. *The Leader's Handbook*. New York: McGraw-Hill (chapter 9).

Appraisals and Their Effects on the Organization and People

Block, Peter. 1993. *Stewardship*. San Francisco: Berrett-Koehler.

Chen, Chao C., and Nancy DiTomaso. 1996. "Performance Appraisal and Demographic Diversity: Issues Regarding Appraisals, Appraisers, and Appraising." In *Managing Diversity*, eds. Ellen Ernst Kossek and Sharon A. Lobel. Cambridge, Mass.: Blackwell, pp. 137–63.

Murphy, Kevin R., and Jeannette N. Cleveland. 1995. *Understanding Performance Appraisal*. Thousand Oaks, Calif.: Sage.

Nickols, Fred. 1997. "Don't Redesign Your Company's Appraisal System, Scrap It! A Look at Costs and Benefits." *Corporate University Review* (May–June). Available on line from nickols@worldnet.att.net.

Smither, James, ed. 1998. *Performance Appraisal: The State of the Art in Practice*. San Francisco: Jossey-Bass.

Communication –Alternative Models

Ellinor, Linda, and Glenna Gerard. 1998. *Dialogue*. New York: John Wiley & Sons.

Janoff, Sandra, and Marvin Weisbord. 2000. *Future Search—An Action Guide to Find Common Ground in Organizations and Communities*. San Francisco: Berrett-Koehler.

Owen, Harrison. 1997. *Expanding Our Now—The Story of Open Space Technology*. San Francisco: Berrett-Koehler.

Owen, Harrison. 1997. *Open Space Technology—A User's Guide*. San Francisco: Berrett-Koehler.

Designing New HR Systems

Gharajedaghi, Jamshid. 1999. *Systems Thinking: Managing Chaos and Complexity*. Woburn, Mass.: Butterworth-Heinemann.

Jenkins, Mary, and Tom Coens. 1999. "Systems Approaches to Human
    Resources Management." Module 21 in *Managing Human Resources in the
    21st Century*, eds. Ellen Ernst Kossek and Richard Block. Cincinnati: South-
    Western. (Module 21 is available separately from the book: 1-800-355-9983.)
Langley, Gerald, Kevin M. Nolan, Thomas W. Nolan, Clifford L. Norman, and
    Lloyd P. Provost. 1996. *The Improvement Guide*. San Francisco: Jossey-Bass.
Ulrich, Dave, Michael R. Losey, and Gerry Lake, eds. 1997. *Tomorrow's HR
    Management*. New York: John Wiley & Sons.

Employee Development Tools and Resources

Career Anchors® (developed by Edgar Schein, Ph.D.). Users of this pro-ac-
    tively plan their future career by understanding past career patterns and de-
    cisions. Available through DBM Publishing at 212-692-7700.
Kolbe Cognitive Index. This tool sheds light on learning styles and skills and
    how they relate to career choices. Available on line at Kolbe.com.
Myers Briggs Type Indicator. Widely used as a supplemental career counseling
    tool. Information available from Consulting Psychologist Press, Inc. 1-800-
    624-1765.
Personal Profile DiSC® System. Inscape Publishing. Enables people to under-
    stand their individual workstyles. 1-763-212-2882.
Self Directed Search (SDS)(developed by John Holland, Ph.D.). This tool
    helps identify job categories based on interests and skills. Available from
    Psychological Assessment Resources. 1-800-331-test.
Tieger, Paul and Barbara Barron-Tieger. 1992. *Do What You Are*. Boston: Little,
    Brown and Company.

Feedback

Feedback Solutions Videos (four videos): *Basic Skills, Receiving Feedback; Basic
    Skills, Giving Feedback; Giving Feedback, Advanced Skills;* and *Receiving
    Feedback, Advanced Skills*. Studio City, Calif.: Ash-Quarry Productions, Inc.
    (12444 Ventura Blvd., Suite 203, Studio City, CA 91604, 1-800-717-0777).
Folkman, Joe. 1996. *Turning Feedback into Change*. Provo, Utah: Novations
    Group.
Maurer, Rick. 1994. *Feedback Toolkit: 16 Tools for Better Communication in the
    Workplace*. Portland, OR: Productivity Press.

Legal Documentation

Patterson, Lee T., and Michael R. Deblieux. 1993. *Supervisor's Guide to
    Documenting Employee Discipline*. Carlsbad, Calif.: Parker & Sons (P.O. Box
    9040, Carlsbad, CA 92018, 1-800-452-9873).

Organizational Change

Bridges, William. 1991. *Managing Transitions—Making the Most of Change*. Reading, Mass.: Addison-Wesley.

Noer, David. 1997. *Breaking Free—A Prescription for Personal and Organizational Change*. San Francisco: Jossey-Bass.

Scholtes, Peter R. 1998. *The Leader's Handbook*. New York: McGraw-Hill.

Motivation

Csikszentmihalyi, Mihaly. 1990. *Flow: The Psychology of Optimal Experience*. New York: Harper.

Deci, Edward. 1995. *Why We Do What We Do*. New York: Penguin.

Frankl, Viktor E. 1984. *Man's Search for Meaning* (rev.) New York: Washington Square.

Herzberg, Frederick. 1966. *Work and the Nature of Man*. Cleveland: World Publishing Co.

Kohn, Alfie. 1993. *Punished by Rewards*. Boston: Houghton Mifflin.

Mahesh, V. S. 1993. *Thresholds of Motivation*. New Delhi: McGraw-Hill.

Maslow, Abraham. 1998. *Maslow on Management*. New York: John Wiley & Sons (reissue of Maslow's earlier work, *Eupsychian Management*).

McGregor, Douglas. 1985. *The Human Side of the Enterprise* (25th anniversary printing). New York: McGraw-Hill.

Rodin, Robert. 1999. *Free, Perfect, and Now*. New York: Simon & Schuster.

Systems Theory and Emerging Organizational Models

Covey, Stephen R. 1992. *Principle-Centered Leadership*. New York: Simon & Schuster.

Deming, W. Edwards. 1993. *The New Economics for Industry, Government, Education*. Cambridge, Mass.: MIT.

Hock, Dee. 1999. *Birth of the Chaordic Age*. San Francisco: Berrett-Koehler.

Jaworski, Joseph. 1996. *Synchronicity: The Inner Path of Leadership*. San Francisco: Berrett-Koehler.

Johnson, H. Thomas, and Andres Broms. 2000. *Profit Beyond Measure— Extraordinary Results Through Attention to Work and People*. New York: Free Press.

Land, George, and Beth Jarman. 1992. *Break-Point and Beyond: Mastering the Future Today*. New York: Harper.

Richards, Dick. 1995. *Artful Work*. San Francisco: Berrett-Koehler.

Senge, Peter M. 1990. *The Fifth Discipline*. New York: Doubleday.

Wheatley, Margaret J. 1992. *Leadership and the New Science*. San Francisco: Berrett-Koehler.

Wheatley, Margaret J., and Myron Kellner-Rogers. 1996. *A Simpler Way*. San Francisco: Berrett-Koehler.

Zohar, Danah. 1996. *Rewiring the Corporate Brain*. San Francisco: Berrett-Koehler.

▪ Notes

Chapter 1

1. *The American Heritage Dictionary of the English Language*, s.v. "performance."
2. Ibid., s.v. "appraise."
3. Eichel, Evelyn, and Harry E. Bender. 1984. *Performance Appraisal: A Study of Current Techniques*. New York: Research and Information Services, American Management Association.
4. Langley, Gerald, et al. 1996. *The Improvement Guide: A Practical Approach to Enhancing Organizational Performance*. San Francisco: Jossey-Bass, p. 4.
5. Schellhardt, Timothy D. 1994. "It's Time to Evaluate Your Work, and All Involved Are Groaning." *Wall Street Journal*, 19 November, p. A1.
6. Bernardin, John H., Christine M. Hagan, Jeffrey S. Kane, and Peter Villanova. 1998. "Effective Performance Management." In *Performance Appraisal*, ed. James W. Smither. San Francisco: Jossey-Bass. p. 3.
7. Gosselin, Alain, Jon M. Werner, and Nicole Halle. 1997. "Ratee Preferences Concerning Performance Management and Appraisal." *Human Resource Development Quarterly*, Vol. 8, pp. 315–33.
8. Imperato, Gina. 1998. "Tales of Tomorrow." *Fast Company*, No. 17 (September), p. 147.
9. Gharajedaghi, Jamshid. 1999. *Systems Thinking—Managing Chaos and Complexity*. Woburn, Mass.: Butterworth-Heinemann, pp. 9–10.
10. Mathews, Jay. 1996. "Do Job Reviews Work?" *The Washington Post*, 20 March, pp. H1–4.
11. Dalessio, Anthony T. 1998. "Using Multisource Feedback for Employee Development and Personnel Decisions." In *Performance Appraisal*, ed. James W. Smither. San Francisco: Jossey-Bass, pp. 287–88.
12. Kozlowski, Steve W. J., Georgia T. Chao, and Robert F. Morrison, "Games Raters Play." In *Performance Appraisal*, ed. James W. Smither. San Francisco: Jossey-Bass, p. 169.
13. The names have been altered to maintain confidentiality.
14. Block, Peter. 1993. *Stewardship*. San Francisco: Berrett-Koehler, p. 23.
15. Bradshaw, John. 1992. *Creating Love*. New York: Bantam, pp. 25–26.
16. Block, p. 26.
17. Maurer, Rick. 1994. *Tools for Giving Feedback*. Portland, OR: Productivity Press, p. 51.
18. Richards, Dick. 1995. *Artful Work*. San Francisco: Berrett-Koehler, p. 65.
19. Ibid., p. 77.
20. Zohar, Danah. 1997. *ReWiring the Corporate Brain*. San Francisco: Berrett-Koehler, p. 25.

Chapter 2

1. Murphy, Kevin R., and Jeannette N. Cleveland. 1995. *Understanding Performance Appraisal*. Thousand Oaks, Calif.: Sage Publications, p. 3.
2. Ibid.
3. Lublin, Joann S. 1994. "It's Shape-Up Time for Performance Reviews." *The Wall Street Journal*, 3 October, p. B1.
4. Tiffin, Joseph, and Ernest J. McCormick. 1958. *Industrial Psychology*, 4th ed., Englewood Cliffs, N.J.: Prentice Hall, citing *Studies in Personnel Policy*, No. 145, National Industrial Conference Board, 1954.
5. Murphy, Kevin R., and Jeannette N. Cleveland. 1991. *Performance Appraisal: An Organizational Perspective*. Boston: Allyn and Bacon, p. 3, citing W. R. Spriegel. 1962. "Company Practices in Appraisal of Managerial Performance." *Personnel*, Vol. 39, p. 77.
6. Ibid.
7. McGregor, Douglas. 1957. *Harvard Business Review*, Vol. 35, No. 3 (May–June), pp. 89–94.
8. Zohar, Danah. 1997. *ReWiring the Corporate Brain*. San Francisco: Berrett-Koehler; Danah Zohar and Ian Marshall. 1994. *The Quantum Society*. New York: William Morrow & Sons; Margaret J. Wheatley. 1992. *Leadership and the New Science*. San Francisco: Berrett-Koehler; Margaret J. Wheatley and Myron Kellner-Rogers. 1996. *A Simpler Way*. San Francisco: Berrett-Koehler; Dee Hock. 1999. *The Chaordic Age*. San Francisco: Berrett-Koehler, and H. Thomas Johnson. 2000. *Profit Beyond Measures—Extraordinary Results Through Attention to Work and People*. New York: Free Press.
9. Wheatley and Kellner-Rogers, p. 97.
10. Loden, Marilyn and Judy B. Rosener. 1991. *Workforce America*. Homewood, IL: Business One Irwin.
11. Scholtes, Peter. 1998. *The Leader's Handbook*. New York: McGraw-Hill, p. 21.
12. Deming, W. Edwards. 1994. *The New Economics*, 2nd ed. Cambridge: MIT Center for Advanced Engineering Study, p. 33.
13. The authors thank Dr. Kim Melton of North Georgia College & State University for this insightful recount.
14. Hendricks, Kevin B., and Vinod R. Singhal. 1999. "Don't Count TQM Out." *Quality Progress* (April), pp. 35–41.

Chapter 3

1. Chen, Chao C., and Nancy DiTomaso. 1996. "Performance Appraisal and Demographic Diversity: Issues Regarding Appraisal, Appraisers, and Appraisal." In *Managing Diversity*, eds. Ellen Ernst Kossek and Sharon A. Lobel. Cambridge, Mass.: Blackwell, pp. 144–46.

2. See Tsui, Anne S., and Bruce Barry, 1986. "Interpersonal Affect and Rating Errors," *Academy of Management Journal*. Vol. 29, No. 3, p. 597, concluding: "This study provided robust evidence that *affect* directly influences the quality of performance ratings. Our results underscore the importance of encouraging raters to segregate objective judgments from subjective feelings when evaluating others. But is this really possible? If affect is in fact inescapable and irrevocable (citing R. B. Zajonc), can we reasonably expect raters to ignore or set aside their feelings when participating in performance appraisals?" These researchers also found that a neutral affect actually *reduced* the quality of rating in some respects. This may suggest that, even if people are capable of changing their affect to neutral, it may still be problematic.

3. While trait ratings, as opposed to behavior or MBO (outcome) ratings, appear to be in decline, the highly subjective categories used in some of the increasingly popular competency model ratings (e.g., leadership and communication competencies) seem to play out like trait measurement. See Gilliland, Stephen W. and Jay C. Langdon. 1998. "Creating Performance Management Systems That Promote Perceptions of Fairness." In *Performance Appraisal*, ed. James W. Smither. San Francisco: Jossey-Bass, p. 237, citing B. R. Nathan, A. M. Mohrman, and J. Milliman. 1991. "Relationships Between Organizational Justice and Organizational Citizenship Behaviors." *Journal of Applied Psychology*, Vol. 76, pp. 845–55.

4. For a sense of how this stereotyping works, see Heilman, Madeline E. 1983. "Sex Bias in Work Settings: The Lack of Fit Model." *Research in Organizational Behavior*, Vol. 5, pp. 269–98.

5. Beauvais, Cheryl, and Janet T. Spence. 1987. "Gender, Prejudice, and Categorization." *Sex Roles*, Vol. 16, No. 1, p. 98.

6. Chen and DiTomaso. p. 145.

7. Halpert, Jane A., Midge L. Wilson, and Julia L. Hickman. 1993. *Journal of Organizational Behavior*, Vol. 14, pp. 649–63.

8. Kraiger, Kurt, and Kevin J. Ford. 1985. "A Meta-Analysis of Ratee Race Effects in Performance Ratings." *Journal of Applied Psychology*, Vol. 70, No. 1, p. 60.

9. For a different view of the Kraiger and Ford meta-analysis (above), see Paul R. Sackett and Cathy L. Z. DuBois. 1991. "Rater-Ratee Race Effects on Performance Evaluation: Challenging Meta-Analytic Conclusions." *Journal of Applied Psychology*, Vol. 76, No. 6, pp. 873–77; race tendency examples are from Chen and DiTomaso, containing numerous additional citations.

10. Cox, Jr., Taylor, and Stella M. Nkomo. 1992 (Summer). "Candidate Age as a Factor in Promotability Ratings." *Public Personnel Management*, Vol. 21, No. 2. Other evidence is found in Chen and DiTomaso, who cite eleven studies, p. 149. Re potential, see Chen and DiTomaso, p. 149, citing G. M. McEvoy and W. F. Cascio. 1989. "Cumulative Evidence of the Relationship Between Age and Job Performance." *Journal of Applied Psychology*, Vol. 74, pp. 11–17.

11. Chen and DiTomaso, p. 147.

12. Effects of method, format, and training are referenced in Chen and DiTomaso, with supporting citations.

13. Chen and DiTomaso, pp. 145, 151, 152, and 155. The listed conclusions are reworded slightly for format and abbreviation.

14. Tsui and Barry, p. 588.

15. Greenberg, Jerald. 1991. "Motivation to Inflate Performance Ratings: Perceptual Bias or Response Bias." *Motivation and Emotion*, Vol. 15, No.1, pp. 93–96.

16. See, e.g., Atwater, Leanne E. 1998. "The Advantages and Pitfalls of Self-Assessment in Organizations." In *Performance Appraisal*, ed. James W. Smither. San Francisco: Jossey-Bass, p. 350.

17. Referencing the research findings of Stanford psychologist Felicia Pratto, see "What's So Good About Remembering the Bad?" 1992. *Newsweek*, 2 November, p. 83.

18. Dalessio, Anthony T. 1998. "Using Multisource Feedback for Employee Development and Personnel Decisions." In *Performance Appraisal*, ed. James W. Smither. San Francisco: Jossey-Bass, p. 288, citing A. J. Wohlers and M. London. 1989. "Ratings of Managerial Characteristics: Evaluation Difficulty, Subordinate Agreement, and Self-Awareness." *Personnel Psychology*, Vol. 42, pp. 235–61.

19. Dalessio. p. 287, citing Wohlers and London.

20. See Kozlowski, Steve W. J., Georgia T. Chao, and Robert F. Morrison, "Games Raters Play." In *Performance Appraisal*, ed. James W. Smither. San Francisco: Jossey-Bass, pp. 163–205, regarding the results of their study and many others. It provides an excellent overview of the depth of political distortion in ratings.

21. Ibid., p. 173.

22. Ibid., p. 180.

23. Ibid., pp. 172–90.

24. Bernardin, H. John, Christine M. Hagen, Jeffrey S. Kane, and Peter Villanova. 1998. "Effective Performance Management." In *Performance Appraisal*, ed. James W. Smither. San Francisco: Jossey-Bass, p. 41, concluding: "(P)erformance appraisals are widely used to achieve political purposes rather than to accurately report a record of performance outcomes (citation). This is largely due to the fact that existing PM systems, including the plethora of competency-based systems being marketed today, are so readily amenable to such distortion, as well as to the prevalence of organizational cultures that tacitly approve of it. We believe that such manipulation of appraisals leads not to enhanced organizational effectiveness, but rather the opposite effect."

25. Kozlowski et al., p. 199.

26. Ferris, Gerald R., and K. Michele Kacmar. 1992. "Perceptions of Organizational Politics." *Journal of Management*, Vol. 18, No. 1, p. 113; also see Kozlowski et al., pp. 189–90; 197–200.

27. Kozlowski et al., p. 192–93.
28. Bartol, K. M., and D. C. Martin. 1990. "When Politics Pays: Factors Influencing Managerial Compensation Decisions." *Personnel Psychology*, Vol. 43, pp. 599–614.
29. Graddick, Miriam M., and Pamela Lane. "Evaluating Executive Performance." In *Performance Appraisal*, ed. James W. Smither. San Francisco: Jossey-Bass, pp. 370, 382, citing D. A. Gioia and C. O. Longenecker, "The Politics of the Executive Appraisal." *Organizational Dynamics*, pp. 47–57.
30. Deming, W. Edwards. 1994. *The New Economics*. Cambridge: MIT Center for Advanced Engineering, pp. 25–26.
31. Bernardin et al., pp. 35–40.

Chapter 4

1. Block, Peter. 1993. *Stewardship*. San Francisco: Berrett-Koehler, p. 152.
2. Adler, Alfred. 1964. *The Individual Psychology of Alfred Adler*, eds. Heniz L. Ansbacher and Rowena R. Ansbacher. New York: Harper Torchbook, pp. 116–17.
3. Ibid., p. 457.
4. Atwater, Leanne E. 1998. "The Advantages and Pitfalls of Self-Assessment In Organizations." In *Performance Appraisal*, ed. James W. Smither. San Francisco: Jossey-Bass, p. 342, citing H. H. Meyer. 1980. "Self-Appraisal of Job Performance." *Personnel Psychology*, Vol. 33, pp. 291–95; similarly, see, Paul H. Thompson and Gene W. Dalton. 1970. "Performance Appraisal: Managers Beware." *Harvard Business Review* (January–February), p. 155, reporting that only 2 out of 92 engineer participants saw themselves as below-average performers.
5. Pearce, Jone L., and Lyman W. Porter. 1986. "Employee Responses to Formal Appraisal Feedback." *Journal of Applied Psychology*, Vol. 71, No. 2, p. 217, reporting that Meyer, in different samples, found from 70 to 80% of employees seeing themselves in the top quarter, citing H. H. Meyer. 1975. "The Pay for Performance Dilemma." *Organizational Dynamics*, Vol. 3, pp. 39–50. Also see Thompson and Dalton (note 4), reporting that self-appraisals of General Electric employees averaged at the 77th percentile.
6. Bernardin, John H., Christine M. Hagan, Jeffrey S. Kane, and Peter Villanova. 1998. "Effective Performance Management: A Focus on Precision, Customers, and Situational Constraints." In *Performance Appraisal —The State of the Art*, ed. James W. Smither. San Francisco: Jossey-Bass, p. 33.
7. Glasser, William. 1994. *The Control Theory Manager*. New York: Harper Business, p. 23.
8. Kohn, Alfie. 1993. "Punished by Rewards." Ohio Quality and Productivity Forum Conference, 23 August. Cincinnati, Ohio.

9. Levering, Robert. 1988. *A Great Place to Work*. New York: Avon, pp. 153–54.

10. Rosener, Judy. 1992. "Ways Women Lead." *Harvard Business Review* (November–December), pp. 119–25.

11. For example, consider Fred Fiedler's situational leadership model, which works around three variables: (1) leader-employee relations; (2) the need for task structure; and (3) level of formal power of the leader. See Jerald Greenberg and Robert A. Baron. 1993. *Behaviors in Organizations*. Boston: Allyn and Bacon, pp. 459–61.

12. Gordon, Judith. 1993. *A Diagnostic Approach to Organizational Behavior*. Boston: Allyn and Bacon, pp. 343–45.

13. Hammond, Josh, and James Morrison. 1996. *The Stuff Americans Are Made Of*. New York: Macmillan, pp. 19–21.

14. Ibid., p. 68, italics in original.

15. Adams, Scott. 1996. *Dogbert's Top Secret Management Handbook* (audio cassette).

16. Greenberg, Jerald, and Robert A. Baron. 1995. *Behavior in Organizations*, 5th ed. Englewood Cliffs, N.J.: Prentice Hall, p. 136.

17. Levinson, Harry. 1976. *Psychological Man*. Cambridge, Mass.: Levinson Institute, p. 105.

18. Kreitner, Robert, and Angelo Kinicki. 1995. *Organizational Behavior*, 3rd ed. Chicago: Irwin, p. 187.

19. Ibid., p. 189, citing S. W. Gilliland and R. S. Landis. 1992. "Quality and Quantity Goals in a Complex Decision Task: Strategies and Outcomes." *Journal of Applied Pyschology* (October), pp. 672–81; and J. Bavelas and E. Lee. 1978. "Effects of Goal Level on Performance: A Tradeoff of Quantity and Quality." *Canadian Journal of Psychology* (December), p. 219–39.

20. Deci, Edward L., and Richard Flaste. 1995. *Why We Do What We Do*. New York: Penguin, p. 31.

21. The authors thank author and psychologist Joseph Bailey for information on this study.

22. Greenberg, Jerald, and Robert A. Baron. 1993. *Behaviors in Organizations*, (4th ed.). Needham Heights, Mass.: Allyn and Bacon , p. 124, citing K. G. Smith, E. A. Locke, and D. Barry. 1990. "Goal Setting, Planning, and Organizational Performance: An Experimental Simulation." *Organizational Dynamics and Human Decisions Processes*, Vol. 46, pp. 118–34, confirming an earlier hypothesis of T. Peters and R. Waterman (*In Search of Excellence*, Pub. 1982).

23. The study looked at a number of larger cities (e.g., Chicago, New York) and smaller cities such as Tucson, Kansas City, Spokane, Knoxville, Springfield, and Savannah). Bureau of Justice Statistics. 1999. *Criminal Victimization and Perceptions of Community Safety in 12 Cities*, 1998. Washington, D.C.: U.S. Department of Justice, p. 25.

24. Plan-Do-Check-Act, sometimes known as Plan-Do-Study-Act, is discussed in Peter Scholtes' book referenced in *Further Reading and Resources*. SARA is derived from the work of Herman Goldstein, according to Captain Michael Masterson, Madison Police Department.

Chapter 5

1. Senge, Peter. 1990. *The Fifth Discipline*. New York: Doubleday, p. 75.
2. Imperato, Gina. 1998. "Tales of Tomorrow." *Fast Company*, No.17 (September), p. 147.
3. Karp, Hank, Danilo Sirias, and Kristen Arnold. 1999. "Teams: Why Generation X Marks the Spot." *Journal for Quality and Participation*, Vol. 22, No. 4 (July–August), p. 31.
4. Deci, Edward L., and Richard Flaste. 1995. *Why We Do What We Do*. New York: Penguin, pp. 66–71.
5. Kohn, Alfie. 1999. *Punished by Rewards*. Boston: Houghton Mifflin, p. 114.
6. Farson, Richard. 1996. *Management of the Absurd*. New York: Touchstone, pp. 64–66.
7. Deci and Flaste, p. 71.
8. Bernardin, John H., Christine M. Hagan, Jeffrey S. Kane, and Peter Villanova. 1998. "Effective Performance Management." In *Performance Appraisal*, ed. James W. Smither. San Francisco: Jossey-Bass, p. 33.
9. "What's So Good About Remembering the Bad?" 1992. *Newsweek* (2 November), p. 83 (discussing research by Stanford psychology professor Felicia Pratto).
10. Squires, Paul, and Seymour Adler. 1998. "Linking Appraisals to Individual Development and Training." In *Performance Appraisal*, ed. James W. Smither. San Francisco: Jossey-Bass, p. 486.
11. Imperato, p. 154.
12. Squires and Adler, p. 486, citing A. N. Kluger and A. S. DeNisi. 1996. "Effects of Feedback Interventions on Performance." *Psychological Bulletin*, Vol. 74, pp. 657–90.
13. Dalessio, Anthony T. 1998. "Using Multisource Feedback for Employee Development and Personnel Decisions." In *Performance Appraisal*, ed. James W. Smither. San Francisco: Jossey-Bass, p. 279, citing C. Romano. 1994. "Conquering the Fear of Feedback." *HR Focus*, Vol. 71(3), pp. 9–19.
14. Ibid., p. 282.
15. Ibid., p. 297.
16. The Canadian Conference Board found in 1995 that 15 of 27 companies were using 360-degree to evaluate employees. A year later, however, it found that 7 of the 15 had dropped it altogether and, reportedly, most of the remaining 8 were leaning toward discontinuing 360 as an evaluation tool. Information at www.conference.ca and information regarding the remaining 8 from Bob Hughes on perfmgt@egroups.com (5/8/2000).

17. Burke, W. Warner. 1995. "Organization Change: What We Know, What We Need to Know." *Journal of Management Inquiry*, Vol. 4(2), pp. 158–71.

18. Senge, Peter. 1999. *The Dance of Change*. New York: Currency Doubleday, p. 13.

19. Bernardin, H. John. 1979. "Competitive Human Resource Advantage Through the Strategic Management of Performance." *Human Resources Planning* (15 November) Vol. 12, pp 179–94.

20. Covey, Stephen R. 1996. "To Live, To Love, To Learn, To Leave a Legacy." Presentation at Robert K. Greenleaf Center's 1996 Annual International Conference (14 June).

21. Covey, Stephen R. 1990. *Principle-Centered Leadership*. New York: Simon & Schuster, pp. 205–08.

22. Deming, W. Edwards. 1994. *The New Economics for Industry, Government and Education*, 2nd ed. Cambridge, Mass.: MIT Center for Advanced Engineering Study, p. 128; *Out of the Crisis*. 1986. Cambridge, Mass.: MIT Center for Advanced Engineering Study, p. 128.

23. Moen, Ronald. 1989. "The Performance Appraisal System: Deming's Deadly Disease" *Quality Progress*, Vol. 22, No. 11 (Nov.), p. 63.

Chapter 6

1. Kohn, Alfie. 1999. *Punished by Rewards*. Boston: Houghton Mifflin, pp. 124–25.

2. Kohn, Alfie, and Jennifer Powell. 1998. "How Incentives Undermine Performance." *Journal for Quality and Participation* (March–April), p. 8; also see Note 1 and Kohn, 1993. "Why Incentive Plans Cannot Work." *Harvard Business Review* (September–October), p. 55; and reply article, "Rethinking Rewards." *Harvard Business Review* (November–December), pp. 37–49.

3. Gupta, Nina, and Atul Mitra. 1998 (Autumn). "Value of Financial Incentives: Myths and Empirical Realities." *American Compensation Journal* (Autumn), pp. 62.

4. Kohn, *Punished by Rewards*, p. 119.

5. Ibid., pp. 119–41; 181–86; and 257–271.

6. Rodin, Robert. 1999. *Free, Perfect, and Now*. New York: Simon & Schuster.

7. In her *equity theory* of motivation, J. Stacey Adams says that people compare their inputs to the outputs they receive. Greenberg, Jerald, and Robert A. Baron. 1995. *Behavior in Organizations*, 5th ed. Englewood Cliffs, N.J.: Prentice Hall, pp. 137–139.

8. Author (T.C.) interviews with Dr. Beer during June 1999.

9. Hammond, Josh, and James Morrison. 1996. *The Stuff Americans Are Made Of*. New York: Macmillan, p. 87.

10. Herzberg, Frederick. 1987. "Workers' Needs: The Same Around the World." *Industry Week* (21 September), p. 30.

11. Csikszentmihalyi, Mihaly. 1990. *Flow: The Psychology of Optimal Experience*. New York: Harper Perennial, pp. 49–53, 152–57.
12. Hammond and Morrison, p. 305.

Chapter 7

1. Milkovich, George T., and John W. Boudreau. 1997. *Human Resource Management*, 8th ed. Boston: Irwin McGraw-Hill, p. 360.
2. *Webster's New Universal Unabridged Dictionary*. 1996. s.v. "objective" and "subjective."
3. Kruger, Pamela. 1999. "A Leader's Journey." *Fast Company*, No 25 (June), p. 118.
4. Early seminal case was *Brito v. Zia Co.*, 478 F2d 1200 (10th Cir. 1973).
5. *Price Waterhouse v. Hopkins*, 109 S.Ct. 1775 (1989).
6. 41 Code of Federal Regulations 60, *et seq.*
7. *Ward's Cove Packing Co. v. Atonio*, 109 S. Ct. 2115 (1989).
8. Kozlowski, Steve W. J., Georgia T. Chao, and Robert F. Morrison. 1998. "Games Raters Play." In *Performance Appraisal*, ed. James W. Smither. San Francisco: Jossey-Bass, pp. 167–69 (and citations).
9. Milkovich and Boudreau, pp. 379–83.
10. Ibid., p. 381.
11. Ibid., p. 262 (citing *Employee Selection Procedures*. Washington, D.C.: Bureau of National Affairs).
12. Ibid., pp. 262–63.
13. Quoting Michael Ray. Maslow, Abraham. 1998. *Maslow on Management*. (Deborah C. Stevens and Gary Heil, eds.) New York: John Wiley & Sons, p. 222.
14. Turner, Chris. 1999. "The Art of Smart" (Article ed., Anna Muoio). *Fast Company* (July-August), p. 96.
15. Scholtes, Peter. 1998. *The Leader's Handbook*. New York: McGraw-Hill, p. 354.
16. Buckingham, Marcus, and Curt Coffman. 1999. *First, Break All the Rules— What The World's Greatest Managers Do Differently*. New York: Simon & Schuster.
17. Milkovich and Boudreau, p. 371.
18. GM's dual ladder practices come from personal knowledge; the others are referenced in Milkovich and Boudreau, pp. 384–85.
19. Fishman, Charles. 1999. "Engines of Democracy." *Fast Company*, (October), pp. 174–202.
20. Dalessio, Anthony T. 1998. "Using Multisource Feedback for Employee Development and Personnel Decisions." In *Performance Appraisal*, ed. James W. Smither. San Francisco: Jossey-Bass, pp. 281–88. When used for appraisal and connected to personnel decisions such as career advancement, significant distortion of ratings can be expected.

21. Many good-sized organizations have functioned well despite no-layoff poli-
    cies, including Haworth, GB Fuller, Lincoln Electric, and Northwestern
    Mutual Life. (Robert Levering and Milton Moskowitz. 1994. *The 100 Best
    Companies to Work for in America*. New York: Plume.) In Japan, Nippon
    Steel avoided layoff by letting surplus steel workers create an Aero-Space
    Amusement Park that has become a major tourist attraction in Japan. Some
    manufacturers reduce wages or hours across the company to avoid layoff.
    The public sector has used furloughs as a way to cut labor costs without ex-
    tended layoffs or RIFs.
22. Jenkins, Mary, and Tom Coens. 1999. "Systems Approaches to Human
    Resources Management—New Assumptions." In *Managing Human
    Resources in the 21st Century*, eds. Richard Block and Ellen Ernst Kossek.
    Cincinnati: South-Western College Publishing, pp. 21.17–21.18.

Chapter 8

1. Delaney, John T., David Lewin, and Casey Ichniowski. 1989. *Human
   Resources Policies and Practices in American Firms*. Bureau of Labor-
   Management Relations and Cooperative Programs, U.S. Department of
   Labor, BLMR 37, p. 56.
2. Kelly, H. David. 1996. "Merit Matters" (private paper), Sterling Heights,
   Mich., p.16 (referencing Lexis database).
3. 29 U.S.C. Section 623(f)(3) (1967).
4. Davidson, John Edward. 1995. "The Temptation of Performance Appraisal
   Abuse in Employment Litigation." *Virginia Law Review*, Vol. 81, p. 1615.
5. U.S. Dept. of Justice study. 2000. Sniffen, Michael. J. "Private Job Bias
   Lawsuits Skyrocketed in '90's." *Lansing State Journal* (17 January), p. A-3.
6. Criteria are loosely derived from commonly cited arbitration cases, decided
   by Carroll R. Daugherty, *Enterprise Wire Co.*, 46 BNA Labor Arbitration
   Cases 359 (1966).
7. Panken, Peter M., and Starr, Michael. 1985. "Termination Without Tears:
   Avoiding Litigation Risks in Reductions in Force." 2 *Employment and Labor
   Law* (ALI-ABA Resource Materials) 7th ed., p. 988.
8. Survey taken at the Michigan Bar Association Winter update conference,
   January 30, 1999, and its Labor and Employment Law Seminar, April 23,
   1999. Surveyed attorneys were not aware of this book or of the authors' view
   on this subject.
9. Ibid. (survey responses on attorney recommendations regarding appraisal).
10. In Michigan, for example, see *Chamberlain v. Bissell, Inc.* 547 F.Supp 1067
    (W.D. 1982) and *Schipani v. Ford Motor Co.*, 302, NW2d 307 (1981), recog-
    nizing the tort of "negligent evaluation" (though in the latter case, the court
    cautioned that its application should be limited to the particular facts of the
    case). The tort has been rejected by several Michigan cases as well, e.g.,
    Mitchell v. General Motors Acceptance, 439 NW2d 261(1989).

11. For example, see published decision, *Ton v. Information Resources, Inc.*, 70 BNA *Fair Employment Practices Cases*, 355 (N.D. Ill. 1996).
12. *Ryther v. KARE 11*, 864 F. Supp 1510, 1517–18 (D. Minn. 1994); and *Johnson v. Group Health Plan*, 61 BNA *Fair Employment Practices Cases*, 1591, (8th Cir. 1993).
13. For example, see *Mann v. E. J. Baker Co.*, 52 BNA *Fair Employment Practices Cases*, 1111 (D. Pa. 1990).
14. See discussion of *Matthewson v. Aloha Airlines*, 152 LRRM 2986 (Haw. 1996) in Stanley B. Malos, "Current Legal Issues in Performance Appraisal." In *Performance Appraisal*, ed. James W. Smither. San Francisco: Jossey-Bass, p. 53.
15. Malos, p. 67, citing 72 *Fair Employment Practices Cases*, 980 (5th Cir. 1996).
16. Farson, Richard. 1996. *Management of the Absurd*. New York: Harper Touchstone, pp. 154–55.
17. Author (T.C.) interview with Dr. Beer in June 1999. The Organizational Fitness Profiling Process information comes from a paper by Dr. Beer and Russell A. Eisenstat, Center for Organizational Fitness, May 27 (1999).

Chapter 9

1. Gharajedaghi, J. 1999. *Systems Thinking: Managing Chaos and Complexity*. Woburn, Mass.: Butterworth-Heinemann, p. 23.
2. Condensed from: Scholtes, Peter. 1998. *The Leader's Handbook*. New York: McGraw-Hill, p. 327.
3. In organizing a team with nonsupervisory and nonmanagerial participants, you may run up against a highly controversial provision of the National Labor Relations Act. Section 8(a)(2) makes it unlawful for an employer (including non-union employers) to control, dominate, or finance an employee committee that deals with wages, hours, working conditions, or terms and conditions of employment. Some state labor laws governing public employees have similar provisions. With thoughtful planning, however, serious risk to violation can easily be minimized. Accordingly, legal advice should be sought on this issue *before* structuring or assigning issues to an employee committee.
4. Farson, Richard. 1996. *Management of the Absurd*. New York: Harper Touchstone, p. 46.
5. Langley, Gerald, Kevin M. Nolan, Thomas W. Nolan, Clifford L. Norman, and Lloyd P. Provost. 1996. *The Improvement Guide*. San Francisco: Jossey-Bass, p. 4.
6. McGregor, Douglas. 1960. *The Human Side of the Enterprise*. New York: McGraw-Hill, p 8.
7. Maslow, Abraham. 1998. *Maslow on Management*. (Deborah C. Stevens and Gary Heil, eds.) New York: John Wiley & Sons, p. 73.
8. Ibid.

9. Jenkins, Mary, and Tom Coens. 1999. "Systems Approaches to Human Resources Management—New Assumptions." In *Managing Human Resources in the 21st Century*, eds. Richard Block and Ellen Ernst Kossek. Cincinnati: South-Western College Publishing Co., p. 21.17.

Chapter 10

1. Barlow, Janelle, and Claus Moller. 1996. *A Complaint Is a Gift*. San Francisco: Berrett-Koehler.

Conclusion

1. Jaworski, Joseph. 1996. *Synchronicity—The Inner Path of Leadership*. San Francisco: Berrett-Koehler, p. 183.
2. Maslow, Abraham. 1998. *Maslow on Management*. (Deborah C. Stevens and Gary Heil, eds.) New York: John Wiley & Sons, p. 73.
3. Eliot, T. S. 1952. "Little Gidding." *T. S. Eliot—The Complete Poems and Plays*. New York: Harcourt Brace Jovanovich, pp. 144–45.

What the Sages Say

1. Imperato, Gina. 1998. "Tales of Tomorrow." *Fast Company*. No. 17 (September), p. 147.
2. Beer, Michael. 1997. "The Transformation of the Human Resources Function: Resolving Tension Between a Traditional Administrative and a New Strategic Role." In *Tomorrow's HR Management*, eds. Dave Ulrich, Michael R. Losey, and Gerry Lake. New York: John Wiley & Sons, p. 89.
3. Crosby, Philip C. 1995. *Quality Without Tears*. New York: McGraw-Hill, p. 16.
4. Deming, W. Edwards. 1986. *Out of the Crisis*. Cambridge, Mass.: MIT, p. 102.
5. Glasser, William. 1994. *The Control Theory Manager*. New York: Harper Business, p. 23.
6. Maister, David H. 1994. "The Value of Intolerance." *The American Lawyer* (September).
7. McGregor, Douglas. 1957. "An Uneasy Look at Performance Appraisal." *Harvard Business Review*, Vol. 35, No. 3 (May–June), p. 91.
8. Peter Scholtes. 1993. "What's Wrong with Performance Appraisal. What to Do Instead." Presentation before Ohio Productivity and Quality Forum, Cincinnati, Ohio (23 August).
9. Wheatley, Margaret, and Myron Kellner-Roger. 1996. *A Simpler Way*. San Francisco: Berrett-Koehler, p. 26.

▪ Index

■ About the Authors

Tom Coens is a writer, organizational trainer, public speaker, attorney, and educator, with more than thirty years of experience in dealing with human resources, labor law, organizational transformation, and quality management issues. He has provided training and facilitation for hundreds of organizations across the United States and abroad, including Chem-Trend International, Delta Dental, Detroit Edison, Mead, Sears, Sparrow Health Systems, the State of Illinois, the State of Michigan, U.S. Department of Labor, and Voyager Information Services.

Mr. Coens also practices in the area of labor and employment law as *of counsel*, with the Lansing, Michigan law firm of Knaggs, Harter, Brake, and Schneider, P.C. Over the years, his law practice has encompassed a wide range of industries including healthcare, manufacturing, retail, service, media, utilities, and the public and non-profit sectors. Mr. Coens' background further includes ten years with the U.S. Department of Labor and the U.S. Equal Employment Opportunity Commission, where he was Assistant Director of the Wage-Hour Division's Chicago Office and directed the EEOC's Equal Pay Unit of the Chicago Regional Office. He previously served as Staff Director of the Michigan State Employees Association and Executive Director of Human Resources at Lansing Community College. He has taught graduate courses in the area of human resources at Michigan State University, Loyola University (Chicago), DePaul University, and Aurora University.

Mary Jenkins, a private consultant, previously spent 18 years with General Motors Corporation in progressively responsible human resources positions. Before entering private consulting with Emergent Systems in 1993, she was Director of Salaried Personnel at the GM–Powertrain division which then employed more than 26,000 employees. Over a period of seven years, Ms. Jenkins worked directly with Dr. W. Edwards Deming in abolishing appraisals and creating alternative systems at GM–Powertrain. Ms. Jenkins also served on the Saturn Corporation start-up human resources team where she helped formulate its innovative human resource strategies.

Ms. Jenkins' consulting practice through her company, Emergent Systems, focuses on human resources design and organizational development issues. She has worked with a diverse range of clients across North America including, including Compaq, Drake, Beam, and Morin, EDS, General Motors, Ingham County (Michigan) Intermediate School District, Kodak, Mobil Oil, National Steel, Saturn, U.S. General Accounting Office, Wheaton Franciscan Services, and the City of Winnipeg, Manitoba. Ms. Jenkins has taught graduate courses with the School of Labor and Industrial Relations at Michigan State University and consulted with the University's H.R. department.

Both Mr. Coens and Ms. Jenkins have authored numerous articles in various business and industry periodicals. Together they wrote a chapter about designing HR systems in Managing Human Resources in the 21st Century (South-Western Publishing Co.). *Abolishing Performance Appraisals* is their first book.

Both authors may be contacted through their website:
abolishappraisals.com